Advanced Systems Design with Java, UML and MDA

Kevin Lano

ELSEVIER
BUTTERWORTH
HEINEMANN

AMSTERDAM ● BOSTON ● HEIDELBERG ● LONDON ● NEW YORK ● OXFORD
PARIS ● SAN DIEGO ● SAN FRANCISCO ● SINGAPORE ● SYDNEY ● TOKYO

Elsevier Butterworth-Heinemann
Linacre House, Jordan Hill, Oxford OX2 8DP
30 Corporate Drive, Burlington MA 01803

First published 2005

British Library Cataloguing in Publication Data
A catalogue record for this book is available from the British Library

Library of Congress Cataloguing in Publication Data
A catalogue record for this book is available from the Library of Congress

ISBN   0 7506 6496 7

For information on all Elsevier Butterworth-Heinemann
publications visit our website at www.books.elsevier.com

Printed and bound in Great Britain

Working together to grow
libraries in developing countries

www.elsevier.com | www.bookaid.org | www.sabre.org

ELSEVIER   BOOK AID
            International   Sabre Foundation

Contents

Preface

The world of software development is experiencing dramatic growth and diversification, with a multitude of new languages and technologies continually being introduced and elaborated: XML, .Net, web services, mobile computing, etc. It therefore becomes increasingly difficult to keep up to date with even the technologies in one particular area.

At the same time, important steps towards unification and standardisation of notations and methods are taking place – the new UML 2.0 standard is the prime example of these, and provides a common notation and set of concepts which can be used in any object-oriented development for any kind of system. The MDA[1] (Model-driven Architecture) likewise provides a general strategy for separating platform-independent specifications of systems from their platform-specific implementations.

In this book we cover the key languages and techniques for object-oriented software design of a wide range of systems:

- UML 2.0: we introduce the core concepts and notations of UML, and show how they can be used in practice.
- MDA: we describe the key elements of this approach, and transformations of models using UML Profiles, XSLT, JMI and REI.
- Internet system design: how to use JavaScript, Flash, XHTML, JSP and Servlets to produce modular, usable, portable and accessable web systems.
- Web Services: including technologies such as J2EE, JavaMail, .Net, SOAP, WSDL and streaming.
- E-commerce: including the Semantic Web, FTP, WML and Bluetooth.

A catalogue of UML model transformations is also provided. The supporting website contains the UML-RSDS tool to support the MDA process, and the UML2Web tool for the synthesis of web applications from UML descriptions.

Examples of the use of these techniques are given throughout the book, with three large case studies being used:

---

[1]MDA is a registered trademark of the OMG.

- A system to play Scrabble.
- An internet jukebox using data streaming.
- An online estate-agent system.

Acknowledgements

Kelly Androutsopoulos, David Clark and Pauline Kan contributed to the program synthesis concepts used in the book. Runa Jesmin contributed the material on usability design of web systems. The internet jukebox case study is due to Ruth O'Dowd, Taherah Ansari contributed the case study of XSLT and REI transformations, and numerous other students at King's College have also helped in providing feedback on courses in which the material presented here has been taught.

Chapter 1

The Challenges of Software Design

This chapter surveys current issues in software construction, the problems caused by the pace of technological change, and the need for improved maintainability and portability of software. In particular we consider the need for software development to focus more resources on construction of platform-independent models to reduce the effort in recreating a system for a new platform or technology.

1.1 Software development

The purpose of software[1] remains the same today as it was at the beginning of computing in the 1940s: to automate the solution of complex problems, using computers. However the nature of the problems to be solved has changed dramatically, and so have the programming techniques employed: the first computers were used for highly critical and specialised tasks such as decryption, and 'programming' them meant reconfiguring the hardware (vacuum tubes or 'valves') of these huge and massively expensive devices.

Today, the variety of tasks for which computational power is used spans the whole range of business, social and creative endeavours. Increasingly, instead of performing some isolated computation, software systems form active or passive elements in a communicating network of services and agents, each new system depending essentially on existing capabilities of previously developed systems, whose services it uses.

Programming techniques have also advanced in the decades that followed the 1940s, through the use of languages of increasing power and abstraction: Assembly languages, FORTRAN, C, C++, and now Java and C$^\#$. Instead of manipulating instructions at the level of the hardware, programmers specify data and algorithms in terms of the problem domain. The rise of object-orientation as a language for problem description and solution is the prime

---

[1]The name 'software' for computer programs seems to have been used for the first time by John Tukey in the January 1958 edition of the *American Mathematical Monthly* journal [50].

present-day example of this progression. Object-oriented languages have become the dominant trend in software development, and even archaic languages such as FORTRAN, BASIC and COBOL have been extended with object-oriented facilities.

The software development activities undertaken by companies today have also changed. Instead of building new stand-alone systems, software development is often used to enhance a company's enterprise information capabilities by building new functions into an already existing infrastructure, or by gluing together existing systems to carry out new services. In general, the emphasis in software development is increasingly on systems as *components* in larger systems, components which interact and combine with each other, perhaps in ways that were not envisaged by their original developers.

For example, in the jukebox audio streaming case study of Chapter 8, existing web services specialised for streaming audio data need to be combined with a playlist database, control unit and a device for playing the downloaded data.

Another factor has arisen, of profound significance for the software industry, which is the *pace of change and introduction of new technologies*. Although the rate of progress in the computer industry has always been rapid compared to other fields, since the advent of the internet, the dissemination and uptake of new languages and techniques has reached a level that seems to put any system more than a year old in danger of obsolescence, and requires continual revision in education and training of developers.

For example, it took over a decade for object-orientation to emerge from research and niche application areas to become the pervasive feature of modern programming languages, yet more recently XML [53] has made the same scale of transition in under five years.

The rapid change and introduction of new software technologies and languages, whilst obviously bringing benefits in enhanced capabilities, has also resulted in expense and disruption to companies using software, due to the need to continually upgrade and migrate applications.

The concept of *Model-driven Architecture* (MDA) [28] aims to alleviate this problem by focusing developer effort at higher levels of abstraction, in the creation of *platform-independent models* (PIMs) from which versions of the system appropriate to particular technologies/languages can be generated, semi-automatically, using *platform-specific models* (PSMs). This means that companies can retain the key elements of their software, especially the *business rules* or logical decision-making code, in a form that is independent of changes in technology, and that can be used to generate, at relatively low cost, new implemented systems for particular technologies.

The MDA approach (Figure 1.1) can be seen as a continuation of the trend towards greater abstraction in programming languages. In this case, the 'programming' is intended to take place at the level of diagrammatic UML models and constraints on these models. Executable versions of the system are then generated, as an extension of the compilation process.

This book will describe one approach for making this vision of reusable

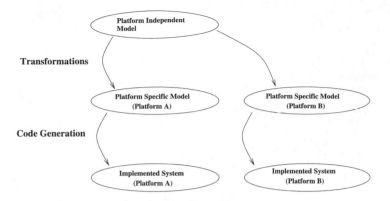

Figure 1.1: The MDA process

software a practical reality. In the remainder of the chapter we survey existing software development methods and the key concepts of software development processes, and discuss how these relate to the MDA.

1.2   Software development methods

A *software development method* is a systematic means of organising the process and products of a software construction project. A software development method typically consists of:

- *Notations* or languages to describe the artifacts being produced, for example UML [51] can be used to describe requirements, analysis or design models.
- A *process*, defining the sequence of steps taken to construct and validate artifacts in the method.
- *Tools* to support the method.

Some popular development methods are the *spiral model*, the *waterfall model*, the *rational unified process*, and *extreme programming*.

1.2.1   The Waterfall model

In the waterfall model [41], the stages of development such as requirements definition, design and implementation are separated into complete tasks which must be fully carried out and 'signed off' before the next task can be started (Figure 1.2). Each stage produces a deliverable (eg, a complete requirements specification, complete system design) which is intended to not need much further revision.

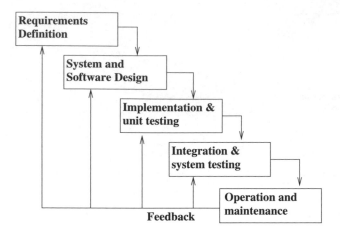

Figure 1.2: Waterfall model process

1.2.2   The Spiral model

The spiral model [5] is based on an iteration of incremental development steps (Figure 1.3). Each iteration (cycle of the spiral) produces a deliverable, such as an enhanced set of models of a system, or an enhanced prototype of a system. In each iteration a review stage is carried out to check that the development is progressing correctly and that the deliverables meet their requirements. Unlike the waterfall model, the deliverables produced may be partial and incomplete, and can be refined by further iterations.

1.2.3   The Rational Unified Process (RUP)

The Rational Unified Process [43] defines four phases in the development process:

1. *Inception*: definition of project scope, goals of the system, evaluation of its feasibility and general estimates of project cost and time. A prototype may be built to assist in checking if the project is viable. The main process in this phase is requirements definition, producing initial use cases in agreement with the users.
2. *Elaboration*: requirements analysis and definition of architectural design. The use cases are elaborated and structured, forming a starting point for the design of the overall architecture of the system.
3. *Construction*: design and implementation through the development of prototypes, culminating in the delivery of a beta version of the system to user sites.
4. *Transition*: testing, correction of defects detected by users, rollout of new versions until a production version is reached.

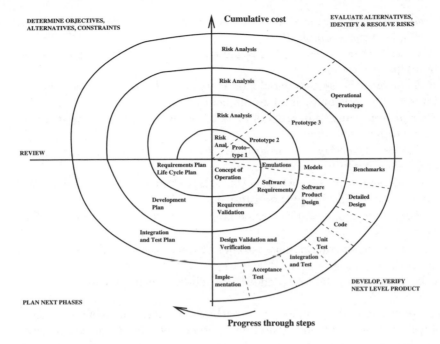

Figure 1.3: Spiral model process

The major milestones in development are the progression from one phase to another: the decision to commit to the project in the *Inception → Elaboration* progression, an accepted first revision of the requirements document in the *Elaboration → Construction* progression, and a beta release in the *Construction → Transition* progression.

The process is *use-case driven*: each design module should identify what use cases it implements, and every use case must be implemented by one or more modules.

1.2.4   Extreme Programming (XP)

Extreme programming tries to minimise the complexity of following a particular development process [4]. Instead of prescribing a rigid set of development steps and milestones, it emphasises a number of *practices*:

- *Realistic planning*: customers make the business decisions about a system, the developers make the technical decisions. Plans are reviewed and revised as necessary.
- *Small releases*: release a useful system quickly, and release updates at frequent intervals.
- *Metaphor*: all programmers should share an understanding of the purpose and global strategy of the system being developed.

- *Simplicity*: design everything to be as simple as possible instead of preparing for future complexity.
- *Testing*: both customers and programmers write tests. The system should be frequently tested.
- *Refactoring*: the system should be restructured whenever necessary to improve the code and eliminate duplication.
- *Pair programming*: put programmers together in pairs, each pair writes code on the same computer.
- *Collective ownership*: all programmers have permission to change any code as necessary.
- *Continuous integration*: whenever a task is completed, build a complete system containing this part and test it.
- *40-hour week*: don't work extreme hours to try to compensate for planning errors.
- *On-site customer*: an actual customer of the system should be available at all times.
- *Coding standards*: follow standards for self-documenting code.

XP is a lightweight development approach which aims to avoid the time-consuming documentation and structures of other methods. Code can be written immediately after definition of use cases (together with test plans for each use case). The code produced can then be refactored and restructured to produce a more efficient and maintainable implementation.

1.2.5   Which method to choose?

The waterfall model has often been criticised for its rigid progression from one task to the next, which can lead to a progressive build-up of delays, as one task cannot begin until its predecessor has completed. On the other hand, it imposes greater discipline than more evolutionary incremental approaches, where 'completion' of a task is left open-ended, and indeed, may not end.

   The cumulative iterations and reviews of the spiral model can lead to earlier detections of errors, and therefore lower costs and reduced risks of failure than monolithic methods such as the waterfall model.

   The Rational Unified Process, like the waterfall model, also has an emphasis on development phases with milestones as the progressions between them. Some software engineers believe that, in contrast, an *architecture-driven* approach is necessary for object-oriented development, whereby global phases are replaced as the focus by the modular construction of systems, component by component and layer by layer. For each layer there are separate specification, design and implementation activities. XP may be a better fit for this approach than phase-centred methods.

   In principle, any of the above development methods can be used in a MDA development, although the end product of the process may be a PIM or a PIM plus PSMs, instead of executable code. With the MDA, the progression from specification to design, and from design to implementation, may be partly automated. This enables developer effort to be concentrated on producing high-quality and correct PIMs. Refactoring transformations and design patterns are of particular importance in this respect, and we describe how these can be used for PIM to PIM mapping and PIM to PSM mapping in Chapter 5.

1.3 Software development steps

A number of stages are typically present in any software development project, regardless of the development model and methods chosen. We will illustrate these stages for two different projects: (i) a system to play Scrabble against human players, and (ii) a system to stream music from a server to a home entertainment system.

1.3.1 Feasibility analysis

This stage evaluates the technical options for implementing the system, determining if it is feasible to implement it, and if so, if there is a cost-effective implementation. Background research may be needed to investigate similar systems that already exist, and what services are available to carry out parts of the required functionality. Trial implementation/prototyping could also be carried out, or mathematical estimation (eg, of bandwidth or data storage requirements).

This stage can be carried out as part of the risk analysis phase in the earliest iteration of the spiral model, or as the first step in the waterfall model. In the spiral model a developer could recheck the feasibility of the system after each iteration as part of the review task.

For example, in the case of the Scrabble playing system, this stage would investigate the rules of Scrabble, existing AI techniques and programs such as Maven [46] and the feasibility of different memory storage and lookup schemes for dictionaries.

For the Jukebox project, this stage would involve investigating the state of available music streaming technologies, for example, streaming servers such as Helix (http://www.realnetworks.com/) and checking that these support the required functionality of the system.

1.3.2 Requirements definition

Provided that it has been determined that there is some feasible and cost-effective way of constructing the system, the development process can advance to elicit in detail the required functionality of the system.

This stage systematically records the requirements that the customer(s) of the system have for it, and the constraints imposed on the system by existing

systems that it is required to operate with, including existing work practices.
For the Scrabble system, the list of requirements could include:

1. The system must enable between one and three human players to play, together with the computer player.
2. Standard Scrabble rules for moves and the validity of moves should be enforced.
3. The system should check all words formed in each move, and only accept the move if all the words appear in its dictionary.
4. The system should keep a history of all valid moves made in a game: the letters played, the player who moved, and the score of the move.

For the Jukebox, the requirements could include:

1. The server should be capable of storing 100 tracks.
2. The user can add a track to the server from a CD, by inserting the CD into their computer and following on-screen instructions from the system.
3. The user interface can be on a separate device to the server. The UI provides an index of tracks, a way to select tracks and playback control (play, stop, fast forward, rewind).

Use-case models in UML can be drawn for either system, to make clear what users or external systems are involved in each functional requirement. Figure 1.4 shows some use cases for the Scrabble system, and Figure 1.5 those for the jukebox.

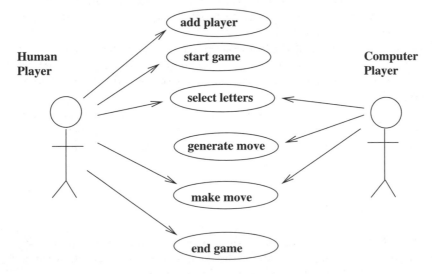

Figure 1.4: Use cases for Scrabble player

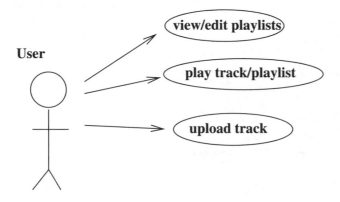

Figure 1.5: Use cases for internet jukebox

1.3.3 Analysis

This stage builds precise models of the system, using suitable graphical or mathematical notations to represent its state and behaviour in an abstract, platform-independent manner. In a critical system, such as a railway signalling system, formal validation that the analysis models satisfy required properties would be carried out.

For the Scrabble system a fragment of the class diagram is shown in Figure 1.6. A fundamental property is that the total number of letters in the game is always 100, these may be distributed between the player's racks, the bag, or the board. Hence the annotation in the top corner of the *Letter* class.

For the Jukebox, the core data model is much simpler (Figure 1.7). There will also be other web forms associated with the system, for logging in, viewing and creating playlists, etc.

1.3.4 Design

This stage defines an architecture and structure for the implementation of the system, typically dividing it into subsystems and modules which have responsibility for carrying out specific parts of its functionality and managing parts of its data. The activities in design include:

1. *Architectural design*: define the global architecture of the system, as a set of major subsystems, and indicate the dependencies between them.

   For example, partitioning a system into a GUI, functional core, and data repository. The GUI depends on the core because it invokes operations of the core, and the core may depend on the GUI (if it invokes GUI operations to display the result of computations, for example). The core depends on the repository. There may be no other connections. Such an architecture is termed a *three tier architecture*. Figure 1.8 shows such a design architecture for the Scrabble system.

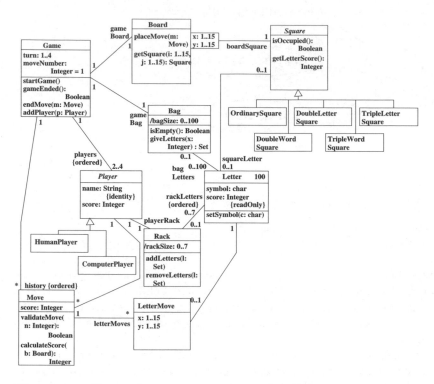

Figure 1.6: Extract from analysis model of Scrabble player

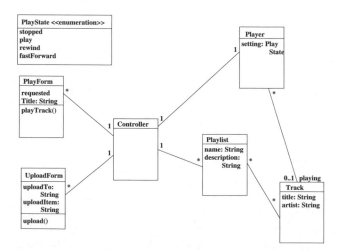

Figure 1.7: Analysis model of jukebox

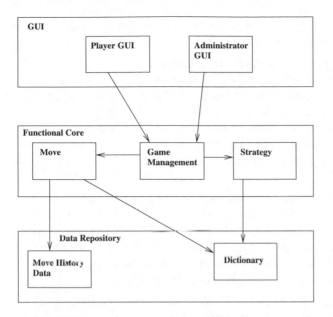

Figure 1.8: Architecture of Scrabble system

MDA may be applied only to the functional core of a system, which contains the business rules of the system, or to all tiers, provided suitable models of these tiers can be defined.

2. *Subsystem design*: decomposition of these global subsystems into smaller subsystems which each handle some well-defined subset of its responsibilities. This process continues until clearly identified *modules* emerge at the bottom of the subsystem hierarchy. A module typically consists of a single entity or group of closely related entities, and operations on instances of these entities.

3. *Module design*: define each of the modules, in terms of:

   (a) the data it encapsulates – eg: a list of attributes and their types or structures;

   (b) the properties (invariants or constraints) it is responsible for maintaining (ie, for ensuring that they are true whenever an operation is not in progress);

   (c) the operations it provides (external services) – eg: their names, input and output data, and specifications. This is called the *interface* of the module.

4. *Detailed design*: for each operation of the module, identify the steps of its processing.

Specialised forms of design include *interface design*, to plan the appearance and sequencing of dialogs and other graphical interface elements for user interaction, and *database design*, to define the structure of a database for the system, and what queries/updates will take place on it.

Pure top-down design, in which a system is hierarchically divided into subsystems, and these in turn into further subsystems and modules, is an idealistic model which can lead to expensive backtracking and rework if applied without regular review. The structure of the design may need to evolve as experience with prototypes of the system grows, for example, and the hierarchical structure may lead to duplication of effort (eg, two teams developing different parts of the system could create similar modules, which a review may detect and merge into one module).

For the Scrabble player, design could partition the system into a GUI to manage the display of the board and racks (bearing in mind the constraint that only the rack of the current turn player should be visible), a module to check the correctness of moves, and (the most technically challenging) a module to generate moves automatically. There will also be data management modules, to hold dictionary data and game history data (Figure 1.8).

For the jukebox, design will identify the client and server program components required: the components to be executed on the client will essentially be web pages containing forms, the server components will be modules handling requests from these pages and performing actions on the database of tracks, and controlling the downloading of tracks. User interface design would sketch out the appearance and format of the interface, for example, to imitate the appearance of a real jukebox (Figure 1.9).

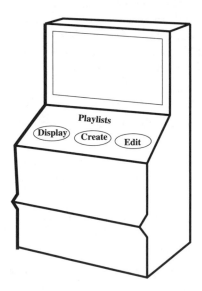

Figure 1.9: Interface design of jukebox

1.3.5 Implementation

This stage produces an executable version of the system by translating the design modules into program language code. Implementation may initially be performed for a small part of the system which acts as a 'template' or 'proof of concept' for the remainder of the implementation.

For the Scrabble player, implementation of the dictionary could consist of representing it as a set of word sets $a2$, $a3$, ..., $a15$, $b2$, ..., $z15$, where each an is the set of words that contain the letter α, and that are of length n. This facilitates lookup of candidate moves for the computer (eg, to find all words of four letters containing 'b', 'r', 'k' and 'i', the intersection $b4 \cap r4 \cap k4 \cap i4$ would be constructed and searched).

For the jukebox, a particular streaming server would be adopted, and the database design implemented in tables in a particular database. The server processing components could be implemented as Servlets [44] or as JSP [23] files, etc.

1.4 Summary

In this chapter we have given an overview of the issues currently affecting software development, and the main processes of software development have been described. In the following chapter we introduce the UML notation and show how it may be used throughout development.

Chapter 2

The Unified Modelling Language

In this chapter we introduce the UML as a means of precisely expressing requirements, analysis models and designs, in a platform-independent manner.

2.1 Introduction

The UML [51] is the result of a successful unification of the many object-oriented analysis and design notations which arose during the 1980s and 1990s. In 1994 work began on unifying the widely-used OMT [42] and Booch [6] methods into what became UML, with OOSE [22] also integrated in 1995. From version 1.1 UML was endorsed by the Object Management Group (OMG), representing many companies and organisations, as a standard for object-oriented analysis and design, and it has now become the primary notation in this field. A major revision of UML, to version 2.0, was published in 2004. UML consists of a large number of different modelling notations:

- Use case diagrams;
- Class diagrams;
- Object diagrams;
- Statecharts;
- Collaboration diagrams;
- Sequence diagrams;
- Activity diagrams;
- Deployment diagrams.

In addition, there is the Object Constraint Language (OCL) which enables precise assertions to be made about elements of particular UML models.

All these notations form different views of a software system, which are intended to be complementary and consistent with each other. Some notations are much more complex than others, for example the use case notation is used at the requirements definition stage of development and so does not express much detail in terms of the internal functioning of the system. In contrast,

14

class diagrams and statecharts may be used at any development stage and are very expressive languages which can describe a level of detail close to that of program code.

In this book we will focus on class diagrams and statecharts as the most generally useful UML notations, especially when enhanced with OCL assertions.

2.2   Use case diagrams

A use case model [22] describes (1) the system to be constructed, (2) the *actors* – representing a role played by a person or other entity that interacts with the system, and (3) the *use cases* – families of usage scenarios of the application, grouped into coherent cases of functionality. A use case is a generalisation of the scenarios of use of the system: technically, a scenario is an *instance* of a use case.

Figure 2.1 shows a generic use case diagram, where actor *A* participates in two use cases and actor *B* in one. The arrows indicate the direction of interaction – this is not part of official UML use case notation but can be helpful in indicating the intention of the use case. Figure 2.2 gives the use

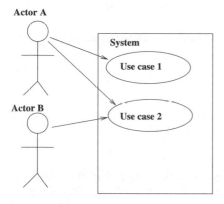

Figure 2.1: Simple use case model

cases for a share management system, where price changes are informed to the system from a stock exchange, and the trader using the system may receive alerts from it when share price changes pass some preset limits. The trader can also use the system to sell shares.

Use cases can have additional textual descriptions. A complete textual description of a use case includes:

1. *Summary* – description of the purpose of the use case.
2. *Start of the use case* – the trigger event: 'the use case begins when *e* occurs'.

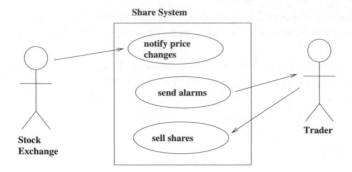

Figure 2.2: Share system use cases

3. *End of the use case* – the termination event: 'when *f* occurs the use case terminates'.
4. *Interaction between the use case and the actors* – this identifies what activities should be inside the system and which outside.
5. *Exchanges of information* – what data items are passed between the system and the actors.
6. *Chronology and origin of information* – identifies when the system requires internal or external information and when it records it.
7. *Repetitions of behaviour.*
8. *Optional situations* – points where an actor or the system may choose different behaviours within the use case.
9. *Capacity* – number of concurrent executions of the use case that the system may have to handle.

An example from the Scrabble project could be the use case for a human player making a move, which has agent *HumanPlayer*, and the detailed description:

- *Summary:* A complete move by a human player, involving the letter-by-letter construction of a new word or words on the board. The move is checked for validity when it is completed, and the board is permanently updated if it is valid, and the player's score incremented.
- *Initiation event:* Player presses 'start move' button when it is their turn and the game has not finished.
- *Termination event:* Player presses 'end move' button.
- *Interaction:* Player clicks on an enabled letter button in their rack and then on a vacant square on the board, to move the letter from the rack to the square. The rack letter button and the square button are disabled by the system and the letter is shown on the square button.
- *Exchanges of information:* The system informs the player if their move is an error, otherwise it gives the score when the move is completed.
- *Repetitions:* Individual letter moves are performed until the whole move is complete.

- *Optional situations:* The system may reject a move, if the letter moves are not co-linear and connected, or if (for the first move) the move does not include the centre square, or (for later moves) if it does not cover a square adjacent to a square that was already occupied by a letter before the move began.
- *Capacity:* 1.

Use case diagrams can also express relationships of *inclusion* and *extension* between use cases:

Includes Use case *uc*1 *includes* use case *uc*2 if doing *uc*1 always involves doing *uc*2. This relationship is particularly useful if *uc*2 is a common subtask of two or more use cases: an example of *factoring* out functionality from several locations and placing it in a single component.

For example, in the jukebox, editing a playlist and viewing a playlist both involve retrieving it from the playlist database server. In the Scrabble game, verifying a human player move and generating a computer player move both involve looking up a word in the dictionary (Figure 2.3 shows the notation for inclusion and extension relationships between use cases).

Extends Use case *uc*1 *extends* use case *uc*2 if *uc*1 provides additional functionality that may be used to carry out *uc*2 in certain cases. For example, calculating a bonus score in Scrabble could be an extension of a calculate score use case (Figure 2.3).

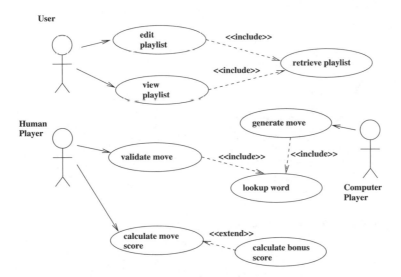

Figure 2.3: Inclusion and extension of use cases

The direction of the arrows in this notation illustrates a common principle that is used across all the UML notations: an arrow from model element *me*1 to model element *me*2 indicates that *me*1 depends on *me*2 in some sense, eg, by

*me*1 invoking operations of *me*2 or by referring to its data. In the case of
≪ include ≫, the use case at the source of the arrow depends on the functionality of the use case at the target. For ≪ extend ≫, the use case at the source
only has a meaning with respect to the use case it extends (the use case at the
target).

A use case may also depend on another, for example by needing a result
produced by another use case before it can operate itself. This type of relationship could be indicated by an unspecialised dependency arrow (dashed line,
≪ *use* ≫ stereotype).

One use case may inherit another, if it is a specialised form of the other.
One actor may also inherit from another actor, this means that the specialised
actor can participate in all the use cases of its ancestor, and possibly additional
use cases. Figure 2.4 shows an example of actor inheritance: the *Administrator*
actor (in an estate agency system) can perform all the use cases that a *Staff*
can, but in addition can modify *Staff* data.

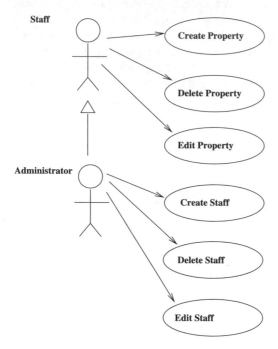

Figure 2.4: Inheritance of use case actors

2.3   Class diagrams

Class diagrams represent the classes (the types of objects) in a system, together
with relationships that exist between them. Class diagrams can be used at
different stages of development:

- Conceptual modelling of the problem domain, possibly including entities that are external to the final developed system, but that interact with it.
- Analysis modelling, recording in a precise but implementation-independent manner the agreed requirements of the system.
- Design modelling, detailing the design structures of the system, dependencies between classes, etc.

Generally more detail is introduced at successive levels. The earlier models should ideally be *declarative*, emphasising *what* the system will do, free from implementation details of *how* it will achieve these functionalities.

Figure 2.5 shows a very small extract from the class diagram of the Scrabble system, in which there are two classes, *Letter* and *Bag*, and a relationship *Bag_Letter* between them, representing the fact that between 0 to 100 letters may be contained in the Scrabble bag at any point in time. This simple model

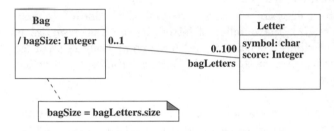

Figure 2.5: Class diagram of letters and bags

has four kinds of element in it[1]:

- *Classes*, represented as rectangles with the name of the class at the top of the rectangle. For example: *Letter*.
  Class names are normally written in bold face, begin with a capital letter and are centred in their rectangle.
- *Attributes*, represented inside the box of the class to which they belong, and written as *name : type* where *name* is the attribute name, and *type* its type. For example: *symbol* is an attribute of *Letter*, describing the printable character of the letter, and so it has type *char*.
  Attribute names should start with a lowercase letter.
- *Relationships*, represented as lines between classes. The UML term for the simple form of relationship shown here is *association*. Associations have names, by default we will take this to be $C_1\_C_2$ where C_1 and C_2 are the names of the classes at the ends of the association. Each end of the association can have:
  - A multiplicity indication, defining how many objects of the class at that end of the association can be associated, via the association, at any one time with a single object of the class at the other end.

---

[1]These four elements are the only UML notation needed for purely declarative UML class diagrams.

      – A role name, or association end name, by which the collection of
objects at this end, associated with a single object at the other, can
be named.

In the example, *Bag_Letter* is an association, with two ends:

      – The *Bag* end has multiplicity 0..1 (for each letter there is either no
bag associated to it – if it is not in a bag – or one – if it is in a bag).
There is no role name at this end.

      – The *Letter* end has multiplicity 0..100 (each bag can contain between
0 and 100 letters) and a role name *bagLetters*. If *b* is a *Bag*,
b.bagLetters refers to the set of letters in the bag.

- *Constraints*, written in 'dog-eared' boxes and attached to the elements
they constrain by dashed lines. Constraints give detailed properties that
the model is intended to satisfy.

  In the example the constraint on *Bag* says that the value of *bagSize*
  is always *bagLetters.size*, the number of letters in the bag. *bagSize* is
  termed a 'derived attribute', because it is defined completely in terms of
  the values of other features of the model. Such attributes are prefixed
  with / on the diagram.

The easiest way to think about the meaning of a class diagram is in terms
of sets of objects. Figure 2.5 describes some properties of the sets of *Letter*
and *Bag* objects in the Scrabble system, and how these objects relate to each
other. Figure 2.6 illustrates one possible arrangement of objects that is allowed
by the class diagram. There are two *Bag* objects, *b*1 and *b*2, and ten *Letter*
objects. Five letters are associated with *b*1 and three with *b*2. Two letters do
not belong to any bag. The symbol and score of each letter object are written
on it, and the size of a bag is written in it.

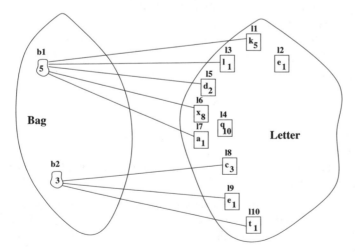

Figure 2.6: Example of letter and bag model

An attribute of an object is a property that is permanently attached to it, and cannot be removed. So each letter object *lett* will always have a *symbol*, written as *lett.symbol* 'the symbol of *lett*', and this will be a character. Also, each letter object will have an integer *score*: *lett.score*. The values of these attributes may change over time (a blank square in Scrabble can be assigned a symbol of any letter before it is placed on the board, in particular), but each letter must have *some* value for each of its attributes. An attribute is rather like a function in this respect: given an object, *obj*, *obj.att* will evaluate to a particular value, if *att* has been declared to be an attribute of the class of *obj*. This value will be in the declared type of *att*.

Rule

If *att* : *T* is listed in a class diagram as an attribute of class *C*, and *obj* is an object of *C*, then *obj.att* is a value of type *T*.

Attributes may be defined as *derived*, meaning that their values can be determined from the values of other features of the class. For example, *bagSize* is a derived attribute of *Bag*, defined to have value *bagLetters.size*, the number of letters of the bag. Derived attributes are written with a forward slash / preceding their name.

Finally, we can give default initial values to attributes. These are written after the type and an = sign in the attribute declaration, for example

$$moveNumber : Integer = 1$$

in *Game* in Figure 1.6. The value of the attribute is set to the default initial value on creation of a new object of the class, unless a more specific constructor operation is used.

At each point in time there will be a set of instances of each class. In Figure 2.6 the set of *Bag* instances is $\{b1, b2\}$, for example. An association is also a set, a set of pairs or *links* of objects of the classes at the ends of the association. In the above example *Bag_Letter* has the value

$$\{b1 \mapsto l1, b1 \mapsto l3, b1 \mapsto l5, b1 \mapsto l6,$$
$$b1 \mapsto l7, b2 \mapsto l8, b2 \mapsto l9, b2 \mapsto l10\}$$

$x \mapsto y$ denotes a link between x and y.

This value for the association obeys the multiplicity assertions on the association ends: each letter is associated with zero or one bag (no letter is associated to both $b1$ and $b2$), and each bag is associated with at most 100 letters (in fact, no more than five).

Like attributes, role names are also functions, but they can yield, for each object at *the other end* of the association, a set of objects at their own end – the set of all those objects that are associated to the object at the opposite end. For example

$$b1.bagLetters = \{l1, l3, l5, l6, l7\}$$
$$b2.bagLetters = \{l8, l9, l10\}$$

The role name describes the role played in the association by the class at its end.

The concepts of attribute and association end are quite similar, and have been converged into the concept of a *property* in UML 2.0.

Rule

If an association between classes C_1 and C_2 is given in a class diagram, and there is a role r at the C_2 end, then for each object *obj* of C_1, *obj.r* is a set of C_2 objects. If the multiplicity at the C_2 end is 1, *obj.r* is considered to be a single C_2 object.

Common mistake: putting the multiplicities on the wrong end of an association. They must go on the end nearest the class whose number of instances in the relation are being constrained. A role name must go on the association end *opposite* to the class of which it is a property.

The multiplicity constraints can define any interval of natural numbers (possibly with no upper bound). The following standard notations are used to describe these sets (Table 2.1).

UML Notation	Meaning
*	any number of objects allowed (including zero)
1..*	at least one object
1	exactly one object
n	exactly n objects
a..b	at least a and at most b

Table 2.1: Multiplicity annotations

The most common form of association is a *many-one* association, with a $*$ multiplicity at one end and a 1 multiplicity at the other. Such an association acts like a function of the class at the many end, associating to each instance of this class *exactly one* instance of the class at the other. Figure 2.7 shows another example of a simple class diagram, with two many-one associations.

Figure 2.7: Employment class diagram

This model contains a self-association on *Person*, associating to each person their boss (and, in the other direction, their set of subordinates). The other association maps each person to the company they work for, and each company to its set of employees.

Figure 2.8 gives an example of a situation that satisfies this diagram: there are five persons, of which $p5$ and $p1$ are their own boss, $p2$ has boss $p1$ and $p3$ and $p4$ have boss $p2$. $p5$ works for company $c2$, the others work for company $c1$. The arrows point in the direction of the 1-multiplicity association ends.

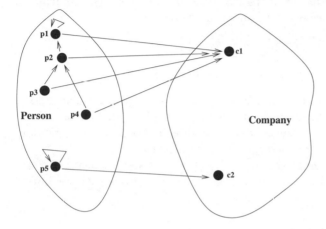

Figure 2.8: Example of Person-Company situation

Associations can also be derived, in this case the role names of the association are written with a prefix '/' in the class diagram.

Associations can have a *navigation direction*, indicating the direction in which the system is expected or intended to navigate. This is indicated by putting an arrow on the end of the association which will be navigated to (Figure 2.9). This means that an instance of *Board* can refer to and call

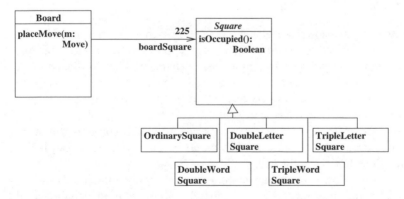

Figure 2.9: Navigation example

methods on instances of its squares, but that the squares are not expected to refer to/invoke methods on their board. Arrows can be placed on both ends if bidirectional reference is required (this should usually be avoided as it complicates system logic). An association without arrows on either end simply means that no information about navigation is being provided (eg, because it is not yet known or has not yet been decided). Explicitly forbidding navigation in a direction can be achieved by placing a diagonal cross on the end to which navigation is not possible.

If class *A* can call operations of class *B* via a navigable association from *A* to *B*, then *A* is termed a *client* of *B*, and *B* is a *supplier* of *A*.

2.3.1   Operations

In addition to attributes, classes may have *operations* or *methods*. The attributes and operations/methods together make up the explicit *features* of a class. Operations are used to specify the behaviour of objects of a class, in particular, how they respond to events or messages directed at them.

Operations are listed in a section of the class rectangle beneath the attributes (Figure 2.10). Operation names are usually written with an initial

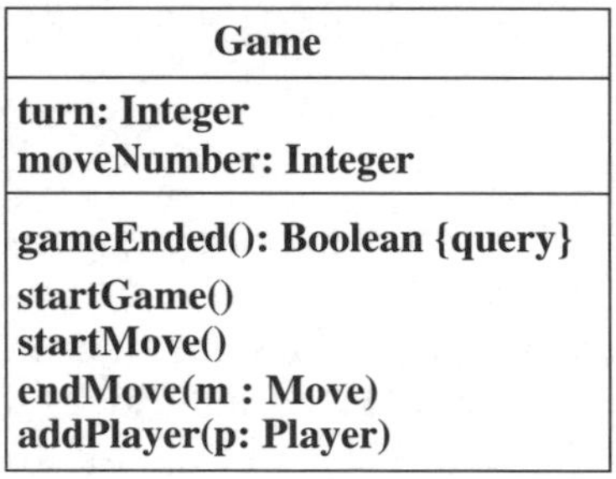

Game
turn: Integer   **moveNumber: Integer**
gameEnded(): Boolean {query}   **startGame()**   **startMove()**   **endMove(m : Move)**   **addPlayer(p: Player)**

Figure 2.10: Operation example

lowercase letter. Operations can either be *query*, if they do not modify the internal state of the object, or *update*, if they do. Query operation declarations can be written with a {*query*} constraint beside them, on a class diagram. A query operation usually returns some property of the object state, and is quite similar to a (derived) attribute in this respect. If *g* is a *Game* object in Figure 2.10, then *g.gameEnded*() is a boolean value, for example.

In contrast, *startGame*() is an update operation, which changes the state of the game it operates on, to initiate the game by choosing the first player, etc, but which does not return a value.

An operation can have input parameters, which supply information to it. Any number of input parameters can be listed, although it is usually good practice to try to minimise the number. *endMove*(*m* : *Move*) is an example of an operation with a parameter, it supplies the move *m* which has been constructed during the move, to the game, for evaluation of its validity and to update the game board and player scores if it is valid.

> **Rules**
> If $op(x : T) : S$ is a query operation of class C, *obj* is an object of C, and e is a value of type T, then *obj.op(e)* evaluates to a value of type S.
> If $op(x : T)$ is an update operation of class C, *obj* is an object of C, and e is a value of type T, then *obj.op(e)* represents the invocation of *op* with parameter e on *obj*.

The effect of an operation on the internal state of an object is usually specified by a *postcondition* constraint, as described in Chapter 3 below.

We will say that an operation is *declared* in a class if it is written, together with its parameters and their types, and its result type, if any, in the class box. It is *defined* in a class if in addition a specification of its effect is given in that class. Operations may be declared without being defined, this is particularly the case for *abstract* operations, discussed in Section 2.3.3 below.

2.3.2 Enumerations

An enumeration is a simple enumerated type, such as $\{on, off\}$ for the set of states of a switch. It is represented as a rectangle in a class diagram, with stereotype[2] $\ll$ *enumeration* $\gg$ and with its values listed. Figure 2.11 shows a basic example. If an enumeration E is defined in a class diagram then it can be used as the type of an attribute of a class in the diagram, for example *Direction* is used as the type of *orientation* in *Word* in Figure 2.11.

Figure 2.11: Enumeration example

2.3.3 Inheritance

The modelling of inheritance is one of the characteristic aspects of object-oriented notations, which distinguishes them from earlier modelling languages such as entity-relationship diagrams. Figure 2.12 shows a simple example of inheritance: there are two classes, *Player* and *HumanPlayer*, linked by an inheritance relationship. The meaning of this is that every *HumanPlayer* is

---

[2]A stereotype is a marker which may be placed on any model element, to indicate that it is a specialised kind of that element. Stereotypes are written between double angle brackets.

also a *Player*: inheritance corresponds to an 'is-a' relation between objects, in contrast to an association, which usually represents a 'has-a' relation. Semantically, the set of objects of *HumanPlayer* is always a subset of those of *Player*.

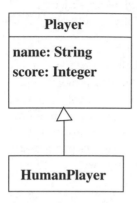

Figure 2.12: Player and Human Player

   Player is called the *superclass* and *HumanPlayer* the *subclass* in this relationship, and *HumanPlayer* is said to *inherit from Player*: each feature (attribute, operation or association) of *Player* is also implicitly a feature, with the same name and type, of *HumanPlayer*, and does not have to be repeated explicitly on the subclass.
   Common mistake: repeating all features of superclass on a subclass.
   Figure 2.13 shows an example of a situation that satisfies Figure 2.12. There are four *Player* objects, of which *p1*, *p3* and *p4* are also in *HumanPlayer*.

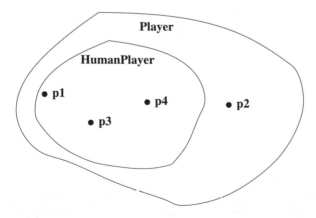

Figure 2.13: Player and Human Player example

   Classes may have several subclasses, for example in Figure 2.14, the class *Square* has five subclasses corresponding to the five different types of square on a Scrabble board: ordinary, double letter, triple letter, double word and triple word. All of these may have a letter on them, so the *Letter_Square* association only needs to be written once, on the superclass.

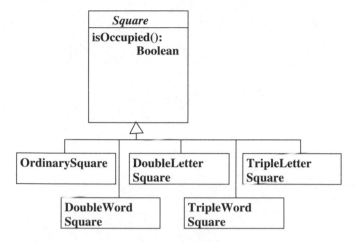

Figure 2.14: Subclasses of Square

Because *every* square must be one of these five kinds, the superclass *Square* itself has no direct instances (all its instances are actually also instances of *OrdinarySquare* or *DoubleLetterSquare*, etc). *Square* is termed an *abstract* class, and its name is written in italic/slanting font on the class diagram to indicate this. An abstract class cannot have direct instances created for it (cf, in Java, *new* $C(...)$ cannot be executed if C is abstract). Non-abstract classes are termed *concrete*.

Like associations, an inheritance is a special kind of relationship, indeed an inheritance can be thought of as a 0..1 to 1 association (Figure 2.15): for each instance of the subclass there is (it is) a corresponding instance of the superclass (cf the 'super' keyword in Java), and each superclass instance may correspond to (may also be) an instance of the subclass.

Abstract superclasses may have abstract operations, operations for which a specific definition cannot be given in the superclass, instead the individual subclasses will give their own definitions. For example, a superclass *Person* could have an abstract operation *alcoholLimit*() : *Integer* which returns the weekly alcohol limit of the person in units. In subclasses *Male* and *Female* this operation can be given specific definitions: to return 28 in the first case and 21 in the second. In such a situation the operation is written both on the superclass and on the subclass, since the subclass is providing a definition of the operation. An operation is also written in the class box if it redefines an ancestor definition. Abstract operations are written with italic font (Figure 2.16).

Cycles of inheritance are disallowed: if A inherits from B, then B cannot inherit directly or indirectly from A. *Multiple inheritance* means that a class may directly inherit from more than one other class, eg, *HouseBoat* inherits

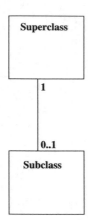

Figure 2.15: Subclassing as association

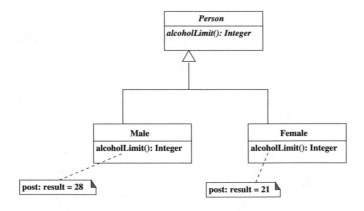

Figure 2.16: Defining methods in subclasses

from *Residence* and *WaterCraft*. UML permits this, but some languages, such as Java, restrict inheritance to *single inheritance*: where each class can only have at most one immediate superclass.

2.3.4   Ordered and qualified associations

The end of an association may have an annotation {*ordered*} beside it (see Figure 2.17), if the multiplicity at the end is not one. The *ordered* annotation means that the set of objects at the role end have an ordering on them, ie, they form a *sequence*, instead of an unordered set. Duplicates are not normally allowed in such a sequence, since association links are considered to be uniquely defined by the pair of objects that they connect.

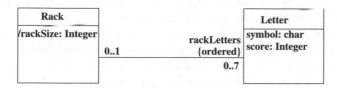

Figure 2.17: Ordered association

An ordered association end can be thought of as an array or list: the elements of the sequence occur in a definite order and can be referred to by their index in this order. In particular the value of *r.rackLetters* for a rack *r* is a sequence: the letters occur in some order left-to-right on the rack. Our notation for accessing the first element of a sequence is *r.rackLetters*[1], *r.rackLetters*[2] for the second, etc.

Associations may also be *qualified*, which means that they act like maps from a certain set of feature values, together with an object at one association end, to identify an object or set of objects at the other end. For example each square on the board of the Scrabble game has a unique *x*, *y* coordinate pair, so these can be used, given a board object, to specify the square. Figure 2.18 shows the notation for this. Given a board *b*, and $x : 1..15$, $y : 1..15$, the square with these coordinates is referred to as *b.boardSquare*[*x, y*].

If a qualified association role is used without qualifier values, then all objects associated at the role end are returned, regardless of index value. Thus *b.boardSquare* is the set of all squares on the board *b*. Similarly for ordered associations.

2.3.5   Aggregation and composition

A normal association represents the concept of 'has' between entities: 'a bag has between 0 and 100 letters', 'a player has a game', and inheritance represents the concept of 'is a': 'a human player is a player', 'a double word square is a square',

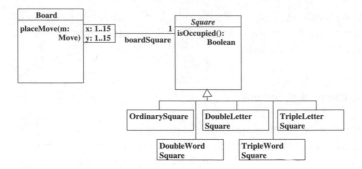

Figure 2.18: Qualified association

etc. UML also has a variation on associations which represents the concept of one object being a 'part of' another. For example 'a wheel is part of a car', or 'a square is part of a board'. The distinction between this form of association, called *aggregation* or *composition* and ordinary associations is that it expresses a binding/ownership between objects of one class and objects of another. The strong form of aggregation is termed *composition* and is represented by a filled diamond at the 'whole' (owner) end. It implies a constraint on the lifetimes of the linked objects: the parts cannot exist without the whole, and vice-versa. For example, a Scrabble board and its squares are strongly bound together in this manner.

UML also has a weaker concept, simple aggregation, represented by an open diamond at the 'whole' end. The meaning of this relationship is deliberately left open by the UML definition, so that modellers can use it as required. At most one end of an association can be an aggregation or composition.

A composition association from *A* (whole) to *B* (part) should be:

1. transitive (a part of a part is also a part of the whole)
2. irreflexive (an object can't be a part of itself)
3. one-many (no sharing of parts between different wholes)
4. deletion propagating from *A* to *B*: deleting a whole deletes all its parts.

Figure 2.19 shows the distinction between ordinary associations, aggregation and composition. The difference between (c) and (a) is that in (a) an object of *Cat* can only have one owner at any given time, but it may change to a different owner over the course of its life. In (c) a *Square* cannot move to a different board: it only exists while it is part of the board it was created with, and while that board exists.

2.4   Object diagrams

An object diagram is a variant of a class diagram in which *instance specifications* are drawn, representing detailed specifications of objects of particular

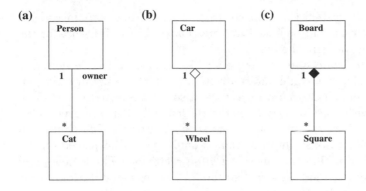

Figure 2.19: Association, aggregation and composition

classes. Both instance specifications and classes can be represented together in the same diagram. Instance specifications usually have a name and a class, and are represented in the diagram as a class rectangle with the name and class underlined, for example: *g : Game*. Inside the rectangle the value of attributes can be given by equalities. Figure 2.20 shows an example of an object diagram, representing the GUI of the Scrabble system, which specifies a *mainFrame : Frame* object and subordinate panels, buttons and labels linked to this. A line between instance specifications represents a description of an

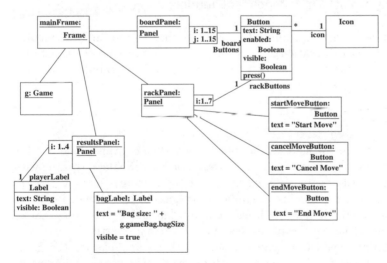

Figure 2.20: Object diagram of Scrabble GUI

instance of an association, that is, a link, or pair of objects in the association. Role names are not needed unless there is ambiguity about which association the link belongs to.

For example, the object specification of *startMoveButton* defines that this is an instance of *Button*, and has the value "Start Move" for its *text* attribute.

This means that in a system that satisfies this diagram, there should be such an object, and that it should be linked to a *rackPanel* object. Likewise for the other object specifications in the model.

There are usually many ways to express a situation in a class/object diagram. For example, we could alternatively model the *startMoveButton*, *cancelMoveButton* and *endMoveButton* as three associations from the *rackPanel* object to *Button*, with these rolenames on the *Button* end. This however makes the expression of button-specific constraints such as *text* = "*End Move*" on *endMoveButton* less obvious: the constraint would have to be placed on the association instead of within the *endMoveButton* rectangle. The benefits and drawbacks of alternative modelling choices should be considered during review and analysis steps in a development.

Common mistake: confusion between objects and classes, and object diagrams and class diagrams. Object diagrams only describe one particular arrangement of specific objects of classes, each class diagram could have a large number of object diagrams which are instances of it, ie, that describe arrangements of objects and links that satisfy the class diagram properties.

Figures 2.6 and 2.13 can be directly recast as object diagrams that satisfy the class diagrams 2.5 and 2.12 respectively.

2.5   Creating a platform-independent model

The previous sections have introduced a large amount of notation for modelling systems – how can this notation be used in practice to create precise, detailed but platform-independent models of a system such as the Scrabble player?

2.5.1   Defining use cases

The first step is to go through all the information that is available about the requirements of the system, from documentation or 'stakeholders' (people with an involvement in the commissioning or use of the system), making this information systematic by defining a number of coherent and distinct use cases to describe the required functionalities, and by defining a class diagram to capture the conceptual entities of the system and their properties.

For the Scrabble system we can use the existing rulebooks for the game (summarised in Appendix A), together with practical experience of playing it, to determine that there are only a few basic operations:

Add player Add a new player, up to a total of four, the player must be given a unique name.

Start game For each player, randomly choose a letter from the bag. The player with the alphabetically lowest letter (blank being before 'a') is given the first turn. The selected letters are returned to the bag.

Choose letters The turn player is given a set of p random letters (or as many letters as are in the bag, if the bag has fewer letters than this in it), where $p = 7 - r$ and r is their current rack size. The selected letters are placed on the rack.

Make move The turn player selects letters from their rack and places them on the board. The move is checked for validity and committed to the board if valid, and the player's score is updated.

End game Occurs when the bag is empty and one of the players has an empty rack, or by agreement between the players. The final score of each player is decreased by the sum of the letters remaining on their rack – the player who has an empty rack gets their score increased by all the letters from the other players.

Figure 2.21 shows the use cases. We have divided the make move use case into two, since the behaviour in the human and computer player cases will be quite different.

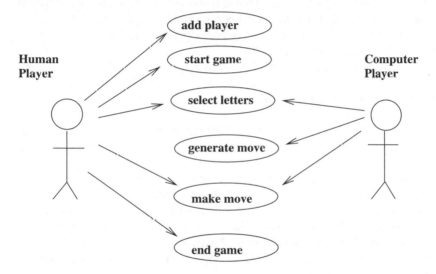

Figure 2.21: Use cases for Scrabble player

2.5.2 Defining entities and associations

For the data model, the first step is to identify the entities in the system – a basic way of doing this is to list the nouns in the requirements statement and discard those that are non-specific to the system. For the Scrabble system the key nouns appear to be:

> player, game, score-keeper, score, turn, score sheet, tile, bag, blank, rack, board, word, square, line, dictionary, double letter square,

centre square, row, column, premium square, triple word square, double word square.

The software itself will play the role of the score-keeper and score sheet, so these entities are not explicitly needed. Score and turn are attributes rather than entities in their own right (each player and played word has a score, for example). There are many kinds of square mentioned, suggesting already that inheritance will be useful to describe these.

Having identified the main candidates for entities, we can start to determine what attributes and properties they have, and what relationships they have with each other:

Board: Consists of 15 by 15 squares, with certain positions identified as premium squares of various kinds (Figure 2.22). Therefore there is an association to the *Square* entity of multiplicity 225 at the *Square* end and 1 at the *Board* end.

Square: Several kinds are needed: ordinary, double letter, double word, triple letter, triple word. Each has a different visual icon (an attribute or association of *Square*) and each may contain a tile (an association from *Square*, 0..1 at the *Tile* end).

Tile: Each is marked with a letter 'a' through to 'z' plus a blank, and with a score (integer 0..10). These are both attributes of a tile. There are exactly 100 tiles, with the number of each letter specified (eg, 12 'e's in English Scrabble).

Rack: One for each player. A rack may hold up to seven tiles (ie, there is an association to *Tile* of multiplicity 0..7 at the *Tile* end). There must be an operation to add a set of tiles to a rack.

Bag: Initially contains all 100 tiles. It must have an operation to remove and output randomly-selected sets of tiles from itself.

Game: Has between two to four players, one board and one bag (associations from *Game* to these entities). There is a current turn player once the game has started (an association to *Player*).

Player: Has a rack (association) and a score (attribute). Can be either a human or computer player.

Dictionary: Contains a set of words, which is used to decide if a played word is valid – so it must have a *lookup*(*w* : *Word*) : *Boolean* operation.

Putting all these facts together, we can draw an initial class diagram (Figure 2.23).

To refine this model we consider what other information and properties will be needed in the software system (as opposed to what information is present in the physical board game). For example, it will be useful for each player to be given a name, so their score can be displayed on the system GUI. In addition, one of the requirements specified that a history of moves should be kept, so this needs to be added as an extra association from *Game*. Attribute types could be made more precise, for example the score of a tile must be between 0 and 10, so we could write *score* : 0..10 in the *Tile* class. This could be over-specific,

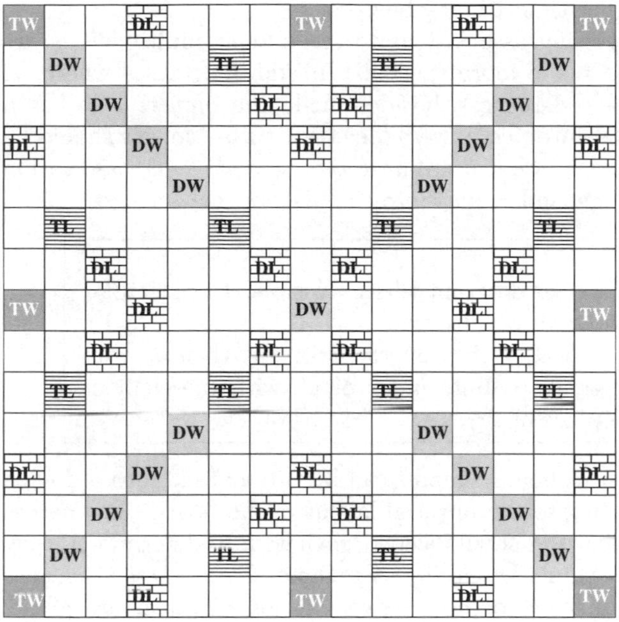

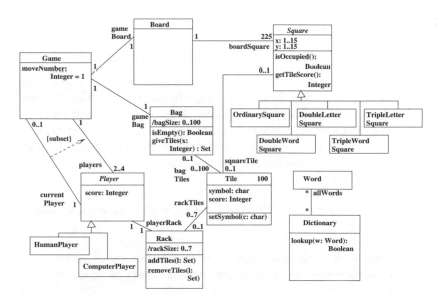

Figure 2.22: Scrabble board

Figure 2.23: Initial Scrabble class diagram

however, preventing our specification being used for non-English versions of Scrabble where scores higher than 10 may be possible.

We should examine existing associations to see if their multiplicities are precise enough, or can be made more specific. In addition, cases where an association end should be ordered can be identified: the *players* role has a natural ordering – the order in which players take their turn – so this should be documented. Having done this we can optimise the *currentPlayer* association and replace it with an integer index *turn* into the *players* sequence.

Guideline
Simplify the data of a class diagram where possible. In particular if a class C has an ordered role dr_1 from itself to a class D, and a 1-multiplicity role dr_2 to D, with property $dr_2 : dr_1$, then dr_2 can be replaced by an integer attribute *index* of C, with the element $dr_1[index]$ taking the place of dr_2.

Similarly, the linear list of board squares can be rationalised into a double array structure corresponding to the physical layout of the board. The names used for classes and class features should also be reviewed, to determine if they can be improved. In this system we decide to rename *Tile* to *Letter* because 'tile' is a technical term specific to the physical version of the board game, which is not as implementation-independent or as generally comprehensible as the name 'letter'.

Figure 2.24 shows the class diagram after these rationalisations.

2.6   Exercises

1 Draw a use case diagram and class diagram to represent the following system.

- Over the summer holiday, university students can book college hall accommodation online. They must specify their name, student number, course, year, and identify three college residences as their preferences.
- The system makes an allocation of students to rooms before the start of term, trying, where possible, to allocate students to a room in one of their preferred halls.

2 Is it possible to create an object of class A in Figure 2.25? Give an argument to justify your answer.

3 In Figure 2.26, what is the maximum number of users that can be given aliases, given that each user has five aliases, and there are at most 100 user names available?

4 Draw a class diagram for a conservatory design system: this system enables the planning of proposed conservatories in terms of their dimensions (height,

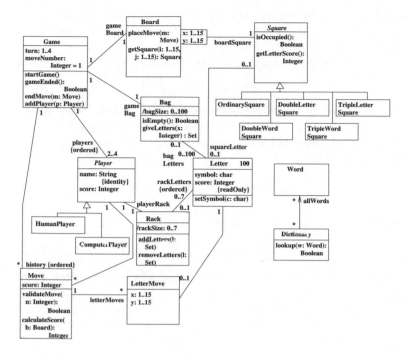

Figure 2.24: Refined Scrabble class diagram

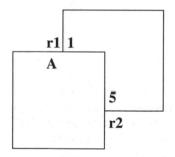

Figure 2.25: Self association

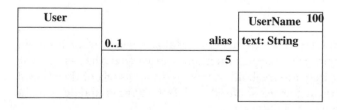

Figure 2.26: Users and aliases

width and depth, all in millimetres), style (Victorian or Contemporary), glass
type (single or double glazed) and number of doors. Each conservatory will be
constructed from a number of modules, which can be either door, window or
wall modules, and which have a fixed height and width, and a style and glass
type (as for conservatories).

5 Draw a class diagram for a conference centre booking system, which allows
customers to book conference rooms for specified time slots (given by a date
and start and end time). A room has an integer capacity and a set of facilities,
such as projectors and PA.

6 Express Figure 2.8 as an object diagram.

7 Express Figure 2.13 as an object diagram.

8 Define a use case diagram for the following ambulance dispatch system:

- The system receives notification from the emergency services when a new
  incident occurs requiring ambulance attendance.
- The system then tries to find a free ambulance which is sufficiently near
  to the incident and then to a hospital so that the patients can be delivered
  to hospital within 30 minutes (15 for a serious emergency).
- If an ambulance can be found, the one with the shortest distance to the
  incident is dispatched.
- Ambulance crews notify the system when they reach an incident and
  complete their journey delivering the patients to hospital, and on return
  to their ambulance station.

9 Draw a class diagram for a multi-language translation dictionary, which
represents words in (for example) English, Russian, Spanish, French, etc, and
records which words translate to which others. A word consists of a sequence of
letters, and a letter has a symbol. A word has properties such as the language
to which it belongs, its gender (some languages have two or three 'genders'
for their words), the *case* of the word (eg, imperative case for words that issue
commands), and the *tense* of the word (eg, future, past, etc). A translation may
have a *hint* string, which is supposed to help the user remember the translation.
Eg, the translation of the Russian word безобразный into the English 'ugly'
could have the hint 'Beelzebub', which is approximately what the Russian word
sounds like.

10 Draw a class diagram for an estate agents' database, which records details
of properties, their asking price and the minimum price that the vendor will
accept, their location, if they are freehold or not, and the details of their seller.
The size of the property in metres squared and feet squared should also be
given (one square metre is ten square feet).

The contents of the property are described as a set of *spaces*, which can be
either rooms, hallways, roof terraces, garden areas, outbuildings, etc. Each has

a textual description, possibly a photograph, and a size specification (width and depth in metres and feet).

11 What are the multiplicities of the role ends (both called *spouses*) of an association representing the relationship of marriage (under UK or USA law), between subclasses *Male* and *Female* of *Person*?

What additional constraint should be added if the association is viewed as a self-association on *Person*?

Chapter 3

The Object Constraint Language

In this chapter we describe the UML constraint language, OCL, and a subset, LOCA, of OCL. OCL is a means to express more complex properties of diagram elements, and interrelationships between elements. OCL is defined for version 2.0 of the UML [34], and this is the version we will base our own constraint language, LOCA, on.

3.1 Using OCL and LOCA Constraints

In a class diagram, constraints are used to:

1. Express invariants of classes – properties relating the attributes and rolenames of the class, which are expected to be true for each object of the class, at all times when the object is not executing a method.
2. Express preconditions of operations of a class – properties of the object responding to the operation, and of the operation input parameters, which are required to be true when it starts execution.
3. Express postconditions of operations of a class – properties of the object responding to the operation, and of the operation output parameter *result*, if present, which are required to be true when the operation completes execution.

To these we add a further category:

- Properties which relate the state of several classes, in particular, the states of objects of these classes which are linked by specific associations between them.

Full OCL notation is itself a complex language [34] which contains four different forms of collection: sets, ordered sets (sequences without duplicates), sequences and bags (multisets), many operations on these and on single valued data, quantifiers, and the capability for auxiliary and recursive definitions. Here we will use a simplified subset of OCL which is adequate for most purposes.

Table 3.1 shows the syntax of this subset, which is known as *LOCA* (Logic of Objects, Constraints and Associations). A *valueseq* is a comma-separated

< value >	::=	< ident > | < number > | < string > | < boolean >
< objectref >	::=	< ident > |
		< objectref >.< ident > |
		< objectref > | (< expression >)
< arrayref >	::=	< objectref > |
		< objectref >[< value >]
< factor >	::=	< value > | { < valueseq > } |
		Sequence{ < valueseq > } | < arrayref > |
		< factor > op1 < factor >
< expression1 >	::=	< factor > op2 < factor >
< expression >	::=	< expression1 > | (< expression >) |
		< expression1 > op3 < expression >
< invariant >	::=	< expression > |
		< expression > => < expression >

Table 3.1: LOCA syntax

sequence of values, an *op1* is a factor-level operator such as $+$, $-$, $*$, $/$, $\,\hat{}\,$, $/\backslash$ or $\backslash/$, an *op2* is a comparator: $=$, $/=$, $>$, $>=$, $<$, $<=$, $:$, $/\,:$, $<:$ or $/<:$, an *op3* is $\&$, *or*.

There are also several built-in constraints for class diagrams, expressed as keywords written between curly brackets. {*ordered*} and {*query*} are two examples we've already seen. Table 3.2 lists some others, and what model elements they apply to. To indicate that a class or operation is abstract, its name is written in italic font. To indicate that an attribute or operation has class scope (ie, it is static), its name and type are underlined in a class diagram.

An example of the union constraint could be an association from a *Letter* to a *Container* in the Scrabble system (Figure 3.1), where *Container* generalises *Rack*, *Bag* and *Square*, and the *Letter_Container* association is the union of the specific 'containment' associations between letters and their containers. What this expresses is that each letter can be held in *only* one of these three locations. Formally:

$$holds = rackHolds \,\backslash/\, bagHolds \,\backslash/\, squareHolds$$

is an invariant of *Letter*. The notation {*subsets holds*} expresses the subset constraint. A union association is analogous to an abstract class: each link in the union association must actually be a member of one of its subset associations (italic font could be used for such 'abstract' roles to emphasise this, perhaps).

We will also use additional constraints, defined in Table 3.3.

We will use *subset* as a constraint between association ends at the same class to indicate that the set of objects at one end is always a subset of those at the other, and use *disjoint* on association ends to indicate that two association

Keyword	Constrains	Meaning
subset	two associations r_1, r_2	Every link in r_1 is in r_2.
addOnly	an association end	Objects cannot be removed from the end.
union	an association	Association is union of all associations that subset it.
query	an operation	Operation does not modify object state.
unique	a multivalued attribute or role	The value of the feature (a collection) has no duplicates.
readOnly	attribute or role	The element cannot be modified after it is initially set. UML 1.*: 'frozen'.
abstract	class operation	Has no instances of its own. Has no implementation in this class.
leaf	class operation	The class cannot have any subclasses. Operation cannot be overridden in any subclass.
sequential	operation class	Concurrent executions of operation should not occur on a particular object. Only one operation of the class should be executing at any time on any specific object of the class.
static	attribute or operation	Feature belongs to class, not to object. That is, there is only one copy of it in the system, not one copy for each object of the class. UML 1.*: 'classScope'.

Table 3.2: Built-in constraints

Keyword	Constrains	Meaning
identity	an attribute	any two different objects of the class have different values of the attribute.
?	an attribute	attribute represents an input to system, eg, a sensor reading.
!	an attribute	attribute represents an output of system, eg, an actuator setting.

Table 3.3: Additional constraints

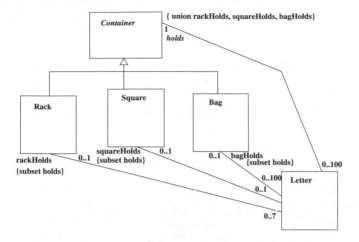

Figure 3.1: Example of union constraint

ends never have a common object at the same time: *bagLetters* is disjoint from *rackLetters* in Figure 3.2, for instance. We also define *cardinality* constraints on classes to indicate the total number of objects of the class (including objects of its subclasses) which can exist. This is written in the top right hand corner of the class. For example the total number of letters must be 100.

Examples of each of the general kind of constraints discussed above are shown on Figure 3.2.

Class invariants: The constraint *endx = startx or endy = starty* on *Word* means that a word object must be either vertical (the first case) or horizontal (the second).

Preconditions: The constraint *pre : score = 0* on *setSymbol(c : char)* expresses the fact that only the blank letter, which has score zero, can be used as any character.

Postconditions: The constraints

$$post : \quad squareLetter = \{\} \; => \; result = false$$
$$post : \quad squareLetter \; /= \; \{\} \; => \; result = true$$

on operation *isOccupied() : Boolean* of *Square* define the value of this query operation. *result* is a special keyword denoting the value returned by a query operation, it can only be used in the postcondition constraints of such operations.

Inter-class The constraint *{subset}* between the *wordsFormed* and *allWords* association ends, which enforces that all words constructed during an accepted move must be in the dictionary.

The final category of invariants are the most expressive and are usually necessary for the platform-independent specification of system functionality and business rules required by the MDA.

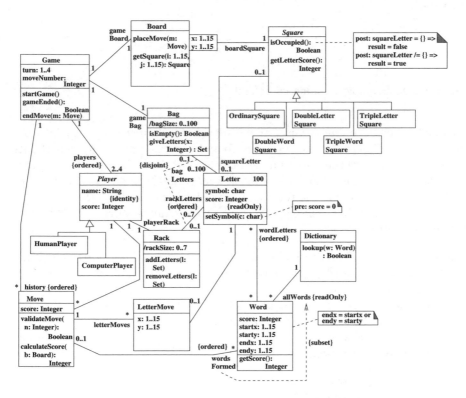

Figure 3.2: Constraints on Scrabble class diagram

As another example of the use of constraints, consider an e-commerce or m-commerce system which allows customers to order meals from a take-away restaurant by using the web or a mobile phone to connect to the restaurant (Figure 3.3). The structure of such a system would consist of three parts:

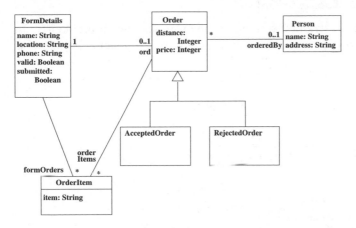

Figure 3.3: Take-away restaurant class diagram

1. client side GUI – consisting of an HTML or WML form that the customer fills in;
2. business rules – the business logic of the system, which enforce constraints such that meals will only be delivered within a radius of ten miles and for orders over fifteen pounds;
3. database – holding the set of current orders and their status.

Each of these parts can be abstractly specified using invariants:

1. constraints describing when a form is valid, ie, that a customer name, location, phone number and orders have been entered:

   ```
   name.size > 0 & location.size > 0 &
   phone.size > 0 &
   formOrders.size > 0  =>  valid = true
   ```

   as an invariant of *FormDetails*.
2. business rules defining when an order is acceptable:

   ```
   distance <= 10 & price >= 15
   ```

   as an invariant of *AcceptedOrder*, and that each valid submitted order will be accepted (this defines that the system must react to a customer pressing the SUBMIT button on the form):

   ```
   valid = true & submitted = true &
   ord.distance <= 10 &
   ord.price >= 15 => ord : AcceptedOrder
   ```

as an invariant of *FormDetails*.

3. Database integrity constraints:

```
orderedBy /= {}
```

as an invariant of *AcceptedOrder*.

We can also add constraints to some of the examples shown previously. In Figure 3.4 the constraint asserts that each person has the same employer as

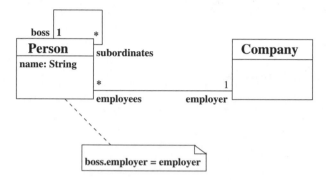

Figure 3.4: Employment class diagram with constraint

their boss. This constraint holds true in the example situation of Figure 2.8.

3.2   OCL operations

OCL has a number of types and operations on these types, which are also present in LOCA:

- The value *self*, which identifies the object being constrained.
- The type *Real*. This is the mathematical concept of real numbers, as opposed to computer approximations such as floating point numbers. Some operations on *Real* are, where $r1$ and $r2$ have values in *Real*:
  - Equality: $r1 = r2$ and inequality $r1 \; / = r2$
  - Arithmetic operators: $r1 + r2$, $r1 - r2$, $r1 * r2$, $r1/r2$
  - Comparators: $r1 < r2$, $r1 > r2$, $r1 <= r2$, $r1 >= r2$
  - Functions returning reals: $r1.abs$, the absolute value of $r1$; $r1.sqr$, the square of $r1$; $r1.sqrt$, the square root of $r1$
  - Functions returning integers: $r1.floor$; $r1.round$.
- The type *Integer*, representing the mathematical concept of integers. It is therefore a subtype (a subset) of *Real* and all the above operators and functions can be used with integers. The operator *div* represents integer division *div* when applied between two integers: a *div* b is the number of times that b fits into a, possibly with some remainder. Eg, 7 *div* 2 is 3. *mod* is the remainder operator between integers: 7 *mod* 2 is 1.

- The type *String*. Literal strings are written between double quotes, eg: "Java". If $s1$ and $s2$ are strings, then:
  - $s1 + s2$ is the concatenation of $s1$ followed by $s2$
  - $s1 = s2$ is true if the strings have exactly the same characters, in the same order
  - $s1.size$ is the number of characters in $s1$
  - $s1.toLower$ and $s1.toUpper$ return strings where all $s1$'s characters have been mapped to lower case and upper case respectively. Eg, *"Java".toLower* is *"java"* and *"Java".toUpper* is *"JAVA"*
  - The comparators $<$, $>$, etc can be used between strings: $s1 < s2$ holds if $s1$ lexicographically precedes $s2$, using a specified character set and ordering, eg, Unicode.

- The *Boolean* type, consisting of values *true* and *false* and with the usual operators & for conjunction, *or* for disjunction, $=>$ for implication.

Enumerated types defined in a UML model can be used in OCL expressions within the same model, as can class types defined in the model. The = operator on objects can be used: by default it means the objects are identical.

Collection types represent multiple data items grouped together. These can either be unordered and not allowing duplicates of elements within them (sets) or ordered and allowing duplicates (sequences). Two other kinds, *bags*, unordered and allowing duplicates, and *ordered sets*, ordered and not allowing duplicates, exist in OCL but will not be considered here. Ordered sets can be represented as sequences plus a constraint $sq.asSet.size = sq.size$ expressing the no duplicates property. Bags can be represented by sequences in which the ordering is disregarded.

The following operators apply to both sets and sequences:

- $s1 = s2$ – for sets this is true if the sets have exactly the same elements, for sequences the order of elements must also be identical (as with string equality)
- $s.size$ – the number of elements in the set or the length of the sequence s, depending on what s is
- $x : s$ – true if x occurs in s
- $x\ /\ : s$ – the negation of $x : s$
- $s1 <: s2$ – '$s1$ is a subset of $s2$' – true if every element of $s1$ occurs in $s2$
- $s1\ /\ <: s2$ – the negation of $s1 <: s2$
- $s.max$, $s.min$ for non-empty collections s of elements supporting comparator operators between themselves
- $s.sum$ for collections of elements supporting the + operator
- $s \mid P$ for a boolean-valued expression P which may use the feature names of objects in s. This is read as 's filtered by P' or 's select P'. If s is a set it returns the set of all elements in s that satisfy P. If s is a sequence it returns the subsequence of s of elements that satisfy P, retaining the same order that they had in s.

In a filter expression the objects being iterated over can be referenced using *self*. So, for example,

$$Integer \mid (self > 0)$$

is the set of positive integers.

On sets there are the special operators:

- $s1 \setminus / s2$ – the union of $s1$ and $s2$, the set that consists of all elements that are in either set. This can also be written as $s1 \cup s2$
- $s1 / \setminus s2$ – the intersection of $s1$ and $s2$, the set that consists only of those elements that are in both sets. This can also be written as $s1 \cap s2$
- $s1 - s2$ – the difference of the sets: $s1$ with all elements of $s2$ removed
- Literal sets are written between curly brackets: $\{x, y, z\}$ is a set with three elements.

For sequences there are the special operators:

- $s1 \frown s2$ – the sequence constructed by following all elements of $s1$ by those of $s2$
- $s[i]$ – the ith element of s, with numbering starting from 1 and ending at $s.size$
- $s.asSet$ – the set of elements in s, with ordering and duplicates discarded.
- Literal sequences are written as $Sequence\{v1, v2, ..., vn\}$ where $v1$ is the first element, $v2$ the second, etc.

Some examples of true formulae involving these operators are:

$$3 : \{5, 3, 6\}$$
$$4 \ / : \{5, 3, 6\}$$
$$\{6\} <: \{5, 3, 6\}$$
$$\{4, 6\} \ / <: \{5, 3, 6\}$$
$$\{5, 3, 6\}.sum = 14$$

Table 3.4 shows the correspondence between the standard OCL notation and LOCA. LOCA notation is closer to conventional mathematical notation and has been found to be easier to use than OCL as a specification and reasoning language.

3.3   Navigation expressions

A very important mechanism in OCL and LOCA are *navigation expressions*. These enable assertions to be made about compositions of associations and attributes across a diagram. There are two variants of these:

OCL	LOCA	Meaning
r1.max(r2)	{ r1, r2 }.max	Maximum of $r1$ and $r2$
set->union(set2)	set \/ set2	union of *set* and *set2*
set->intersection(set2)	set /\ set2	intersection of *set* and *set2*
set->includes(elem)	elem : set	test if *set* contains *elem*
set->including(elem)	set \/ { elem }	add *elem* to *set*
set->excludes(elem)	elem /: set	test if *set* does not contain *elem*
set->excluding(elem)	set - { elem }	remove *elem* from *set*
set->isEmpty()	set = {}	test if *set* has no elements
set->select(P)	set | (P)	those *set* elements that satisfy P
seq->at(i)	seq[i]	ith element of *seq*
C.allInstances()	C	set of all currently existing instances of class C

Table 3.4: Correspondence of OCL and LOCA

1. Object (or object set or sequence) references: *rolename* or

   obj.rolename

   where *obj* is an object or collection of objects, and *rolename* is a role name of an association, at the opposite end of the association to the class of *obj*/the class of the elements of *obj*. The result is the collection of all objects related by the association to *obj*/to any element of *obj*.

   For example, if *b* is a *Board* object, *b.boardSquare*[8, 8].*squareLetter* is the set of *Letter* objects on the centre square of *b* (this is either a singleton set or the empty set).

2. Value (or value set or sequence) references:

   obj.att

   where *obj* is an object reference evaluating to a single object or set or sequence of objects of a class C with attribute *att*. The result is the collection of *att* values of each of the objects in *obj*.

   For example, *m.letterMoves.x* is the collection of x-coordinate values of all letter moves of a *Move* object *m*.

   If *obj* denotes a sequence, then *obj.att* is a sequence, possibly with duplicate elements (Figure 3.5).

The following rules determine whether the result of a navigation expression is a set or sequence:

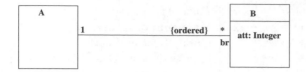

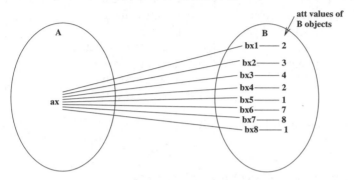

Figure 3.5: Object sequence navigation through an attribute

Rules

obj.role is a sequence if *role* is ordered and *obj* is a single object
or a sequence, or if *obj* is a sequence and *role* is single-valued. In
the case that both *obj* and *role* are ordered and many-valued, the
result is the concatenation of the *x.role* sequences for $x : obj$, in
the order that the *x* occur in *obj* (Figure 3.6):

$$obj[1].role \frown \ldots \frown obj[obj.size].role$$

obj.role is a set if *role* is set-valued (not ordered, and not of 1
multiplicity) or if *obj* is set-valued.
obj.att is a sequence if *obj* is a sequence. The order of *obj* is
preserved in the result.
obj.att is a set if *obj* is.

This means that if we want to form a sum of a collection, *objs.att*, and we
want duplicate values of *att* for different elements of *objs* to be summed, then
objs needs to be a sequence, otherwise the duplicate values will be discarded
in *objs.att*.

An example of a constraint using navigation expressions is

$$letterMoves.x.size = 1 \ or \ letterMoves.y.size = 1$$

as an invariant of *Move*. This states that the set of letters placed in the move
must either all have the same *x* coordinate (a vertical move) or all have the
same *y* coordinate (a horizontal move).

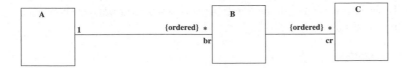

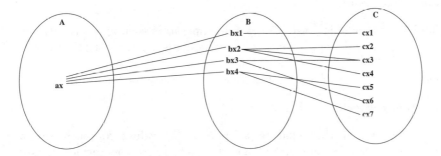

Figure 3.6: Object sequence navigation through ordered role

An invariant of *Game* which expresses that the initial move must include the centre square is:

$$8 : history[1].letterMoves.x \ \& \ 8 : history[1].letterMoves.y$$

The special keyword @*pre* can be appended to a feature name in operation *post* constraints (but not in any other constraints). f@*pre* refers to the value of f at the start of the operation, and is used to specify changes that the operation makes to f. For example:

```
addEmployees(c: Company, p: Person)
post: c.employees = c.employees@pre \/ { p } &
      p.employer = c
```

could be a specification of an operation to add a new employee to a company in the system of Figure 2.7.

Filter expressions allow constraints to be placed on subsets of associations. For example, in English-language Scrabble there can be at most twelve 'e' letters in the bag:

$$(bagLetters \mid (symbol = \ 'e')).size \ \leq \ 12$$

'The set of elements of *bagLetters* whose *symbol* is 'e' has size at most 12' as an invariant of *Bag*. In standard OCL notation this is:

$$bagLetters{\rightarrow}select(symbol = \ 'e'){\rightarrow}size() \ \leq \ 12$$

Alternatively, to avoid the use of filter or select completely, a new derived association *eLetters* could be defined, linking a bag to the 'e' letters within it.

As in OCL, we can treat single elements as sets when comparing them to a set: an equality such as

$$bagLetters.symbol = \,'e'$$

'every letter in the bag is an 'e", actually means

$$bagLetters.symbol = \{'e'\}$$

since the left hand side is a set. Comparator operators such as $<$ can also be used between sets and single values: $s < y$ where s is a set, means that $x < y$ for every x in s.

Query operations can be used in navigation expressions, for example

$$wordsFormed.getScore(b).sum$$

computes the sum of the separate $wd.getScore(b)$ values for each wd in $wordsFormed$, where b is the current board object. Query operations behave in the same way as attributes (if they have a single-valued result) or as *-multiplicity roles (if they have a collection as their result) with regard to the rules on ordering, so $wordsFormed.getScore(b)$ is a sequence of integers.

A set of useful algebraic laws relate filtering and navigation expressions, for example:

$$
\begin{aligned}
(x \cup y).f &= x.f \,\cup\, y.f \\
(x \cup y) \mid (P) &= x \mid (P) \,\cup\, y \mid (P) \\
x \mid (true) &= x \\
x \mid (false) &= \{\} \\
x \mid (P) \mid (Q) &= x \mid (P \,\&\, Q) \\
x \mid (P \,\&\, Q) &= x \mid (P) \,\cap\, x \mid (Q) \\
x \mid (P \; or \; Q) &= x \mid (P) \,\cup\, x \mid (Q)
\end{aligned}
$$

3.4   Quantifiers

OCL contains two *quantifier* expressions: $s \rightarrow forAll(P)$ and $s \rightarrow exists(P)$ for a collection s and predicate P.

These have the meanings:

$s \rightarrow forAll(P)$ 'P is true for every element of the collection s'.
$s \rightarrow exists(P)$ 'P is true for at least one element of the collection s'.

P typically involves features of the class of the objects of s, or navigation expressions starting from this class.

For example:

$$gameBag.bagLetters \rightarrow forAll(score \le 10)$$

says that every letter in the game bag has a score at most 10.

These expressions can be alternatively expressed using filtering:

$$s \rightarrow forAll(P) \quad \text{is the same as} \quad s \mid (P') = \{\}$$

where P' expresses the negation of P, or as $s \mid (P) = s$, or as $x : s \Rightarrow P(x)$ where features f of the class of elements of s, occurring in P, are replaced by $x.f$ in $P(x)$. x is a new variable.

So the above example of *forAll* could be written as

$$gameBag.bagLetters \mid (score > 10) = \{\}$$

or more simply as

$$gameBag.bagLetters.score \leq 10$$

$$s \rightarrow exists(P) \quad \text{is the same as} \quad s \mid (P) \; / = \{\}$$

A class invariant is implicitly quantified by *forAll* over the objects of the class: it is intended to hold for all of these objects. In LOCA, quantifiers can also be implicitly written by attaching a constraint to an association: the constraint is required to hold for all pairs of objects in the association.

3.5 Association constraints

Association constraints are constraints that are attached to one or more associations, instead of to classes (such as class invariants), or to operations (operation pre and postconditions). Association constraints can refer directly to the attributes of all the classes at the ends of the association(s), and so can express properties that span two or more classes – these properties, also called *inter-class constraints*, are asserted by the constraint to be true for all instances of the classes which are related at any particular time by the associations.

Although inter-class constraints are static in their form (ie, they refer to single time points and state), they are extremely powerful and expressive as a means of specifying functionality and dynamic behaviour, in a platform-independent manner. For example, consider the class diagram of Figure 3.7, showing part of a PIM for a home security system.

Figure 3.7: Class diagram of security system

The central controller has a set of connected sensors, and it moves into the alarm on state *alarm = true* if any of its sensors are triggered by an intrusion.

This behaviour is completely described by the constraint

$$triggered = true \implies alarm = true$$

attached to the *System_Sensor* association, because this means that for all pairs $sys \mapsto sen$ in this association, if $sen.triggered = true$, then $sys.alarm = true$.

Therefore, if some event sets a sensor to the *triggered* state, the response to this event (whether performed in the *Sensor* class, the *System* class or both) must set the *alarm* on, in order that the constraint remains true.

The constraint could be alternatively expressed as

$$true : allSensors.triggered \implies alarm = true$$

but this is less implementation-neutral: as an invariant of *System* it suggests that the code to maintain it will be in the *System* class.

Rule

If constraint C is attached to a set rs of associations, relating classes E_1 to E_n, the meaning of C is that, for all objects $x_1 : E_1, ..., x_n : E_n$ related by elements of rs, $C(x_1, ..., x_n)$ is true, where this formula is C with each feature f of E_i replaced by $x_i.f$, for each class E_i.

If two classes E_i and E_j have the same feature name f, these can be disambiguated in C by prefixing the feature by the name of the class as $E_i :: f$ or $E_j :: f$.

If an association r is a self-association on a class E, then association constraints on r can refer to objects at the different ends by the rolenames of these ends – these will denote single objects from the viewpoint of the association and its constraint, regardless of the multiplicities of the ends. Figure 3.8 shows an example.

Likewise, a meaning could be given to constraints attached to a set of classes and associations: a feature name f of a class E is interpreted by $x.f$ in a constraint, where x is the object ranging over class E in the context of the constraint.

Thus very concise formulae can be used to express the properties of possibly very many objects. In this example we also need an invariant to express the converse property: that if all sensors are not triggered, the system is not alarmed:

$$allSensors.triggered = false \implies alarm = false$$

This is a conventional invariant of *System*.

Association constraints can often be used instead of navigation expressions to specify inter-class properties, and have the advantage that they are less dependent on the precise structure of the model, and so are more resilient to model reconfigurations. For example, if a model contains classes A and B with a class invariant *Con*

$$aatt > 0 \implies br.batt = 1$$

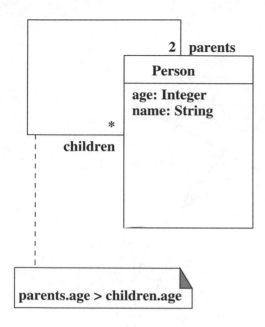

Figure 3.8: Association constraint on self association example

of A (left hand side of Figure 3.9), then this formula would need to change to

$$aatt > 0 \;\Rightarrow\; cr.br.batt = 1$$

if a new intermediate class C was introduced (eg, to eliminate the many-many association). In contrast, if an association constraint

$$aatt > 0 \;\Rightarrow\; batt - 0$$

was used instead, this formula would not need to change for the new model, only the set of associations constrained would change, from $\{A\_B\}$ to $\{A\_C, C\_B\}$.

3.6 Recursion

Although recursive definitions are not presently included in LOCA, some of the power of these can be obtained by a function *closure*, applied to self-associations on an entity. Consider the self-association *parents_children* on *Person* (Figure 3.10). If we keep following the *children* role from a person to their children, to all their grandchildren, and adding all the people we obtain to a set, etc:

$$p.children \;\backslash/$$
$$p.children.children \;\backslash/$$
$$p.children.children.children \;\backslash/...$$

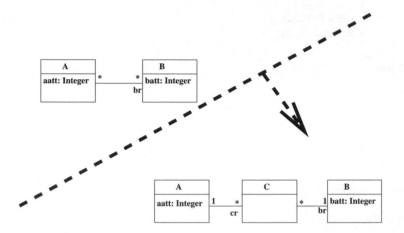

Figure 3.9: Flexibility example

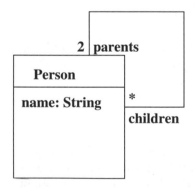

Figure 3.10: Person class

then eventually we will obtain all the descendents of p. This construction is called the closure of *children* and is written as *p.children.closure*. Likewise, in the other direction, *p.parents.closure* is the set of all ancestors of p.

This construction is particularly useful in the Scrabble system, since a key invariant is that all the letters on the board must be in one connected group. This means that for any two letters on the board, it is possible to get to one from the other by moving vertically and horizontally, staying all the time on squares that also have letters on them. Figure 3.11 shows a valid Scrabble board with all letters being connected.

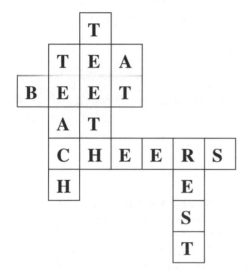

Figure 3.11: Connected Scrabble game

We can formalise this notion of reachability as the closure of a relationship of 'adjacency' on squares, where squares $s1$ and $s2$ are adjacent if both are occupied by letters and $s1$ and $s2$ are next to each other either vertically or horizontally, or are the same square (Figure 3.12). This association is symmetric (if a is adjacent to b, b is adjacent to a) so both ends can have the same rolename. The invariant

$$x : adjacent \Rightarrow squareLetter \mathrel{/}= \{\} \;\&\; x.squareLetter \mathrel{/}= \{\}$$

expresses that adjacent squares must both be occupied. The closure of the adjacency association is the relation of connectedness, and we can therefore express the constraint that all letters on the board are connected by:

$$squareLetter \mathrel{/}= \{\} \;\&\; x : Square \;\&\;$$
$$x.squareLetter \mathrel{/}= \{\} \Rightarrow x : adjacent.closure$$

'if I am occupied, then any other occupied square x is reachable from me'.

Although this is expressible as an invariant of *Square* it will probably be the responsibility of other classes, such as *Board*, *Game*, or *Move* to maintain. This

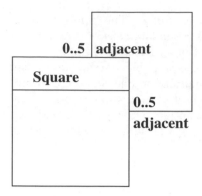

Figure 3.12: Square class with adjacency

is often the case for invariants which refer to two or more different members of a class.

3.7   Identity attributes

If an attribute *att* has the constraint {*identity*} beside its declaration, this means that no two different objects of the class can hold the same value in this attribute. These attribute values can therefore be used as unique identities for objects of the class – if there is an object of the class with that value as the value of its *att*, then no other object of the class can also have *att* equal to the same value.

For example, in the Scrabble system, the name of a player is an identity attribute, because there should not be two different players with the same name (Figure 3.13). So, given a name, such as 'Felix', there will be only one player

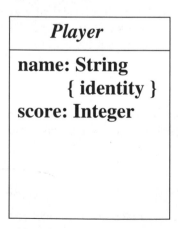

Figure 3.13: Player class

object *obj* with *obj.name* = "*Felix*" (or no such object at all).

More precisely, if class C has identity attribute *key* (Figure 3.14) then the property

$$a : C \ \& \ b : C \ \& \ a.key = b.key \ \Rightarrow \ a = b$$

holds. In other words, if objects a and b of C have equal values for their *key*

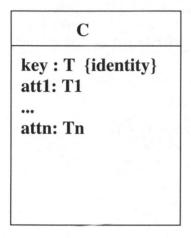

Figure 3.14: Class with identity attribute

attribute, then they must be equal.

The {*identity*} constraint can be considered an abbreviation for the association-style notation of Figure 3.15.

Figure 3.15: Identity attribute as injective association

Identity attributes provide a useful way to define equality for objects, in particular the Java wrapper classes such as *Integer* can be abstractly characterised in this way as classes *IntegerObject*, etc (Figure 3.16). Even though there can be many *IntegerObject* objects with the same *value*, they are all equal under the *equals* method in Java.

For an identity attribute *key* : T of class C, the set

$$C \ | \ (key = val)$$

will always have 0 or 1 element, for each *val* in T – the unique (if any) object of C that has key value *val*. This set is also written as $C[val]$ if *key* is the only identity attribute of C. Likewise for any set e of C objects, $e[val]$ abbreviates $e \mid (key = val)$.

Identity attributes correspond to primary keys in database terminology.

As an example of the use of sets and identity attributes in specification, consider the problem of defining a lottery game, in which the computer generates six random numbers, and the human player then makes six guesses. The system then calculates their score – how many numbers they guessed correctly. Figure 3.16 shows this system. The requirement that six *different* random numbers

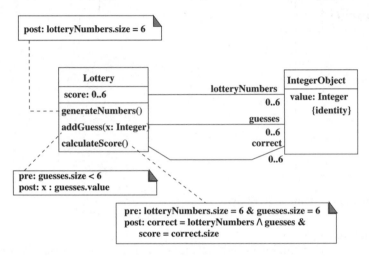

Figure 3.16: Class diagram of lottery system

are generated is expressed by the postcondition of *generateNumbers*: it puts 6 different *IntegerObject* objects into the set *lotteryNumbers*, these objects must also have different *value*s because *value* is an identity attribute.

addGuess adds x to the set of values in the *guesses* set, ie, it must add a new *IntegerObject* object I with $I.value = x$ to this set, if x is not already the value of some member of *guesses*. This can be written more explicitly as:

```
post: I : IntegerObject & I.value = x &
      guesses = guesses@pre \/ { I }
```

(constants, written all in capitals, are used for objects that may be created in a postcondition or constraint conclusion).

To enforce that I is a new object, we could add

```
I /: IntegerObject@pre
```

to the postcondition.

Once six different random numbers and six different guess numbers have been selected, the *calculateScore* operation computes the set of common values, and sets *score* to the number of correct guesses. For example, if

$$lotteryNumbers.value = \{33, 50, 0, 11, 202, 99\}$$
$$guesses.value = \{0, 1, 2, 10, 11, 12\}$$

then

$$correct.value = \{0, 11\}$$
$$score = 2$$

There are several other clever specification tricks that can be performed using identity attributes. See exercise 9 of Chapter 4 below for another example.

The idea of an identity attribute can be generalised to model *compound keys* of an entity (Figure 3.17): each combination of values of the compound key T attributes uniquely identifies some instance of the entity, and each instance of the entity has a value for the compound key. This means

Figure 3.17: Pattern for compound keys

$$e1 : E \; \& \; e2 : E \; \& \; e1.att1 = e2.att1 \; \& \; e1.att2 = e2.att2 \; \Rightarrow \; e1 = e2$$

This constraint can be expressed visually by attaching a single {*identity*} constraint to both the attributes (more generally, to all the attributes involved in a compound key).

3.8 Association classes

Association classes are associations which are also classes: they may have their own set of attributes, operations and roles, in addition to participating in their own association.

Figure 3.18 shows an example, where the *Person_Company* association has been made into an association class and has a *salary : Integer* attribute. Association classes are denoted by separate association and class symbols, connected by a dashed line.

Any association class has two implicit single-valued roles back to the classes it links. These are named after the corresponding classes, with the initial letter

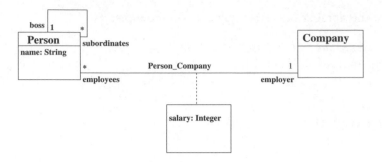

Figure 3.18: Association class example

changed to lower case. So in the example of Figure 3.18, *Person_Company* has roles *person* and *company* of multiplicity one.

These roles also satisfy a uniqueness property similar to that of a compound key:

$j1 : Person\_Company$ & $j2 : Person\_Company$ &
$j1.person = j2.person$ &
$j1.company = j2.company$ $\Rightarrow$ $j1 = j2$

In fact, an association class can always be replaced by a conventional class and a pair of associations, together with this form of uniqueness constraint.

3.9 Implicit and explicit associations

An association may be *implicit* if it represents a conceptual relationship between two entities, which will not be explicitly recorded in implementation data. In programming terms, the fact that two objects obj_1 and obj_2 are linked by the association will not be stored in memory, instead it will be determined by computing some predicate or condition involving the objects. In the UML model this predicate can be attached to the association in order to define what objects it links.

This approach is often necessary if the relation has a very large multiplicity at its ends, for example, making explicit recording of its elements impractical. As an example, consider a *Person* class with forename and surname string data (Figure 3.19) and a relation of $<$ defining an ordering on such objects: $p_1 < p_2$ if p_1's surname precedes p_2's surname, or, if they have the same surname, if p_1's forename precedes p_2's:

$p_1.surname < p_2.surname$ *or*
$(p_1.surname = p_2.surname$ & $p_1.forename < p_2.forename)$

The relation $p_1 < p_2$ is modelled in the diagram by $p_2 : p_1.gt$ (in which case also $p_1 : p_2.lt$).

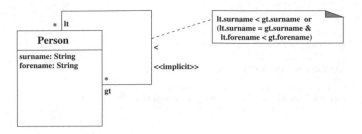

Figure 3.19: Implicit association

In a database of 1000 people, the size of this relation is $\frac{1000}{2} * 999 = 499500$. If an association is not implicit, it is termed *explicit*.

3.10 Interfaces and implementation inheritance

A useful concept which can be used to support abstract specification of a system, and modular development, is the notion of an *interface*. An interface is essentially an abstract class which contains a list of operations, which clients of the interface will require, and which implementations of the interface must implement. Interfaces are written as class rectangles with the stereotype $\ll$ *interface* $\gg$ above or beside the interface name.

An interface cannot inherit from a class, but it can be the endpoint of an association from a class. All features of an interface must be public. Interface inheritance, a form of inheritance of an interface by a class or by another interface, is indicated by a dashed inheritance line[1]. It means that all operations declared in the ancestor interface must also be declared/defined as operations of the subclass/subinterface.

Figure 3.20 shows some examples of interfaces that express Java-style data collections. The *Collection* interface represents any kind of collection, ordered or unordered, and so has only very general operations such as *add*(x : *Object*) or *remove*(x : *Object*). Any other class/interface representing collections of data must be a subclass/subinterface of *Collection*, and hence must support these operations as well. Since these interfaces have no data, we have specified the effect of *Collection* operations in terms of the basic query operation *contains* of the interface. This is a common style for very abstract specification and avoids any commitment to or assumptions about the particular data structures to be used in any implementation.

Additional operations can be declared in subinterfaces such as *List*, which describe more refined data structures, supporting an ordering on their elements.

Concrete classes which implement interfaces, such as *LinkedList*, must provide particular implementations for each operation of all the interfaces they implement. Such classes are said to *realise* their interfaces. In a complete PIM,

---

[1]In UML 2.0 the same notation, a solid inheritance arrow, is used for inheritance of a class and an interface.

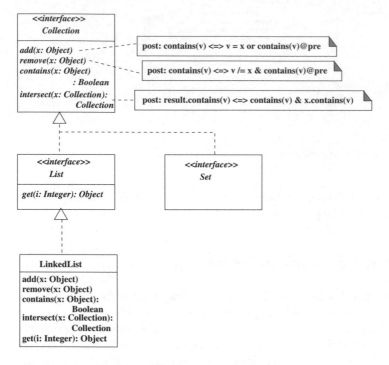

Figure 3.20: Interfaces for collection classes

normally every operation must eventually be defined: all classes at the bottom of the inheritance hierarchies of the system must be concrete.

The importance of an interface is that it allows a client class to make assumptions about what operations can be performed on an object that it accesses (eg, as an operation parameter or role value) without having to declare a precise concrete class as the type of this object.

Thus if our program only needs the *add*(*x* : *Object*), and *intersect*(*x* : *Collection*) : *Collection* operations, then it can be a client of *Collection*, and we have the freedom to choose any concrete subclass of this very general interface to actually implement the data of our system. This is the case for the lottery system, in particular.

Interfaces can also be used to abstractly specify the functionality to be provided by a subsystem, so that clients of the subsystem can be developed independently of its implementation.

Notice however, that inheritance and implementation inheritance do not necessarily preserve the semantics of a class: the postconditions and preconditions of an operation of a subclass can be quite different to those for the same operation in the superclass.

If the superclass semantics *is* preserved, in a specific sense, then we say that the subclass/implementation is a *subtype* of the class/interface it inherits from.[2] In this case clients of the superclass/interface can safely use objects of the subclass, and can rely on all properties of the superclass/interface still being true for such objects.

The conditions for class or interface D to be a subtype of a class or interface C that it inherits from are:

1. Each invariant of C is also a valid invariant of D:

$$Inv_D \;\Rightarrow\; Inv_C$$

2. Each operation of D that redefines an operation of C has a precondition that is at least as general as its precondition in C (so that D can validly execute the operation whenever C can):

$$pre_{C,op} \;\Rightarrow\; pre_{D,op}$$

3. Each operation of D that redefines an operation of C has a postcondition that is as strong, or stronger, than its postcondition in C (so that D's operation achieves all the effects that C's can):

$$post_{D,op} \;\Rightarrow\; post_{C,op}$$

As an example, class D in Figure 3.21 is a subtype of class C. This is true, be-

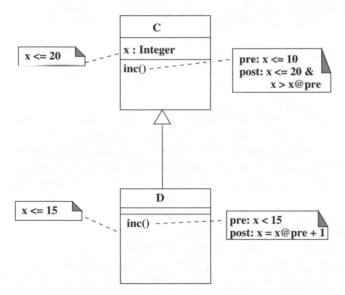

Figure 3.21: Subtyping example

cause the invariant of D is logically stronger than that of C, and the operation precondition of *inc* in D is weaker than that in C, whilst its postcondition is stronger.

---

[2]UML does not distinguish subtyping from ordinary subclassing.

An even stronger notion, of behavioural subtyping or substitutability, adds the further requirement:

- Each execution sequence of D corresponds to an execution sequence of C – in particular no new behaviours/operations can be introduced in D which are not expressible in terms of operations of C.

This means that clients of objects *obj* of C cannot be 'surprised' by state changes in *obj* that arise from subclass operations (when *obj* actually belongs to a subclass): only those state changes already declared in C are possible for *obj*. This condition is also true for the example of Figure 3.21.

The UML notion of an interface is more general than that of a Java interface: in Java an interface may only contain public static final attributes (global constants). This is usually used to facilitate the declaration of enumerated types in Java, so in Java PSMs we will only allow such attributes in an interface.

3.11   Packages, Subsystems and Models

Often, it is necessary to have a higher level of structure than classes and associations, in order to group parts of a system together into separate subsystems. UML provides such a capability via the *package* structuring mechanism, and the related concepts of a *model* and *subsystem*:

Package A grouping of model elements. Packages are represented as a 'folder' rectangle, with a tab at the top left corner containing the name of the package, and the contents of the package drawn inside the main rectangle. Figure 3.22 (a) shows a typical package.

Packages own model elements: each element (such as a class, association, type, package, etc) can only be directly owned by one package, ie, they cannot be shared. Packages can however contain subordinate packages, and dependency relationships such as $\ll$ *import* $\gg$, $\ll$ *access* $\gg$, etc can exist between packages, allowing one package to make use of elements in another.

An unspecialised package is essentially a syntactic grouping of elements, providing a *namespace*. For example, the *java.util* package in Java groups together various utility classes, such as the *List* and *Map* classes.

Model A specialised form (a stereotype) of package, which represents a view of a physical or software system. It can be used to express properties and structure of the context of a system, eg, the entities and procedures involved in ambulance dispatch, for a new dispatch support system.

It is notated using the package symbol with a small triangle in the top right corner. Figure 3.22 (b) shows a typical model package.

Subsystem A specialised form/stereotype of package which represents a behavioural unit. It may be instantiable (have instances in the manner of a class). It is more than simply a namespace, and typically provides a set of operations, which may have both a specification and a realisation (implementation).

Figure 3.22 (c) shows a typical subsystem. Three compartments, for the operations, specifications (eg, use cases, interfaces or statecharts) and realisations, are listed. A 'fork' symbol indicates that the package is a subsystem.

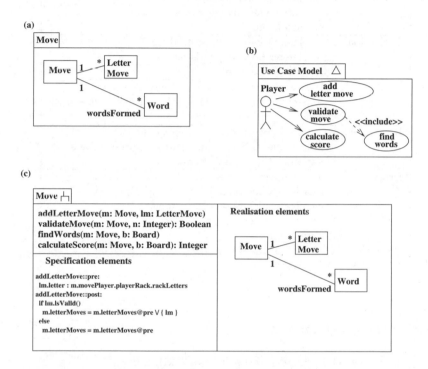

Figure 3.22: Package, Model and Subsystem notation

A feature f owned by package P can be referred to as $P :: f$ in any package that accesses or imports P, if f is public in P. Features of subpackages Q of P can be referred to as $P :: Q :: f$, etc.

When we decompose a system into subparts, these will usually correspond to UML subsystems, in that they will provide a set of services, and will have a specification, and (eventually) an implementation. Thus both modules and subsystems (in the terminology of this book) can be expressed as UML subsystems.

In terms of the MDA, a PIM will typically define the specification elements of UML subsystems, and a PSM will define the subsystem realisations.

In this book we will not use the term 'model' in the technical sense of a specialised form of UML package. Instead, we will use it to denote the general MDA concept of a model, that is, a collection of model elements in whatever modelling notation is being used. Such models could be (sets of) UML packages, models or subsystems if the modelling notation was UML.

Table 3.5 shows some of the kinds of dependency that can exist between
UML elements. These are usually represented by a dashed open-headed ar-
rowed line pointing from the element that depends on another, to the element
it depends on.

Keyword	*Name*	*Meaning*
access	Access	One package can access the public elements owned by the package it depends on.
derive	Derivation	An element can be computed from the element(s) it depends on. Eg a derived attribute.
import	Import	Access, plus the addition of the public elements of the imported package to the namespace of the importing package.
refine	Refinement	Usually between two versions of the same element. The refinement is expressed by a mapping. Eg, a PSM refines a PIM.
use	Usage	One element requires the presence of another in order to function. Includes *call* dependency: one class calls operations of another, *create* dependency: one class creates instances of another, etc.

Table 3.5: UML dependency types

3.12   Other class diagram elements

There are many other class diagram notations in UML 2.0:

- Ternary and higher associations, between three or more classes, represented by association lines from a diamond symbol to each of the associated
  classes.
- Inheritance between associations, allowing a specialisation of an association to be defined, typically where one (or more) end of the association
  is a subclass of an end of the original association and the other ends are
  unchanged. The set of elements in the specialised association are a subset of those in the original association, so the specialised association may
  have stronger multiplicity constraints (eg, it could be one-many even if it
  inherits from a many-many association). A specialisation of a composite
  aggregation must also be a composite aggregation.
- Nested classes: classes which are defined within other classes.
- Templated classes, which carry a type parameter which can be used
  within the class as if it were a specific type, but which will be instantiated
  elsewhere. An example could be a typed *Sequence* $< X >$ construct, with
  parameter X denoting the type of elements of the sequences. X could

be instantiated to *String* to give the class *Sequence* < *String* > of string sequences. Such a mechanism has been introduced into Java from version 1.5.

Figure 3.23 summarises the UML 2.0 class diagram notations that we have introduced.

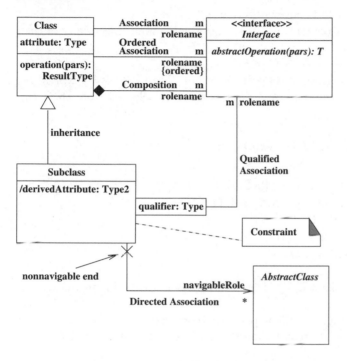

Figure 3.23: Summary of UML class diagram notations

3.13 Exercises

1 Draw a diagram to illustrate a possible set of objects that satisfies the class diagram of Figure 3.24. How are *A.size* and *B.size* related in general for this model?

Figure 3.24: Zero-one to five association

2 If x is an identity attribute of a class C, show that it is also an identity attribute of any subclass D of C.

3 Add an attribute *age* : *Integer* to the *Person* class of Figure 3.10, and define two constraints:

1. To express that *age* is never negative.
2. To express that a person's age is always greater than that of any of their children.

4 Modify the class diagram of the lottery system (Figure 3.16) to express the constraint that lottery numbers and guesses must be selected from the range 1..30 of integers only.

5 Evaluate the following LOCA expressions:

1. $Sequence\{1,4,7\} \frown Sequence\{2,3,5\}$
2. $Sequence\{1,4,7\} <: Sequence\{3,4,1\}$
3. $\{1,3,7,2\} \,/\backslash\, \{2,9,11,0\}$
4. $Sequence\{1\} <: \{2,9,1,0\}$
5. $\{1,4,7\} \,/\backslash\, \{0,1,2,3\}.sqr$

6 Express 'for all integers i, $i*i$ is greater than or equal to i' in LOCA.

7 For the model of Figure 3.25, express the constraint that "there exists an A object whose x value is greater than the y value of any associated B".

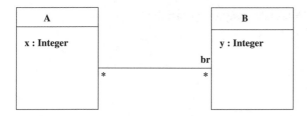

Figure 3.25: Classes A and B

8 Write a LOCA/OCL constraint which expresses that one integer sequence $sq1$ is the reverse of another, $sq2$, ie, that they are the same size but have the same elements in opposite orders.

9 Write a LOCA/OCL constraint to express that a sequence sq of *IntegerObjects* is sorted in descending order of *value*, ie, with the largest element first.

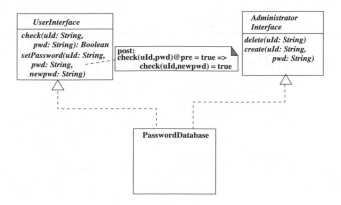

Figure 3.26: Password database

10 Give postconditions for the *delete* and *create* operations of the *PasswordDatabase* in Figure 3.26, using only the *check* query function. *delete* removes a user and their password, *create* creates a new user id and password pair.

11 Explain why

$$(x \cap y).f \; = \; x.f \cap y.f$$

is not generally true, for sets x and y of objects, and an attribute f of the class of these objects. What happens if f is an identity attribute?

12 How is the cardinality of a subclass related to that of its superclass? If A is an abstract superclass of disjoint classes $A1$, ..., An, how is A's cardinality related to those of the Ai?

Provide cardinalities for the *Square* class and its subclasses in Figure 3.2.

Chapter 4

UML Dynamic Modelling Notations

In this chapter we complete the introduction of UML notation by describing the modelling languages used to define dynamic behaviour of a system: statecharts (also called state machines), collaboration and sequence diagrams.

4.1 Statecharts

In contrast to class diagrams, statecharts focus on the dynamic behaviour of objects, and graphically represent the life history of objects over time and their patterns of inter-communication.

Figure 4.1 shows a simple statechart with two states, *On* and *Off* and transitions between them.

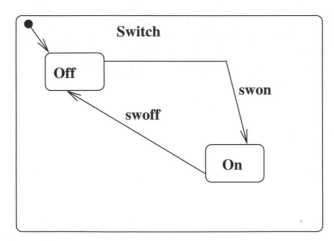

Figure 4.1: Simple statechart

The elements of a statechart are:

States Written as rounded-corner boxes, these have a name.

Transitions Written as arrows from one state, the *source* of the transition, to another, the *target*, they are labelled with the event that causes the transition.

Default initial state The state the object is in at the start of its life history, indicated as the target of a transition arrow with source the initial pseudostate (a black filled circle).

Termination of a statechart can be shown by a 'bullseye' symbol.

UML divides statecharts into two kinds:

1. **Protocol state machines**, which describe the allowed life histories of objects of a particular class. In this case the events on transitions correspond to operations of that class, and transitions may have pre and post conditions (in addition to any that are defined in the class diagram: implicitly the transition precondition is conjoined to that of the operation, for the given starting state. Likewise for the postcondition). Transitions cannot have generated actions (although we will allow this, as discussed below).

2. **Behaviour state machines**, used for describing method execution and the implementation of object behaviour. Transitions of such state machines do not have postconditions, but can have actions.

Thus statecharts describe the behaviour of objects of a particular class, or of a subset of the features of the class (such as the changes in one or two of its attributes) or, at more detailed design stages, the stages of execution of a particular method.

Figure 4.1 is an example of a protocol statechart which describes the behaviour of objects of a *Switch* class (Figure 4.2). This means that the life history of an object *obj* of *Switch* must be a sequence of alternations between the *On* and *Off* states, beginning in *Off*:

$$Off \longrightarrow_{swon} On \longrightarrow_{swoff} Off \longrightarrow_{swon} \cdots$$

The events of a protocol statechart normally correspond to operations or methods of the class whose behaviour the statechart describes. The semantic meaning of a protocol statechart attached to a class is that:

1. Each object of the class begins its life history in the default state of the statechart.

2. If an object *obj* is in state s and an event α occurs on *obj* (eg, because the operation call $obj.\alpha()$ has been made), then if there is a transition labelled with α and with source s, this transition occurs, and the object moves into the target state of the transition.

   If there is no transition for α from state s, then the object remains in state s.

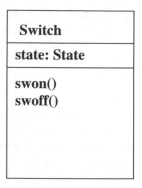

State <<enumeration>>
On
Off

Switch
state: State
swon() swoff()

Figure 4.2: Switch class

Transitions may have *guards* (termed preconditions in the case of a protocol statechart) and *actions*. A guard is a condition (boolean-valued expression) using features of the class, which is evaluated when the event of the transition occurs on a particular object, and the object is in the source state of the transition. If the condition is true, then this transition takes place, otherwise it does not. An action on a transition describes an event or set of events which this statechart generates when the transition occurs. Typically these events are method or operation invocations on objects of supplier classes of the class that owns the statechart.

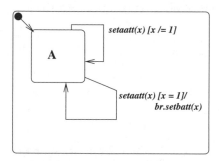 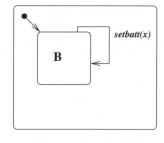

Figure 4.3: Statecharts of classes A and B

Figure 4.3 shows an example of guards and actions, where class A has an integer attribute *aatt* and *-multiplicity role *br* to class B, and B has an integer attribute *batt* (Figure 4.4). This model means that if *setaatt(x)* is invoked on an object a of A, then if $x = 1$, the method *setbatt(1)* is invoked on every

B object in $a.br$, otherwise nothing is done. This behaviour is additional to any postcondition of $setaatt(x)$ (which states that $aatt = x$). Both effects take place when the event happens.

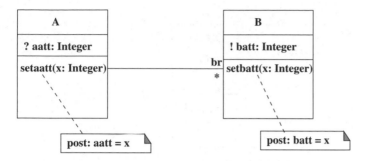

Figure 4.4: Classes A and B

Actions are written following a forward slash, after the event and guard (if present). Multiple actions can be specified, separated by / or ; . Actions can include updates *feature = val* or *feature := val* of local attribute and rolename values, or invocations of operations on objects that can be navigated to from the object of the statechart. Typically, operation postconditions are used to express changes to local features of a class, and state-independent behaviour (which would otherwise have to be duplicated on every transition for the operation in the statechart), transition actions are used to express non-local effects such as invocations of methods on other objects, and state-dependent behaviours.

Rules
For each state s, and event α of a statechart, there can be at most one unguarded transition for α from s. If there are several transitions, these must all be guarded and have disjoint guards, so that it is impossible for more than one guard to be true at any time.

For the simple statecharts described in this section, an object is in exactly one basic state at all times after its creation and before its destruction. It need not visit all states, however it should be possible, in principle, to reach each state from the initial state.

4.1.1 Composite states

States can be *nested* within others to express relationships of generalisation and specialisation, and to reduce the number of transitions in the diagram. Figure 4.5 shows an example of a state *Off*, containing two substates *Standby* and *NoPower*. States such as *Off* are called *composite* states. When the transition *swoff* occurs in state *On*, the system goes to the basic state *Standby*, the default state of *Off*. When *swon* occurs, if the system is in either *Standby*

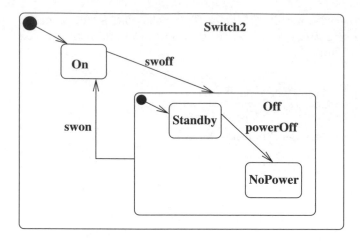

Figure 4.5: Statechart with nesting

or *NoPower*, then the next state is *On*. The nested state notation therefore reduces the number of transition arrows by one in this case.

The rule that an object can be in at most one basic state at a time is still true, however if an object is in a basic state s, then it is also considered to be in every state that contains s – analogously to the sub/super-class relation between classes.

States can have attached constraints, the meaning of these constraints are that they hold true of any object while it is in the state, including in all substates of the state, if it is a composite state. The constraint is written in square brackets after the state name (Figure 4.20).

Finally, if every transition into a state s has the same final action *act*, then we can abbreviate the diagram by defining *act* as the *entry* action of s, and removing it from the incoming transitions. Likewise, if every outgoing transition has the same initial action *act'*, this can be made the *exit* action of the source state. Figure 4.6 shows the use of *entry* and *exit* as abbreviations. The statechart on the right is an equivalent abbreviation for the statechart on the left.

States can also be *concurrent*, consisting of two or more regions which are composite states, which can simultaneously be occupied (Figure 4.7). Here, sensor 1 and sensor 2 can change state independently of each other: *sen1triggered* can take place if sensor 2 is in *sen2undetecting* or *sen2detecting*. Indeed this is often the actual situation if there are several instances of a class existing at the same time: the different instances all pursue their own life-cycles autonomously of each other. With concurrent states there is no longer just one basic state that the system is in at any time, instead the system will be in a *set* of basic states: the members of this set must be from different parts of a parallel

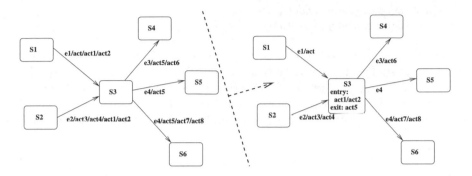

Figure 4.6: Statechart with entry and exit actions

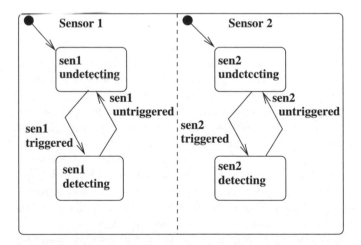

Figure 4.7: Statechart with concurrent states

composition of statecharts. In Figure 4.7 the possible sets of states are

$$\{sen1undetecting, sen2undetecting\}$$
$$\{sen1undetecting, sen2detecting\}$$
$$\{sen1detecting, sen2undetecting\}$$
$$\{sen1detecting, sen2detecting\}$$

When a concurrent composite state is entered, each of its subcomponents is entered, usually at their default state, although it is possible to specify direct entry to specific states. In Figure 4.8 the transition from $E2$ enters the state $\{S1, S4\}$, whereas the transition from $E1$ enters the default initial state $\{S1, S3\}$. Transitions may exit from multiple sources: these sources must

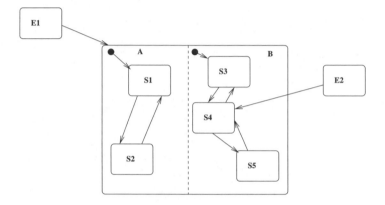

Figure 4.8: Entering a concurrent state

be from different concurrent components of a concurrent composite state, and transitions can enter multiple targets, which likewise must be from different concurrent components of a concurrent composite state. Such multi-transitions are written with a vertical bar joining the exit and entry lines.

It is possible to write quite strange examples of concurrent states, eg, where a transition appears to exit from one subcomponent and enter another (Figure 4.9). It is always possible to work out what actually happens by using the rule that a component of a concurrent state is always entered by its default state unless an explicit transition to a substate (including a history state, see below) is defined. So in this example, t goes from any state of A and any state of B, and $s6$, to $\{s1, s5, s6\}$, whilst t'' goes from $\{s2, s4, s6\}$ or $\{s2, s4, s7\}$ to $\{s1, s5, s7\}$. But please don't write such models in real systems!

If an event has transitions both from a substate of a state and from the state itself, then the substate transition has higher priority and will fire if the event occurs when the substate is occupied and the transition guard is true. In Figure 4.10, if the system is in state $A2$ the transition to $S2$ fires when e occurs, otherwise, in states $A1$ and $A3$, the transition to $S1$ takes place.

History states represent a means for 'remembering' what substate of a composite state was last occupied, when the composite state is exited. A history

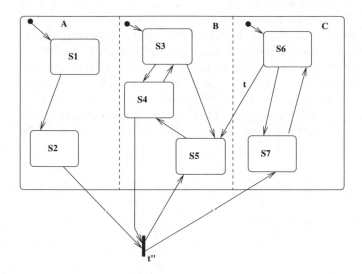

Figure 4.9: Statechart with pathological transitions

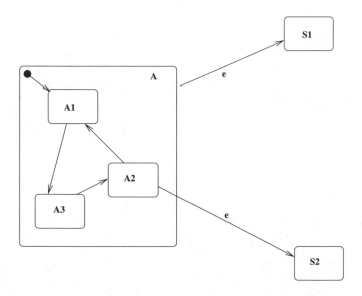

Figure 4.10: Transition priority example

state is written as an *H* within a circle (Figure 4.11). A transition to this circle actually goes to the substate of the closest enclosing (non-concurrent) composite state which was last occupied when the composite state was last exited (ie, to the substate from which the composite state was exited). If the composite state has not previously been occupied, then the default substate of the composite state is entered instead. A history state is not a real state and is never actually occupied. It is therefore known as a 'pseudostate', of which the bullseye symbol is another example. In Figure 4.11, if events α, β and γ occurred in this order, starting from state *S*1, then the resulting state would be *S*2. If events β and γ occurred from state *S*1, the resulting state would be *S*1.

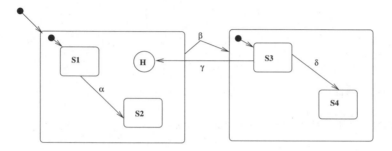

Figure 4.11: History state example

Another variant of a history state is the 'deep history state', notated with an additional $*$ inside the history pseudostate. This means 'recursively enter the most recently vacated substate of every non-concurrent composite substate of the composite state enclosing myself'. Figure 4.12 shows an example of the deep history mechanism. If events α, β, γ, *e*2, *e*4, *e* occurred in that order, the resulting state would be *S*5. If instead, events α, β, *e*1, *e*3, *e* occurred in that order, the resulting state would be *S*4.

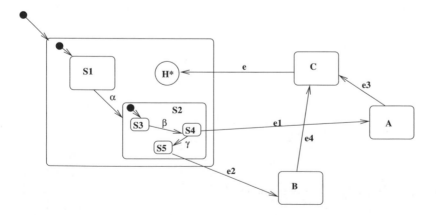

Figure 4.12: Deep history example

Statecharts are particularly useful in expressing the intended order in which events are expected to happen. Although preconditions of operations can also express the expected order of these operations – by only evaluating to *true* in situations where the operation is being invoked in its correct order – it is preferable to use statecharts in addition to preconditions for this because they are a graphical and intuitively simple notation which is immediately comprehensible. For example, Figure 4.13 shows the intended sequence of events for the lottery system of Figure 3.16.

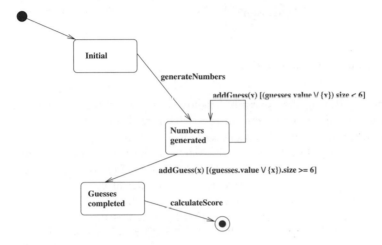

Figure 4.13: Operation ordering in lottery system

4.2   Interaction diagrams

Interaction diagrams show examples (scenarios) of particular use cases. There are two forms of interaction diagram in UML: sequence and collaboration diagrams. *Sequence diagrams* emphasise timing and the history of objects. Sequence diagrams relate an interaction to statechart models of the classes involved, and can be used to give examples of the interactions involved in a particular use case scenario.

Collaboration diagrams in contrast emphasise the connection of the interaction to the class diagram. They show an interaction between objects as a set of messages sent from one object to another to achieve some required unit of functionality (eg, a module operation execution). The diagrams consist of objects, links (instances of associations) and messages, they enhance UML object diagrams by showing explicitly what messages are passed between objects and the order of these messages. An example is given in Figure 4.14.

The features of collaboration diagrams are:

- Objects are represented by rectangles containing the name/identifier of the object, and the name of its class, all underlined: object: Class.

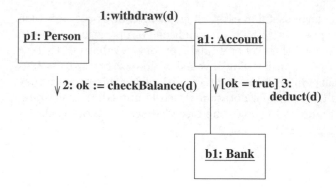

Figure 4.14: Example collaboration diagram

- Objects created during the operation execution are written as {*new*}.
- Objects deleted during the execution are written as {*destroyed*}.
- Objects both created and deleted are written as {*transient*}.
- Links (instances of associations) can have arrows indicating their navigability direction: if a message is sent from object *a* of class *A* to object *b* of class *B* then *a* must have access to *b*, for example by means of an association from *A* to *B* which is navigable in that direction.
- Messages are numbered consecutively starting at 1, nesting of messages is indicated by suffixes: eg: 3.1.4 follows 3.1.3 within subprocedure 3.1.
- Conditions are given in square brackets: the associated message is only sent if the condition is true.

Figure 4.15 shows a possible collaboration for taking letters from the bag in the Scrabble system and putting them in the rack. As in this example,

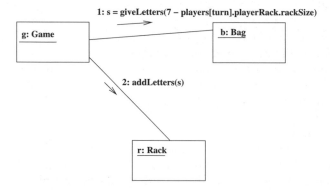

Figure 4.15: Choose Letters collaboration diagram

collaboration diagrams are often used to show the design or implementation of a use case. Here it is the *select letters* use case.

A sequence diagram corresponding to the collaboration diagram of Figure 4.14 is shown in Figure 4.16. In this diagram there are three objects, *p1*, *a1*

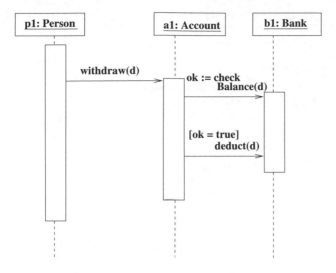

Figure 4.16: Example sequence diagram

and *b*1, which exist throughout the interaction (their lifelines are the vertical dashed lines). The vertical rectangles indicate an activity of the objects (usually an execution of a method on the object) and the duration of this activity. Arrows from one object lifeline to another represent messages, usually method invocations. Parameters, results and conditions are shown as in collaboration diagrams.

Figure 4.17 shows a more complex sequence diagram, for the *play track* use case of the jukebox system. Here, the user operates the remote control to select a song and the 'play track' command. The main application identifies the location of this song on the streaming server, and makes a request for this to stream the song to the media player on the application server.

4.3 The Scrabble system revisited

The constraint and behaviour notations introduced in this chapter and the previous chapter can be used to further refine the Scrabble system specification.

4.3.1 Defining constraints

The next step after derivation of the entities and associations of a system is to look again at the background information on the system, and the use cases, and try to identify precise constraints on the system – on the entities, on relationships between the entities, and for operation pre- and postconditions which are necessary to enable these operations to carry out the use case they are responsible for.

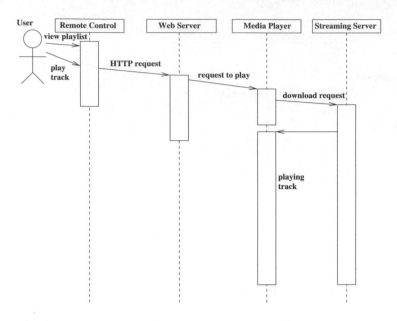

Figure 4.17: Play Track sequence diagram

For Scrabble, many statements in the rules of the game lead directly to constraints in the class diagram:

- 'There are 100 letter tiles'. This is expressed by the cardinality constraint 100 on *Letter*.
- 'All the tiles played in a move must be placed in a straight line vertically or horizontally'. This is expressed by the invariant

```
C1: letterMoves.x.size = 1 or
    letterMoves.y.size = 1
```

of *Move*, and by the postcondition of an operation *addLetterMove(lm : LetterMove)* of *Move*, which only adds *lm* to the move's *letterMoves* if *C*1 is satisfied:

```
addLetterMove(lm: LetterMove)
// pre:
//    lm.letter : m.movePlayer.playerRack.rackLetters
// post:
//    if lm in line with letterMoves@pre
//       letterMoves = letterMoves@pre \/ { lm }
//    else
//       letterMoves = letterMoves@pre
```

(The invariant *C*1 forces such a postcondition to be written, since *Move* would be inconsistent if letter moves that were not in a single line could be added.)

- 'The player removes tiles from their rack and places them on the board'. This is expressed by the *Move* invariant

    ```
    C4: letterMoves.letter :
            movePlayer.playerRack.rackLetters
    ```

    Ie, all letters moved in this move have come from the current player's rack, and by the precondition of *addLetterMove*.

A general principle that is useful to bear in mind during this process is:

> **Guideline**
> Make declarative information (class and inter-class invariants) primary, and as complete and thorough as possible. In many cases operation definitions can be derived from such constraints semi-automatically, so they can be considered after the declarative constraints have been determined.

What is meant by saying that operation definitions are secondary to declarative constraints? Simply that the constraints should be the primary definition of the system behaviour in a class diagram, by specifying how the features of a class, or of several classes, are related to each other. Operations can be viewed as existing for the purpose of ensuring that these constraints remain true when external events occur. In general an operation *op* of a class *E* which might violate an invariant *C* of *E* can do one of three things to avoid breaking the invariant:

1. Include sufficiently strong conditions in its precondition so that any execution of *op* that satisfies these preconditions at its start cannot lead to a state that violates *C* at its end.
2. Change attribute or role values, or call operations of supplier objects, to force *C* to be true when *op* completes execution.
3. Test if *C* would be violated by execution of its normal code, and execute a skip (no update of any data) if this is the case.

These are each appropriate in certain cases. The third case is illustrated by the operation *addLetterMove*(*lm* : *LetterMove*) discussed above – the second approach would be inappropriate here since the player has already decided where they want the letter to go, and the program should not correct this on its own initiative.

On the other hand the condition

$$lm.letter : movePlayer.playerRack.rackLetters$$

is placed in the precondition, because something has gone seriously wrong if a letter is being placed on the board which is not in the current player's rack – ie, an exception should be thrown.

4.3.2   Refinement of data structures

We may add more detail to the data structures of the initial class diagram of the system, in order to support an intended algorithm to carry out system functions. Such detail should be included in a PIM provided it does not bias the PIM unduly to one particular platform (in which case alternative algorithms and data models need to be specified in the PSMs for the different intended platforms).

For the Scrabble system, the dictionary data can be implemented as a map from letters to sets of words (Figure 4.18).

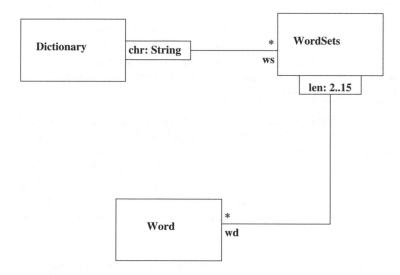

Figure 4.18: Refined data of dictionary

The idea is that *allWords* = *ws.wd*, ie, the original unstructured set of words in the dictionary has been split into sets *ws*["*a*"], *ws*["*b*"], etc, *ws*[*c*] consisting of only those words that contain the letter *c* (as a string), and these in turn have been split up into subsets: *ws*[*c*][*i*] is the set of words of *ws*[*c*] of length *i*.

So, for example:

$$ws[\text{``}a\text{''}][2] \;=\; \{\,\text{``}ad\text{''}, \text{``}as\text{''}, \text{``}pa\text{''}, ...\}$$
$$ws[\text{``}a\text{''}][3] \;=\; \{\,\text{``}air\text{''}, \text{``}arc\text{''}, \text{``}are\text{''}, \text{``}bar\text{''}, ...\}$$

4.3.3   Determine algorithms and sequencing of operations

The final step is to determine how operations should fit together and their executions ordered (sequenced) to carry out the original use cases. This can be done using statecharts, sequence diagrams and collaboration diagrams.

Figure 4.15 shows a collaboration diagram for the Scrabble system, which breaks the 'selection of letters' use case into two steps: producing the random selection of letters from the bag, and then adding them to the rack.

There is a slight inconsistency in the Scrabble rules: they state that a player must always keep seven tiles on their rack, but this is clearly impossible at the end of a game when the bag is empty.

As another example of behavioural specification, illustrating the combined use of statecharts and operation postconditions, consider the problem of specifying the history of a person's marital state over time. We can identify states *single*, *married*, *divorced*, *separated*, *widowed*, at least (Figure 4.19) and the important events *marry*, *divorce*, *separate*, *partnerDies*, etc. Analysis of the situation leads to a certain set of transitions and behaviours. Further analysis

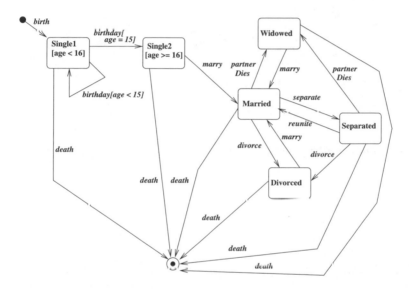

Figure 4.19: Marital status statechart

of the diagram can enable us to group together states, using the 'Introduce Superstate' transformation (Chapter 11): *Divorced*, *Widowed* both have transitions to *Married*, for the event *marry*, with the same guard, so can be grouped and a new superstate *Marriageable* introduced (a state representing the single persons over 16 could also be made a substate of *Marriageable*). Likewise, all the states could be grouped under a single *Alive* superstate with a transition for *death* (Figure 4.20). This has reduced the number of transitions from 18 to 11 and made the diagram more systematic and comprehensible.

The *birthday* event has transitions on every state, but only the transitions on the state where there is a possible change of state due to the event are shown on the statechart. The class description for persons shows the rest of its behaviour (Figure 4.21).

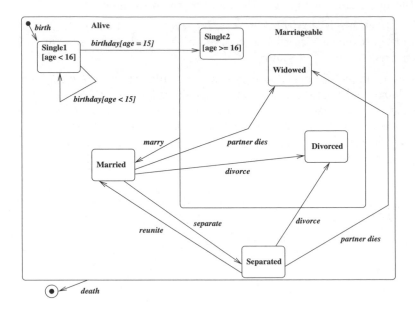

Figure 4.20: Marital status statechart after transformation

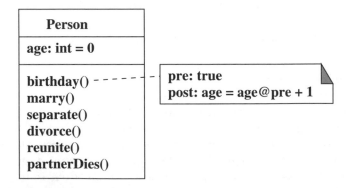

Figure 4.21: Person class

> **Rule**
>
> If an operation is not referred to as the event of any transition of
> a protocol state machine, then the operation can be called in any
> state of the state machine, and it does not change the current state.
> (UML 2.0 Superstructure.)

We could be more explicit about when events are allowed to occur by defining *guard constraints* on the operations. For example:

```
marry()
guard: statePerson = Marriageable
pre: true
post: statePerson = Married
```

A guard constraint expresses that the operation *cannot* occur unless the constraint is true. A precondition constraint simply says that the effect of the operation is undefined if it is executed when the precondition fails.

Guards are mainly used for concurrency control and to enforce orders of events. For example, in a GUI, a command button may be disabled in certain situations to prevent the user selecting the command – this is an implementation of a guard. In the Scrabble system, the *AddPlayer* button is disabled once *Move* is pressed, for instance.

Table 4.1 shows the different possible combinations of a guard and precondition for an operation, and their meaning.

Guard	Precondition	Meaning
false	false	Operation invalid to execute, and cannot be executed
false	true	Operation valid to execute, but blocked
true	false	Operation can execute, but may have erroneous effect
true	true	Operation valid and can execute

Table 4.1: Guard and precondition combinations

The case where an operation is permitted to execute but may execute invalidly is not desirable, and if a guard for an operation is specified, it should normally imply the precondition:

$$Guard \Rightarrow Precondition$$

This rules out the third case in Table 4.1.

Conventions for use of guards

If an operation in a class has an attached *guard* constraint, this gives the definition of the operation guard, and this predicate should imply the operation precondition.

If an operation has a *guard* constraint, and there is a statechart of the class owning the operation, then the guard should be equivalent to the disjunction

$$(stateC = s\alpha_1 \ \& \ G\alpha_1) \ or \ ... \ or \ (stateC = s\alpha_{n\alpha} \ \& \ G\alpha_{n\alpha})$$

of all source states $s\alpha_i$ and guards $G\alpha_i$ of the transitions for the operation, α, in the statechart.

Thus in the example of Figure 4.20, *marry* could be calculated to have guard *statePerson = Marriageable*.

If neither a statechart or a *guard* constraint is defined, the guard is *true*.

4.4   Consistency and completeness checking of UML models

The expressivity and simplicity of UML means that it is very easy to build software models in its notations. Unfortunately it is also easy to build models which are inconsistent or incomplete or that contain other serious flaws.

4.4.1   Reviews

Regular reviews of models produced should take place during their construction, to identify possible mistakes in the use of UML notation, or incorrect understanding by the modeller of the entities and relationships being modelled.

Typical modelling errors, which may be caught by a UML CASE tool, include:

1. Cycles exist in the inheritance relationship.
2. Some attribute is defined both in a class and in an ancestor of that class.
3. An operation is defined twice in the same class, with the same input parameter types, but different result type.
4. Some abstract/interface operation is not eventually implemented in a concrete subclass.
5. An operation is defined with a more restrictive visibility in a descendent class/interface than in an ancestor.
6. An interface is defined to be a subclass of a class.
7. A state in a statechart is unreachable – eg, because it only has outgoing transitions and is not initial.
8. A subset of states in a statechart form a closed cycle, with no outgoing transitions to any other state, so that once the cycle is entered, other states become unreachable.

9. A cardinality q is specified for a subclass of a class with cardinality p, with $q > p$.

These errors are usually simple to correct, and the earlier they can be detected, the less effort is wasted constructing invalid models.

Points to consider for quality improvement and refinement of a model are:

1. That correct multiplicities have been used on associations: not so restrictive that the model excludes some situations that can actually occur, but precise enough to capture the properties of the situation.
   Eg, we could identify that the *wordsFormed* role in the Scrabble system has precise multiplicity 0..8, ie, that no more than 8 new words can be formed in each move.
2. That correct qualifiers have been used on attributes and association ends. For example the {*readOnly*} constraint on a letter score accurately conveys the Scrabble rule that a letter cannot change its score. On the other hand we should not *overspecify* and add constraints that are not an intrinsic part of the problem, eg, putting a {*readOnly*} constraint on player names would be too restrictive and prevents implementations where players can be renamed.
3. That all cases where an association end needs to be ordered have been recognised.
4. That all cases of inheritance have been recognised and expressed in the model.
5. That correct and meaningfully restrictive types have been given to all attributes (eg, using 1..15 as the x-coordinate type in the Scrabble system, instead of simply *Integer*).
6. That suitable states and composite states have been defined which accurately reflect the modes of behaviour and phases that the system can be in: generally, for any two distinct states the system should exhibit different behaviour (otherwise the states could probably be combined).

One dubious aspect of the model in Figure 3.2 is the *Word* class and its incorporation of coordinates *xstart*, *xend*, etc. Such coordinates will not be part of a dictionary word, so it is over-specification to insist that *allWords* is of type *Word* set. Instead it should be just a set of strings.

4.4.2 Consistency

A UML model is *consistent* if there is some possible implementation of it. An inconsistent specification is useless as a prescription for software, since no piece of software can ever be built to satisfy it. For example, if we define a class C with three integer attributes x, y and z, and constraints

$$x < y$$
$$0 \leq y < z$$
$$x = y * z + 1$$

there are no possible implementations of C.

A more subtle error is shown in the model of Figure 4.22. The $a.f$ sets

Figure 4.22: Vacuous UML model

are all of size 3, and form a partition of B, indexed by elements of A (every element of B is in exactly one of the $a.f$), so $B.size = 3 * (A.size)$, similarly $A.size = 5 * (B.size)$. This is only possible if both A and B are empty – ie, no instances of either class exist.

Such consistency problems can be prevented by requiring that the specification includes an explicit setting for all initial values of attributes and associations, or that well-defined and documented default values are used if an initial value is not set. The developer should then check that these initial values meet all the constraints of the model.

In the first example above, the default initialisation of integer variables to 0 clearly fails to satisfy the constraints, and there is no setting of values that does, so the model must be abandoned or modified. In the second example, for each new element of A, three existing elements of B must be provided to initialise the f role. But for these B elements to exist there must already be 15 existing A elements! So it is impossible to create the first A object.

The above are examples of *data inconsistency*. It is also possible for the operations of a class to be inconsistent with its data. An operation op of class C is inconsistent if op can modify C's data in ways that violate the declared types of this data, or that falsifies some constraint of C.

For instance, if class C had an attribute declared as $x : 1..15$ and an operation

```
incx()
post: x = x@pre + 1
```

then *incx* can break the typing restriction of x.

The precondition of an operation can be used to ensure that an operation is only invoked in situations where it cannot break an invariant. The above operation can be rewritten as

```
incx()
pre: x < 15
post: x = x@pre + 1
```

Provided that callers of the operation ensure that the precondition is true before *incx* is called, then it will preserve the typing invariant of x. The precondition of an operation makes explicit what conditions are necessary for correct execution of an operation.

> **Rule**
> A class is *internally consistent* if:
>
> - The initialisations specified for all attributes and roles make all invariants of the class true.
> - For each operation *op* of the class, if the precondition of *op* is true at the start of its execution, and all the class constraints are also true, then *op*'s postcondition also establishes all the constraints of the class on termination of *op*.

If an operation is specified by a statechart instead of a postcondition, then the same principle applies: a transition should be guarded so that it can only take place under conditions which ensure that its actions do not violate constraints.

Statecharts should not specify inconsistent actions or state changes: if two transitions for an event could both fire in some situation, then their generated actions and target states should be consistent.

4.4.3 Completeness

Completeness of a model means that the states and behaviours of the system in all possible cases have been specified. Incompleteness and inconsistency are related problems: an operation may be inconsistent because it sets one attribute *att1* but not another, *att2*, even though these attributes are connected by a constraint which links their values. For example, in the Scrabble system, an operation that adds a letter to a rack must also increment the derived attribute *rackSize*.

Thus some incompleteness can be detected by consistency checking. Another kind of incompleteness may occur in the constraints themselves. For example if a class has two integer attributes *att1* and *att2*, a boolean *att3* and a single constraint

$$att1 > att2 \;\Rightarrow\; att3 = true$$

then the question arises, what is the value of *att3* when $att1 \leq att2$? An implementation would be quite correct to define *setatt1* and *setatt2* as:

```
public void setatt1(int att1x)
{ att1 = att1x;
  if (att1x > att2)
  { setatt3(true); }
}


public void setatt2(int att2x)
{ att2 = att2x;
  if (att1 > att2x)
```

```
  { setatt3(true); }
}
```

But then if *att*1 goes above *att*2 and then later goes below it, *att*3 does not tell us anything about the current value of these variables.

A useful completeness check to do on specification review is to inspect each constraint $A \Rightarrow B$ and consider if the cases where A is false have also been specified, or if absent, if they need to be specified. Another sign of incompleteness is if an attribute does not occur in any constraint.

In a statechart, the set of guards on the transitions for each event α leaving a single state should cover all logical cases, ie, their disjunction should be *true* (unless the cases not covered by guards are being specifically excluded for reasons of concurrency control: an explicit guard constraint for α should be given in this case, equating to the disjunction of conditions under which α is allowed to occur).

Rule
An operation of a class is *complete* if its effect is defined for all possible states which satisfy the class invariant and operation precondition.

4.5   UML tools

A large number of CASE (computer-aided software engineering) tools for UML currently exist, some of the most widely used are:

Rational Rose Offers support with all the UML diagram types, and with management of diagrams into projects. It also provides import and export facilities to transfer models to/from other tools, in text format (XMI), and facilities to build extensions (plugins) to the tool. *www.rational.com*

ArgoUML Supports all UML diagram types, and also provides model analysis facilities to identify possible flaws in a model and alert a user to these (for example, a missing initial state in a statechart). It can export models in XMI format. *argouml.tigris.org*

Together/J Integrates code and diagrams, enabling changes to code displayed in one window to be immediately reflected in changes to a UML diagram displayed in another, and vice versa. Metrics for system quality are also provided. XMI export is supported. *www.togethersoft.com*

Rhapsody Supports statechart modelling, and includes checks on properties such as the existence of isolated states or livelocks (circles of states with no exit transitions). *www.ilogix.com*

4.6 Summary

In the last three chapters we have described the core UML notations of class diagrams, use cases, statecharts and interaction diagrams, and given examples of their use in specifications.

4.7 Exercises

1 How could the marital status statechart of Figure 4.20 be simplified if re-marriage after divorce was not permitted? Draw the revised statechart.

2 Draw a statechart for a set of three radio buttons, $b1$, $b2$ and $b3$. The buttons are all initially off (unpressed). Subsequently, if one button is pressed, it goes on and all the others go off.

3 Simplify the statechart of Figure 4.23 by introducing a suitable composite state.

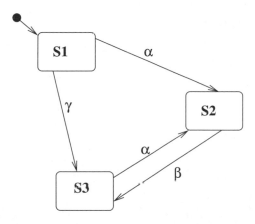

Figure 4.23: Exercise three statechart

4 Use a concurrent composite state to express the behaviour of a light circuit which is controlled by two on/off switches. Whenever any one of the switches changes state, so should the light (from lit to unlit or vice versa).

5 Draw a statechart for a bank account class: the class has attribute *balance* : *Integer* (initially zero) and operations *deposit*(x : *Integer*) to add an amount $x > 0$ to the balance, and *withdraw*(x : *Integer*) to subtract an amount $x > 0$ from the balance. If the account is overdrawn (*balance* < 0) withdrawals are not permitted.

6 Explain why the class in Figure 4.24 is not consistent. How would you modify it to become consistent?

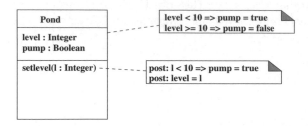

Figure 4.24: Pond pump controller

7 Identify multiplicity bounds on the *history* role of the Scrabble system, if only scoring moves are recorded.

8 Explain why the class diagram of Figure 4.25 is erroneous.

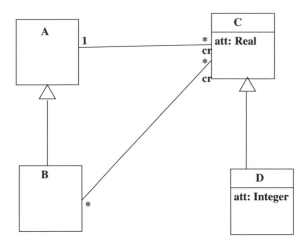

Figure 4.25: Invalid class diagram

9 What is the implication of a class having an attribute which is both an *identity* and of class scope?

10 If an association *r* inherits from an association *s*, how are the multiplicities at the ends of *r* related to the multiplicities of the ends of *s*?

Chapter 5

Platform-Independent Design

This chapter describes techniques for the refinement of analysis models towards platform-independent designs, by model transformation. It also describes platform-independent design structuring techniques such as design patterns and module specifications.

5.1 The design process

Design is concerned with constructing components and organising their interactions in order to achieve the system requirements. This involves:

- Identifying subsystems and modules which have a coherent and well-defined purpose and functional cohesion.
- Identifying the dependencies between modules, and specifying their interfaces and responsibilities (eg, in terms of a set of constraints that they are responsible for).

In a completed design each requirement use case and constraint must be carried out/maintained by some class/module, or by a combination of classes and modules. For example, in the Scrabble system, the 'make move' use case discussed in Section 2.2 will be primarily implemented in the *PlayerGUI* module, which manages all the GUI interaction for constructing a move. The validation and score calculation of the move will be the responsibility of the *Move* module.

Some constraints will be satisfied by the design of an individual module or class, for example the postconditions

$$post : \quad squareLetter \ = \ \{\} \ => \ result \ = \ false$$
$$post : \quad squareLetter \ /= \ \{\} \ => \ result \ = \ true$$

on operation *isOccupied*() : *Boolean* of *Square* can be directly implemented as conditional statements in pseudocode in the definition of this operation.

97

Other constraints, such as the property $C5$ that all occupied squares on the board must be reachable from each other:

$$squareLetter \ / = \ \{\} \ \& \ x : Square \ \&$$
$$x.squareLetter \ / = \ \{\} \ \Rightarrow \ x : adjacent.closure$$

will involve more complex design decisions, and the interaction of possibly several modules. We can use an *inductive* approach to maintain this constraint: to ensure it is true initially, we must enforce (in the *PlayerGUI* or *Move* modules, probably) that all letters placed in the first move must be in a connected line. On subsequent moves it is sufficient to ensure that (i) at least one of the new letters is adjacent to an existing occupied square, and (ii) all the new letters are placed in a connected line. Due to the recursive definition of *adjacent.closure*, this will establish $C5$ for the updated board. The checks (i) and (ii) probably can be implemented in the *Move* module, if the state of the board before the move is provided to this module.

5.2   Model transformations

A number of useful model transformations on UML specifications can be used to improve the structure of a model, or to progress a model towards an implementable form. In terms of the MDA these are PIM to PIM or PIM to PSM mappings. For any model transformation, we must ensure that it preserves all the constraints that were placed on the system as mandatory requirements. A transformation should also not impose additional constraints without a good justification, as these will restrict implementation choices. Thus the best transformations are equivalences. In Chapter 9 we show how to define transformations in terms of constraints between the old and new models, and how to show that they are equivalences. The following are some simple examples of useful transformations:

Removal of many-many associations This transformation (Figure 5.1) replaces a many-many association with a new class and two many-one associations. It is particularly useful as a step towards the implementation of a class diagram in a relational database. If $a : A$ and $b : B$ are related by A_B in the original model, then there is an AB object, call it x, such that $x.ar'' = a$ and $x.br'' = b$, and vice-versa. So the original $a.br$ set can be obtained as $a.xr.br''$ in the new model.

Replace inheritance by association This transformation (Figure 5.2) is useful to remove situations of multiple inheritance from PIMs.

Introduce qualified association This transformation (Figure 5.3) replaces an $\{identity\}$ attribute $att : T$ in a class B by a qualified association, qualified by this attribute, from any class A that has an association to B. The new association A_B'' relates a and x to b exactly when a is related to b by A_B, and $x = b.att$.

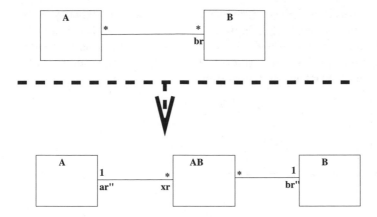

Figure 5.1: Removing a many-many association

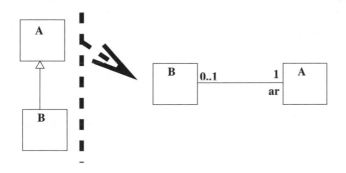

Figure 5.2: Replacing an inheritance by an association

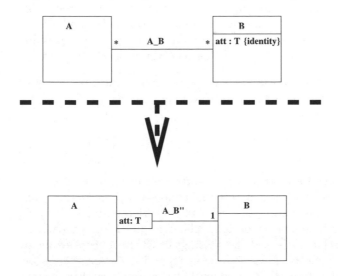

Figure 5.3: Introducing a qualified association

Introducing a superclass This transformation can be applied whenever two
classes have common features (Figure 5.4). The new superclass is usually
abstract, because only A and B instances existed in the original model.
The common features are moved into the new superclass, common operations become abstract in the superclass.

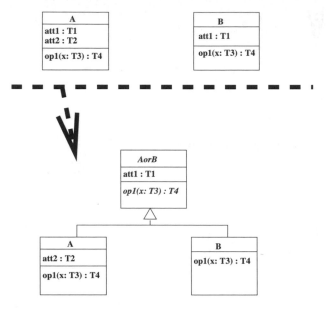

Figure 5.4: Introducing a superclass

Target splitting of statechart transition This transformation refines the
behaviour of a statechart by splitting a transition into two or more disjoint
cases. Figure 5.5 shows an example where $G \equiv G1 \vee G2$ and $G1 \Rightarrow
\neg\, G2$, that is, the guard G is split into two disjoint cases. For example
if G is $x \leq y$, $G1$ could be $x = y$ and then $G2$ would be $x < y$.

The introduction of a qualified association was used to enable the board squares
to be referred to by their coordinates, in the Scrabble system.

5.3   Design patterns

Design patterns are characteristic structures of software which are used to solve
particular design problems. They are mainly independent of programming languages (at least within the general category of object-oriented languages), so
can be used for platform-independent design. The concept of 'design pattern'
originated in building architecture and the writings of Christopher Alexander.
His books included *The Timeless Way of Building* [1] and *A Pattern Language:
Towns, Buildings, Construction* [2]. Subsequently software researchers sought
to apply the concept to program construction and discover 'design patterns'

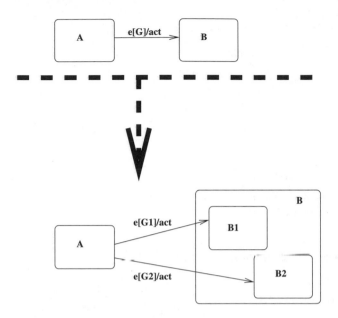

Figure 5.5: Target splitting

of software. The text which popularised the idea in the object-oriented community was the 'Gang of Four' (aka GoF) book [16], which introduced the idea of a design pattern in object-oriented software. GoF divided patterns into three general categories: creational, structural and behavioural, depending on their primary aim (ie, organising object creation, the structure of classes and relationships, or the distribution of behaviour amongst objects).

Subsequently, there has been a considerable amount of research into recognising and cataloguing patterns [17], with many books and papers being published, and a dedicated conference 'Pattern languages of programs' on the issue.

In any significant sized application, it is likely that some patterns will be useful. In the following we will consider the Template Method, Observer, Iterator, Builder, Strategy and Singleton patterns, and their application in the Scrabble project.

5.3.1 The Template Method pattern

This behavioural pattern is used to organise or refactor a design whenever there is a method m which has essentially the same algorithm in two or more classes, but with small variations. The pattern defines a superclass for these classes and places the generic definition of m in this class, meaning that the subclasses only need to define the parts of m in which they differ.

Figure 5.6 shows the general structure of this pattern.

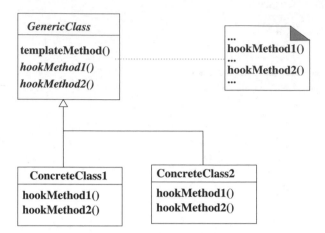

Figure 5.6: Structure of Template Method pattern

The classes involved in this pattern are:

- *GenericClass* – this defines the template method which consists of a skeleton algorithm calling one or more hook methods. It also defines hook methods that subclasses can override.
- *ConcreteClass* – implements the hook methods.

Hook methods may be defined as abstract in *GenericClass*, or given default implementations there.

In the Scrabble system a prime candidate for the use of this pattern is the *Square* class and its subclasses. For example, to calculate the score of a square, we carry out the following algorithm:

```
if the square is empty, return 0
else
      return score of letter, adjusted
              by the kind of square
```

This algorithm applies regardless of the kind of square, so it can be placed in the *Square* superclass, and the part that varies between the subclasses, the computation in the *else* branch, is placed in each subclass:

```
public abstract class Square
{ private Letter squareLetter = null;

  ...

  // Hook method:
  public abstract int getLetterScore(Letter l);

  // Template method:
```

```
    public int getLetterScore()
    { if (squareLetter == null) { return 0; }
      return getLetterScore(squareLetter);
    }
}
```

Each subclass will then define its own version of the hook method *getLetterScore*(*l* : *Letter*):

```
class OrdinarySquare extends Square
{ public int getLetterScore(Letter l)
    { return l.getScore(); }
}
```

```
class DoubleLetterSquare extends Square
{ public int getLetterScore(Letter l)
    { return 2*l.getScore(); }
}
```

```
class TripleLetterSquare extends Square
{ public int getLetterScore(Letter l)
    { return 3*l.getScore(); }
}
```

The same approach is needed to return a graphic icon for a square: an empty square must return the specific icon for that kind of square, an occupied square must return the icon of the occupying letter.

5.3.2 The Iterator pattern

The purpose of this behavioural pattern is to support access to elements of an aggregate data structure (such as a tree or array) sequentially. It is applicable whenever we:

- require multiple traversal algorithms over an aggregate;
- require a uniform traversal interface over different aggregates;
- or when aggregate classes and traversal algorithm must vary independently.

The general structure of this pattern is shown in Figure 5.7.

An iterator object acts like a cursor or pointer into a structure, indicating a current location within this structure and providing operations to move this cursor forwards or backwards in the structure.

Thus normally an *Iterator* class has operations such as *atEnd* / *hasNext* to test if the iteration has reached an end, *advance* / *next* to step forward to the next element, and *current* to obtain the current element.

The classes involved are:

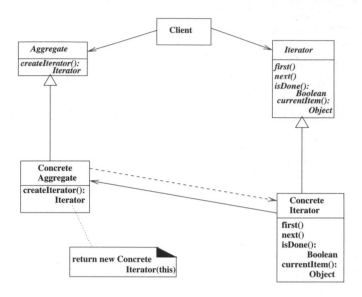

Figure 5.7: Structure of Iterator pattern

- *Aggregate* – the class defining a general composite data structure such as a list or tree.
- *ConcreteAggregate* – specific subclass defining a particular data structure such as a linked list or binary search tree.
- *Iterator* – interface for general iteration operations such as accessing the first element in the collection, stepping through the collection, etc.
- *ConcreteIterator* – iterator subclass specific to a particular data structure. The *createIterator*() method of the data structure returns a *ConcreteIterator* instance for the structure.

The consequences of the pattern are an increase in flexibility, because the aggregate and the traversal mechanism are independent. It is possible to have multiple iterators acting on the same aggregate object simultaneously, possibly with different traversal algorithms: eg, using both a post and pre-order traversal of a tree.

If the iterator pattern was not used, we would require direct access to the private parts of the data structures being iterated over.

5.3.3   Iterators as generators: the permutation iterator

The concept of an iterator is much more general than simply iterating through the elements of a fixed pre-existing data structure. One very important use of iterators is as *generators* of all elements of some collection of objects.

Definition A *generator* for a collection S is a bijective function $g : 1..n \rightarrowtail S$ where n is the size of S.

In other words, $g(1)$, $g(2)$, ..., $g(n)$ are all the different elements of S. S may be too large to represent in memory all at once (eg, if S were all the permutations of 15 letters, the size of S is 15 factorial, approximately 1.3×10^{12}), instead we want to obtain the individual elements one-by-one for use in our program (eg, to allow a Scrabble player to view all permutations of their rack). This concept occurs widely in computer science, in particular the Java database connectivity package, JDBC, uses it when obtaining the results of queries on a database via a *ResultSet* iterator/generator.

Some examples of such generator iterators are:

- *PairIterator*: obtains successively all the C_2^n different pairs of objects from a list of length n.
- *LexicalIterator*: iterates through a list of lists, returning a collection selected from each in lexicographic order. There are $n_1 * ... * n_m$ such collections if these are the size of the lists concerned.
  Eg, for lists $[x, y, x]$, $[a, b]$ and $[p, q]$, there are twelve selections, and the first five selections are:

$$[x, a, p], [x, a, q], [x, b, p], [x, b, q], [y, a, p], ...$$

- *PermutationIterator*: obtains successively all the $n!$ different permutations of a list of length n.
- *SublistIterator*: obtains all the 2^n different sublists (retaining the original list order) of a list of size n.

In the Scrabble project, the *PermutationIterator* is useful to enable a player to shuffle their rack to spot possible words, and it could also be used in a search strategy to find possible computer moves: generate successively all permutations of the rack letters and see if they are valid words and if they fit into available slots on the board. The *SublistIterator* can also be used in searching for possible words: for each sublist of the rack, search for words containing all these letters and test to see if they can be used on the board.

To define such iterators, we need to analyse what the initiation, termination test and advance operations must do. For example, for *PermutationIterator*, we can define the following recursive strategy for generating all permutations:

Given a list $l = [a_1, a_2, \ldots, a_n]$, its permutations are either: (i) a_1 followed by a permutation of a_2 to a_n, or (ii) a_2 followed by a permutation of a_1, a_3, ..., a_n, ..., (n) a_n followed by a permutation of a_1, ..., a_{n-1}.

These n cases are disjoint, and together give all possible permutations of l.

Turning this strategy into a language-independent algorithm, we could have:

- Initiation will be done in the constructor *PermutationIterator* $(l : List)$, which supplies the list to be permuted. The 'first' permutation should be l in its original order, as this is always a valid permutation, even if l is empty. If l is not empty, an *index* variable is set to point to the first element of l. A permutation iterator for the remainder of l is created.

- Termination testing could be done in an operation *hasNext*() : *Boolean*, which is true if further permutations can be generated. If the list is empty, *hasNext*() is false, otherwise it is true if either the *index* is not pointing to the last element of *l*, or if the permutation iterator for the sublist (the list with the index element removed) has a next element.
- Stepping to the next element has two cases:

  1. If the iterator for the sublist has a next element, perform an advance on it.

  2. Otherwise, increment *index*, set the sublist to the list with the index element removed, and create a new permutation iterator for this sublist.

To get the current permutation, we get the current permutation of the sublist, and add the indexed element to its head.

In Java, the complete *PermutationIterator* class is:

```java
import java.util.*;

public class PermutationIterator
{ private List list;     // The list being iterated over
  private Object head;   // The selected list element
  private int index;     // The index of head in list
  private PermutationIterator subpi; // iterator for
                         // list - { head }

  public PermutationIterator(List l)
  { list = l;  // Assumes l instanceof ArrayList
    index = 0;
    if (index < list.size())
    { head = list.get(0);
      List subl = (List) ((ArrayList) l).clone();
      subl.remove(0);
      subpi = new PermutationIterator(subl);
    }
  }

  public boolean hasNext()
  { if (list == null)
    { return false; }
    if (subpi == null)
    { return false; }
    return (index < list.size()-1 ||
            subpi.hasNext());
  }

  public List current()
  { List res = new ArrayList();
    if (list.size() == 0)
    { return res; }
```

```
      res = subpi.current();
      res.add(0,head);
      return res;
  }

  public void next()
  { if (subpi == null)
    { return; }
    if (subpi.hasNext())
    { subpi.next(); }
    else
    { index++;
      if (index < list.size())
      { head = list.get(index);
        List subl = (List) ((ArrayList) list).clone();
        subl.remove(index);
        subpi = new PermutationIterator(subl);
      }
    }
  }
}
```

5.3.4 The Observer pattern

This behavioural pattern is intended for situations where there are multiple views or presentations of a set of data, such as alternative graphical views (pie charts and bar charts of sales figures, for example). In general it defines a one-to-many dependency between objects so that when one object (the data) changes state, all its dependents (the views) are notified and update themselves automatically.

It is applicable whenever there are two entities being represented in software, one dependent on the other, so that a change to one object requires changes to others (its dependents). This pattern can be abstractly expressed (Figure 5.8) by specifying that the state of the observers of the subject are functions of the subject state.

Figure 5.9 shows the typical design and implementation structure of this pattern.

The classes in this structure have the following roles:

- *Subject* – abstract superclass of all classes containing observed data. Provides methods *attach* and *detach* to add and remove observers of a subject, and *notify* to inform all observers that a significant state change has occurred in the observable and that they may need to update their presentation of it.
- *ConcreteSubject* – specific observable data, any method of this class which modifies its state may need to call *notify* on completion.

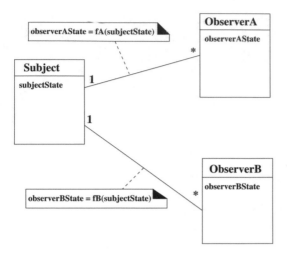

Figure 5.8: Abstract Observer pattern

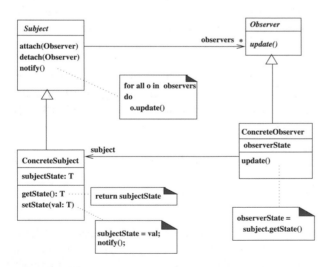

Figure 5.9: Design structure of Observer pattern

- *Observer* – abstract superclass of observers of subjects. It declares an *update* method whose purpose is to adjust the observer's presentation on any subject state change.
- *ConcreteObserver* – class defining a specific view, such as a bar chart. Defines *update* specifically for this view.

It is important to maintain *referential integrity* when using this pattern, this means that for a subject object *s*, its set *s.observers* of attached observers has the property that

$$o : s.observers \equiv o.subject = s$$

That is, these observers are exactly the observer objects whose subject is *s*. This implies that whenever we execute *s.attach(o)* we must also set *o.subject = s*, and whenever we execute *s.detach(o)*, we must also set *o.subject = null*.

The positive consequences of using the pattern are:

- Modularity: subject and observers may vary independently.
- Extensibility: we can define and add any number of observers to a given subject.
- Customisability: different observers provide different views of a subject.

This pattern is widely used in commercial languages and libraries, for example, in the Model-View-Controller (MVC) paradigm. In MVC, the *Model* is the observable data, eg, a logical model of business data in a web system, the *View* is the presentation (observers) of this data, eg, web pages presented to a client. There is an invariant *View = f(Model)* expressing that the views are some representation of the model. The *Controller* is responsible for maintaining this invariant, by coordinating the operations of the model and view.

In Java the Swing event model is also directly related to Observer, with *Listener* objects playing the role of *Observer* for the event source (*Subject*) objects. Java Beans and Jini also use a similar event notification model.

In the Scrabble system, Observer is relevant if we wish to allow multiple human players to play simultaneously via different computers (perhaps remotely via the web). Each player would see a personalised view of the game, which always shows the state of their own rack and not that of any other player. Other parts of the GUI would be seen by all players.

The observer objects in this case are the different player displays, the subject object is an instance of *Game*.

5.3.5 The Builder pattern

This creational pattern allows a client object to obtain complex objects by a declarative specification of their type and content. The details of construction are managed in separate classes, with a different builder subclass for each variant of the object to be constructed.

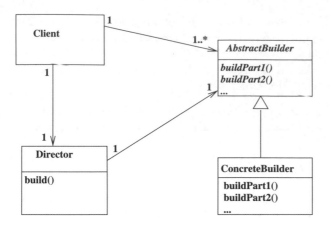

Figure 5.10: Design structure of Builder pattern

Figure 5.10 shows a general structure of this pattern. In the Scrabble system an example where this pattern is useful is in the construction of the board and the letters in the bag. An object of the *Game* class invokes methods on an instance of the *EnglishScrabbleBuilder* class, a subclass of a general *ScrabbleBuilder* class, to construct the board with the correct locations of ordinary and premium squares, and to initialise the bag with the correct numbers of each kind of letter (Figure 5.11).

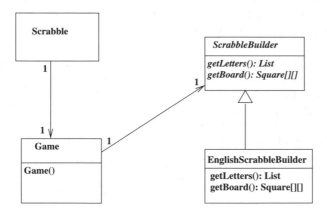

Figure 5.11: Builder pattern for Scrabble system

This makes extension to deal with other language variants of Scrabble quite simple: a new subclass of *ScrabbleBuilder* would need to be defined, but no other part of the system would be changed (if GUI elements and messages also needed to be given in a different language, these could also be constructed by a further *ScrabbleBuilder* method).

5.3.6 The Singleton pattern

This creational pattern is used to define classes which must have only a single instance (eg, mathematical utility classes, a database connection pool, etc). It replaces the use of a global non-object variable. Figure 5.12 shows the structure of this pattern.

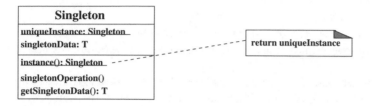

Figure 5.12: Structure of Singleton pattern

Singleton is used when:

- There must be a unique instance of a class, and it must be accessible to clients from a well-known access point;
- when the sole instance should be extensible by subclassing, and clients should be able to use an extended instance without modifying their code.

The involved classes are:

- *Singleton* – defines an operation *instance* that lets clients access its unique instance. *instance* is a class level (static) operation.
- *Singleton* may also be responsible for creating its own unique instance.

The benefits of this pattern are that it:

- provides controlled access to the *Singleton* instance – this can only be accessed via the *instance* method;
- reduces the name space of the program – a class instead of a global variable;
- permits subclassing of *Singleton*;
- it can be adapted easily to give a fixed number $N > 1$ of instances.

In the Scrabble system the *Dictionary* could be made into a *Singleton* class, so that it may be used as a global variable, reducing the number of parameters of operations in the system which need to look up words:

```
public class Dictionary
{ private static Dictionary uniqueInstance = null;
  ...

  private Dictionary() { }

  public static Dictionary getDictionary()
```

```
{ if (uniqueInstance == null)
  { uniqueInstance = new Dictionary(); }
  return uniqueInstance;
}

public boolean lookup(Word w)
{ ... }
}
```

Because the constructor is private, only the *Dictionary* class itself can construct instances of *Dictionary*: this is only done once, when *getDictionary* is called for the first time.

An alternative approach for defining Singleton classes in Java is to define all the features of the class as *static* (the *Math* class is an example of this). However this is less flexible, since it does not permit subclassing, nor the definition of a generalised Singleton with $N > 1$ instances.

5.3.7   The Strategy pattern

This is a behavioural pattern, which defines a common interface for alternative versions of an algorithm, enabling a client to easily select these different versions by varying the object the operation is invoked on.

Figure 5.13 shows the typical structure of this pattern.

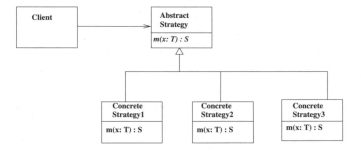

Figure 5.13: Strategy pattern

The elements of the pattern are:

- *Client* – a class which uses the operation via an abstract class or interface.
- *AbstractStrategy* – a class (or interface) that provides a common interface for the different implementations of the operation.
- *ConcreteStrategy* – a class that implements a particular version of the operation.

The benefits of the pattern are that it simplifies the code of the system by separating alternative versions of an algorithm into different classes, and that it allows dynamic selection of these versions by a client.

This pattern can be used in the Scrabble system to structure the alternative computer move strategies. An operation

```
generateComputerMove(g: Game): Move
```

can be defined to use one of several alternative strategies:

1. Find highest scoring word that crosses a new premium square and reaches the covered region of the board, using letters from the rack.
2. Find highest scoring words which are formed by adding letters from the rack alongside existing words.
3. Look for extensions to existing words by suffix *S* or prefix *UN*, etc, if available on the rack.

Each separate strategy could be defined in a separate class.

5.4 System and subsystem design

We will describe some general techniques for platform-independent design structuring using UML, for the functional core of a system. Sections 5.7 and 5.8 consider specific techniques for the GUI and data repository.

The earlier stages of the design process: system design and subsystem design, are already mainly independent of particular platforms, using only architecture description diagrams and textual natural language specifications to identify what are the subsystems of the system under development, and what are the dependencies between them. Figure 5.14 shows an architecture description diagram for the Scrabble system. Components (subsystems and modules) are represented as rectangles. Subcomponents of a component are nested inside it. An arrow from component X to component Y indicates that X *depends on* Y: usually this means that it makes use of Y's functionality, by invoking operations of Y. X is termed a *client* of Y in this case, and Y is called a *supplier* of X.

Such diagrams could also be expressed using UML package notation.

At the module and detailed design level natural-language or UML descriptions can be used to define what are each module's responsibilities, what data it manages, what operations it performs, and what is its interface (the set of operations that it provides to other parts of the system).

A module description of the *Move* module could be:

```
MODULE Move
MANAGES DATA: Move, LetterMove, Word
CONSTRAINTS
   C1: m : Move => m.letterMoves.x.size = 1 or
                   m.letterMoves.y.size = 1
   C2: m is first move => 8 : m.letterMoves.x &
                          8 : m.letterMoves.y
   C3: w : Word => w.xstart = w.xend or
```

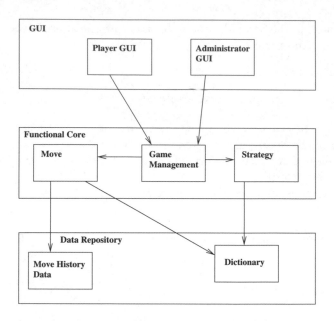

Figure 5.14: Architecture of Scrabble system

```
                  w.ystart = w.yend
  C4: m : Move => m.letterMoves.letter <:
                  m.movePlayer.playerRack.rackLetters
  C6: m : Move & d : Dictionary =>
                  m.wordsFormed <: d.allWords
OPERATIONS
  addLetterMove(m: Move, lm: LetterMove)
  // pre:
  //   lm.letter : m.movePlayer.playerRack.rackLetters
  // post:
  //   if lm valid
  //     m.letterMoves = m.letterMoves@pre \/ { lm }
  //   else
  //     m.letterMoves = m.letterMoves@pre

  validateMove(m: Move, n: Integer): Boolean
  // pre: n >= 1
  // post: returns true if m is valid move, where
  //   n is move number. Otherwise returns false.
  //   Checks constraints C1, C2 and C6

  findWords(m: Move, b: Board)
  // post: m.wordsFormed is set of new
  //       vertical and horizontal words
  //       created when m.letterMoves are
  //       placed on b. Each word satisfies
```

```
//        C3.
```

```
calculateScore(m: Move, b: Board): Integer
// post: m.letterMoves.size < 7  =>
//         result = m.wordsFormed.getScore(b).sum &
//         m.score = m.wordsFormed.getScore(b).sum
// post: m.letterMoves.size = 7 =>
//         result = m.wordsFormed.getScore(b).sum + 50 &
//         m.score = m.wordsFormed.getScore(b).sum + 50
```

A mixture of formal notation and natural language is used to specify constraints and operations. Ideally everything could be expressed formally, although this may be excessive for simple non-critical systems such as this one.

$C4$ could also be written as

```
C4: m : Move => m.letterMoves.letter :
               m.movePlayer.playerRack.rackLetters
```

since *objs*1 : *objs*2 for sets *objs*1 and *objs*2 is taken to mean *objs*1 $<:$ *objs*2.

The second postcondition of *calculateScore* reflects the case that if a player uses all seven of their letters in a move, then they get a bonus score of fifty points.

A module specification such as this description of *Move* is the only definition of a module which other modules should rely on. Other modules should not directly use the internal data of a module, or rely on particular implementations of its operations. This property, of 'loose coupling' between modules, enables modules to be developed and refined relatively independently of each other, and allows the system to be separated into 'layers' which are insulated from changes to other layers.

5.5   Detailed design

For detailed design, statecharts can be used to describe the algorithms and orderings of methods in a platform-independent manner. For the *startGame* operation of *Game* we could define the behaviour given in Figure 5.15.

Similarly, for *startMove* and *endMove* (Figure 5.16). The action of *startMove* says that the turn player's rack is filled up with letters chosen from the bag, when the move starts (eg, if they have three letters on their rack then four are chosen from the bag and added to the rack).

For the *Move* module, the most complex action is determining what are the set of new words produced by the move. A word is a vertical or horizontal sequence of letter-covered squares on the board, which is bounded above (for a vertical word) by the top of the board or by a blank square, and below by the bottom of the board or a blank square. Similarly for horizontal words. Figure 5.17 shows an example midway through a game.

To accumulate all the words for each move we obtain all vertical words, then all horizontal words. If the move itself is vertically aligned there is only

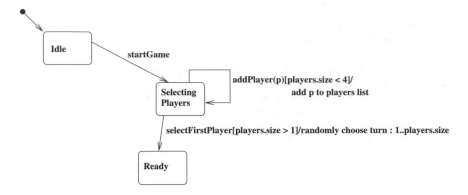

Figure 5.15: Statechart for *startGame*

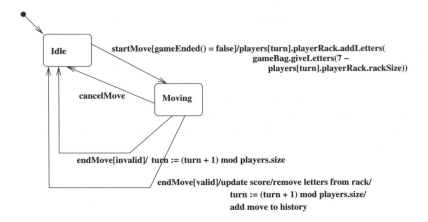

Figure 5.16: Statechart of *startMove, endMove*

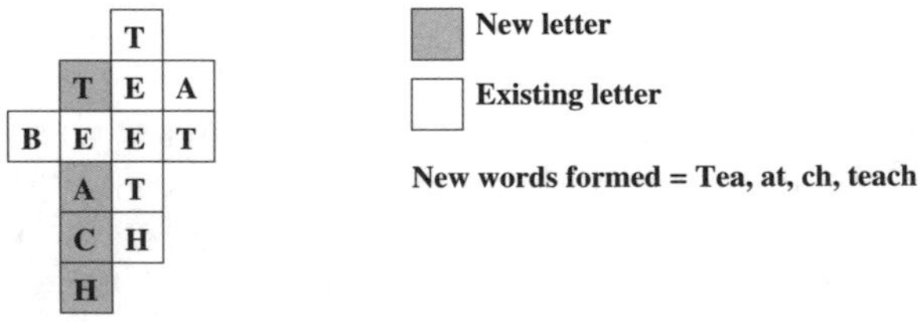

New letter

Existing letter

New words formed = Tea, at, ch, teach

Figure 5.17: Words produced from Scrabble move

one vertical word, but possibly a new horizontal word for each newly placed letter. Similarly if the move was horizontal there is only one horizontal word but possibly many vertical. Therefore the algorithm for *findWords*(*m* : *Move*, *b* : *Board*) is:

```
if (letterMoves[1].x = letterMoves[letterMoves.size].x)
// move is vertical
then
  return letterMoves[1].getVerticalWords(b) \/
       letterMoves.getHorizontalWords(b)
else // move is horizontal
  return letterMoves[1].getHorizontalWords(b) \/
       letterMoves.getVerticalWords(b)
```

where *getHorizontalWords*(*b* : *Board*) : *List* is an operation of *LetterMove* that returns all the new horizontal words created by this letter – there will either be zero or one such word. Likewise for *getVerticalWords*(*b* : *Board*). These two operations can be performed by searching backwards and forwards or up and down from the square of the new letter, finding the maximal contiguous sequence of letters either side of the letter (or above and below it).

5.6 Constructing a design architecture

The general principle for grouping elements of a system into subsystems and modules is that elements in the same group should have 'more in common' with each other than they do with elements in a different group: 'more in common' can mean that they depend on each other's functionality, that they are often involved in the same use cases, that they have similar or closely related functionalities, that they share common data structures or subordinate entities, etc.

A module or subsystem should represent a cohesive set of model elements, with a clear purpose and role in the larger system. Many ways of partitioning a system into subsystems and modules can be used and may produce equally valid, if different, results.

One approach is to start with the initial design class diagram and try to form disjoint groups of classes with the following properties:

Subordinates If class *A* has a directed association to class *B* and class *B* is not an end of any other association, then *B* is probably a *subordinate* class of *A* and *A* and *B* can be put in the same group[1].

Logical coherence More constraints relate classes and associations within the group than between different groups.

Functional coherence Classes are grouped to reduce the number of modules affected by each use case.

---

[1]UML uses the stereotypes *focus* class and *auxiliary* class for master and subordinate classes.

Aggregation Part and aggregate classes of a composition or aggregation are normally put in the same group.

Inheritance A superclass is normally put in the same group as all its subclasses.

No overlap Groups cannot overlap (contain common elements). Any common elements should be put into a separate group, which the remainder of the original groups can refer to/depend on.

Minimise dependencies Groups should be formed so that dependencies between groups are minimised, in particular two-way (bi-directional) dependencies between groups should be avoided if possible.

For example, in the Scrabble system, the *Inheritance* rule means that *Square* and its subclasses belong in the same subsystem. The *Aggregation* rule means *Square* also belongs in the same module as *Board*. *Functional coherence* means *Rack* and *Bag* probably belong in the same group, since several use cases involve transferring letters between the bag and racks. *Logical coherence* implies that *Move*, *LetterMove* and *Word* belong together. *No overlap* means *Letter* should be in a separate group, since it is referred to by several other groups. Figure 5.18 shows an initial partitioning of the class diagram using these heuristics. The dictionary has been placed in a separate module because it is a highly cohesive unit which is likely to be used by other modules if the system was extended (eg, to provide a user with a tool to extend a dictionary).

5.7   User-interface design

Platform-independent GUI design can be carried out by specifying the appearance, layout and behaviour of an interface in terms of generic UI concepts such as 'frame', 'button', 'text field', 'label', 'table', etc, which have similar interpretations in UI technologies such as XHTML and Java Swing.

For example, we can draw diagrams of the intended layout of the Scrabble game interface using only such platform-independent facilities (Figure 5.19).

The mapping of these GUI concepts into XHTML and Java is given in Table 5.1. XML can be used to represent the structure of a GUI, with each kind of GUI component represented by a particular tag, and the nesting structure of the GUI expressed by the nesting hierarchy of XML tags. An example of this is in the XUI toolkit [55], which defines a platform-independent GUI description language using XML, defining generic GUI elements in XML tags.

The behaviour of a GUI can be expressed in terms of constraints, operation specifications and statecharts. In the Scrabble system the GUI structure can be expressed as an object/class diagram (Figure 2.20), and its state expressed as a function of the state of the functional core data:

- If a move is not in progress, then each *boardButtons*$[i, j]$ displays the state

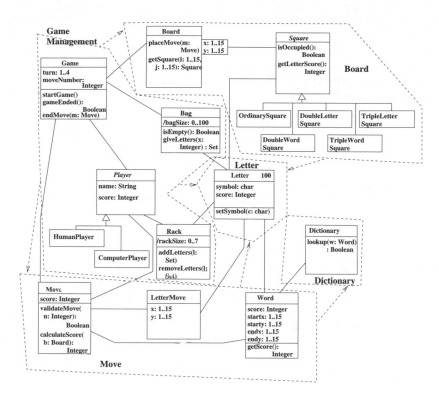

Figure 5.18: Scrabble modules from class diagram

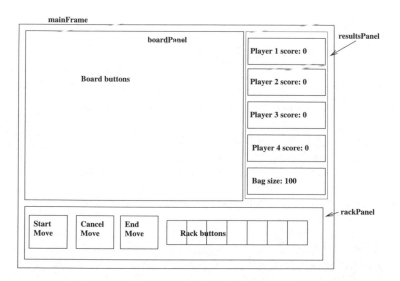

Figure 5.19: Scrabble GUI

GUI concept	XHTML	Java Swing
button	button	JButton
text field	<input type="text"/>	JTextField
checkboxes	<input type="checkbox"/>	JCheckBox
radio buttons	<input type="radio"/>	JRadioButton
selection lists	<select .... />	JComboBox
table	table	JTable
label	text	JLabel
frame	frame	JFrame
dialog	form	JDialog

Table 5.1: Mapping of GUI concepts

of $boardSquare[i,j]$:

$$i : 1..15 \ \& \ j : 1..15 \ \Rightarrow$$
$$boardButtons[i,j].icon \ =$$
$$g.gameBoard.boardSquare[i,j].icon$$

This is an invariant of $boardPanel$.
Each of the rack buttons is blank:

$$i : 1..7 \ \Rightarrow \ rackButtons[i].icon = BLANK\_ICON$$

(An invariant of $rackPanel$.)
Each player label displays the current score of that player:

$$i : 1..g.players.size \ \Rightarrow$$
$$playerLabel[i].text \ =$$
$$\text{“Player ” } + g.players[i].name + \text{“ score : ”}+$$
$$g.players[i].score$$

This is an invariant of $resultsPanel$.

- During a move, the rack displays the rack of the current player:

$$i : 1..g.players[g.turn].playerRack.rackSize \ \Rightarrow$$
$$rackButtons[i].text =$$
$$g.players[g.turn].playerRack.rackLetters[i].symbol$$

When no move is in progress, the rack is blank and each button is disabled:

$$i : 1..7 \ \Rightarrow$$
$$rackButtons[i].text = \text{“} - \text{”} \ \&$$
$$rackButtons[i].enabled = false$$

This is an invariant of $rackPanel$.

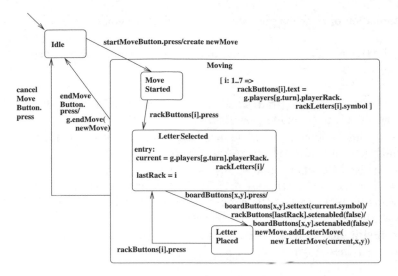

Figure 5.20: Statechart of move creation

This situation is an example of the abstract observer pattern (Figure 5.8). Details of the behaviour of the GUI when a move is being created can be specified in terms of the effect of GUI events such as *startMoveButton.press* (Figure 5.20). During a move, the rack buttons display the letters in the turn player's rack (invariant of *Moving* state), and when one of these buttons is selected, its index is stored in *lastRack* and the corresponding letter is stored in *current*. The next action must be to press one of the board buttons (or to press cancel or end). When a board button is pressed, the rack and board buttons are disabled, the board button is set to display the symbol of *current* and the letter move is added to the move that is being defined. Once all letters in the move have been transferred from the rack to the board in this manner, *endMoveButton* can be pressed to commit the move, it is then checked for validity by the game object.

5.8 Data repository design

This form of design identifies what data needs to be stored persistently, and what structure and organisation of this data will be used. Various technologies can be used for the actual implementation of a data repository: a relational database such as MySQL (http://www.mysql.com) or PostgreSQL (http://www.postgresql.org), an object-oriented database (such as ObjectStore: http://www.objectstore.net), or structured text such as XML (http://www.w3.org/XML/). Ideally the design of stored data should be mappable without excessive work to any of these implementations.

5.8.1   Transformation of class diagrams to relational data-schemas

To translate a UML class diagram to a relational database schema, the following transformations can be used:

1. Identify which entities, attributes and associations are to be stored in the repository, ie, are to be made *persistent*.
2. Introduce primary keys as new *identity* attributes, for every persistent class which does not already possess an *identity* attribute.
3. Replace persistent explicit many-many associations by two many-one associations and a new class (Figure 5.1). In database terms, the new entity will have as its primary key the combination of the primary keys of the entities at the ends of the original association.
4. Replace inheritance by many-one associations, or amalgamate subclasses into the superclass (Figure 5.21).

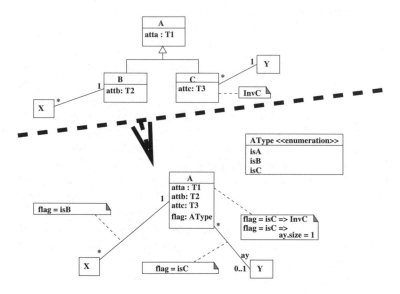

Figure 5.21: Amalgamation of subclasses transformation

The resulting class diagram can then be directly translated into database tables:

1. Each transformed persistent class C is represented as a table with a column for each attribute, and with primary keys the identity attributes, or (producing a compound key) a group of attributes stereotyped as *identity*.
2. Each persistent explicit many-one association from A to B is represented as a foreign key from the table for A to the table for B.

3. Each persistent implicit association will be represented by an SQL predicate which is used to calculate the entity instances in the association by a *SELECT* query.

In the Scrabble system, we only need to store data about moves, consisting of each *Move* object in the history, together with its attached *Player*, *LetterMove*s and their *Letter*. The resulting database schema is shown in Figure 5.22. The 'crows foot' symbol indicates a many multiplicity ∗ at that end

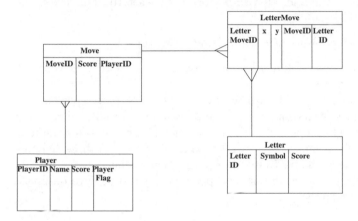

Figure 5.22: Scrabble database schema

of the relationship. In the table at that end there will be a foreign key to the table at the opposite end, where the association must have a '1' multiplicity.

5.8.2 Structured Query Language (SQL)

The standard notation for describing operations on relational data is SQL, which uses a small set of declarative OCL-like statements to express queries or updates on entities stored as tables and relationships expressed via foreign keys.

The most frequently used SQL statements are:

- SELECT columns FROM tables WHERE condition
- INSERT INTO table (column$_1$, ..., column$_n$) VALUES (val$_1$, ..., val$_n$)
- DELETE FROM table WHERE condition
- UPDATE table SET column$_1$ = val$_1$, ..., column$_n$ = val$_n$ WHERE condition

The *SELECT* statement searches through the *tables* and produces a result table whose columns are the named *columns* of the *tables*, with rows made up of these column values from those rows of the tables that satisfy the *condition*. In the condition, columns (attributes) occurring in two or more tables must be qualified by the name of the table (entity). For example,

```
SELECT Name, Move.Score, Symbol
FROM Player, Move, LetterMove, Letter
WHERE Move.PlayerID = Player.PlayerID AND
  Move.MoveID = LetterMove.MoveID AND
  LetterMove.LetterID = Letter.LetterID AND
  Letter.Score >= 10
```

lists the player name, the player's move score and letter symbol for any player who has a move containing a letter with a score of at least 10. This is akin to a filter expression

$$players \mid (10 : playerMoves.letterMoves.letter.score)$$

although more general, in enabling selective presentation of only some columns (attributes) from the result.

The *INSERT* statement adds a new row to the *table* (corresponding to creating a new instance of the entity the table represents). Usually all columns (attributes of the entity) are listed, with the corresponding values for the new instance, although the primary key may be omitted if the database handles the allocation of a new unique (unused) primary key value itself[2]. In this book we will create and maintain our own primary keys to achieve database independence in this respect.

For example:

```
INSERT INTO Move (MoveID, Score, PlayerID)
VALUES (11, 24, 1)
```

would add a row for a new *Move* object for player 1 to the move table.

DELETE removes all rows from *table* that match (satisfy) the *condition*. For example:

```
DELETE FROM Move WHERE PlayerID = 1
```

removes all move data for player 1.

UPDATE modifies all existing rows of *table* that match *condition*, by setting their *column$_1$* column to *val$_1$*, etc. For example,

```
UPDATE Player
SET PlayerFlag = 'ComputerPlayer'
WHERE Name = 'Felix'
```

turns the player 'Felix' into a computer. String data is normally written between single quotes in SQL.

Some features of SQL are platform dependent, for example some databases do not support the *LIKE* option (a regular expression matching facility) for a WHERE clause. Either the SQL should be written to avoid the need for this operator, probably implying that program code is written by the developer in their database interface in its place, or separate versions of the database interface specific to different databases should be written, to make full use of particular database features when they are available.

---

[2] As in Microsoft Access for example.

5.9   Exception handling

Programming languages and environments differ widely in how they deal with situations of erroneous execution, such as an attempt to divide by zero, so it is difficult to provide platform-independent specifications of functionality in such cases. The role of the precondition of an operation is to express what conditions are necessary at commencement of an execution of the operation for it to execute without error. The postcondition only expresses the effect of an execution of the operation in cases where the precondition was true at its start. So neither constraint describes the behaviour of the operation in erroneous cases.

Descriptions of error cases can be added to the module definitions as exception clauses, for example:

```
MODULE Move
...
OPERATIONS
...
  validateMove(m: Move, n: Integer): Boolean
  // pre: n >= 1
  // post: returns true if m is valid move, where
  //    n is move number. Otherwise returns false.
  //    Checks constraints C1, C2 and C6
  // exceptions: dictionary not found, or
  //    memory error: inform user and
  //    return false.
```

In general, an exception should be dealt with at the closest point to where it arises, at which an appropriate action can be taken and/or a meaningful error message can be provided to the user of the system. In the above example, the *validateMove* operation can itself generate a message such as 'No dictionary can be found' or 'Insufficient memory to search dictionary', depending on the kind of error encountered. The GUI module which called *validateMove* should then display this message.

5.10   Transforming a PIM to a PSM

In this section we will consider how to map a platform-independent design into platform-specific designs. Both PIMs and PSMs can usually be expressed in UML notations, so that production of a PSM specific to a particular programming language and environment, such as Java, can be expressed in terms of transformations on UML models.

5.10.1 General issues for PIM to PSM transformation

Since programming languages and software platforms differ significantly in their semantics, care needs to be taken that the intended meaning of the PIM is correctly expressed in a PSM. Particular areas where problems may arise are:

- Data types: the PIM may use unbounded integers, for example, and infinite precision real numbers, which are not available in an executable programming language. Either the developer must ensure that bounds on data are enforced so that the PIM and PSM behave in the same way, or suitable extended data types must be used. For instance, *BigInteger* in Java allows integer values much larger than the standard *int* type.

  The evaluation of boolean expressions in OCL is also slightly different to that in programming languages: A & B is *false* if either A or B is false, even if the other argument is undefined. A *or* B is *true* if A or B is true, even if the other argument is undefined. In contrast, in Java, evaluation is left to right, so that if A is undefined in either case (eg, evaluation results in an infinite loop), the whole expression is undefined. By using preconditions to ensure expressions in an operation definition are always defined, we can remove such discrepancies.

- Method semantics, particularly the rules concerning overloading and overriding, which vary significantly between languages.

- Language-specific rules and features, such as the lack of multiple inheritance in Java (in contrast to C++), or built-in *get*, *set* and *let* method forms in Visual Basic and C$^{\#}$ (in contrast to Java). C++ permits overloading of operators such as $\ll$ (this mechanism is not in Java), and the definition of template classes (only supported in Java from version 1.5).

Ideally, the PIM should be designed so that these problems are minimised, by, for example, using only a subset of UML features whose interpretation in different programming languages is equivalent.

In the PSM class diagram the navigation direction of associations needs to be specified, representing the direction in which object references will be followed in an implementation. The visibility of features (eg, public, protected or private) needs to be made explicit if they are not already defined. Additional implementation-level constraints, such as { *sorted* } on ordered association ends, can be specified.

In a class diagram, navigation along an association from class A to class B is indicated by an arrowhead on the B end of the association. This means that, given an A object or set of A objects, our program will need to access the related B objects. Visibility annotations in UML are prefixed before the feature names they constrain, as with the derived prefix /. Table 5.2 gives the notation and meaning of these.

Notation	Meaning
-	private: accessible in the defining class only
#	protected: accessible in defining class and in its subclasses
+	public: accessible in all classes

Table 5.2: Visibility annotations in UML

5.10.2 Producing a Java-specific design

The particular language rules that must be observed in a Java-specific model are:

- Method overloading (the definition of several methods of the same class with the same name but different parameter types) is valid, provided no two methods with the same name differ only in their output types. Thus trying to define two methods

```
public A m() { ... }

public B m() { ... }
```

  in the same class, or in two classes linked by inheritance, is invalid.
  Java uses only the *declared type* of an actual parameter to determine which version of a method to call – runtime polymorphism only applies to the object on which the method executes, not to the arguments of the method.
- static (class scope) methods cannot be overridden (redefined with identical name and parameter types) in a subclass: two different methods result.
- Trying to restrict visibility of a method in a subclass (redefining a *public* method as *protected*, for example) is invalid.
- If a class contains an abstract method, it must be abstract itself.
- Interfaces cannot contain constructors or instance scope attributes.

This means that the PIM must not contain elements which violate these rules, or that they must be eliminated in the mapping to a PSM.

Constructs such as association classes and aggregation which have no direct corresponding language representation in Java must be translated into constructs which can be represented. For association classes, we can introduce a new intermediate class and factor the association into two new associations (Figure 11.20). For aggregations, we must ensure that an operation which deletes a 'whole' object must also delete all of its 'part' objects.

Another important restriction that a PSM for Java must obey is that no multiple inheritance is permitted: a class may only directly inherit from at most one other class. We can use the 'replace inheritance by association' transformation in Section 5.2 above to achieve this, or replace an inheritance by interface inheritance if the superclass has only abstract methods and constant (readOnly) class scope data.

The datatypes in the PIM class diagram of a system also need to be converted into corresponding programming-language specific types (taking account of the finite and imprecise nature of these, in the case of numbers). Table 5.3 gives this mapping for Java. The *String* type remains unchanged in this map-

PIM type	Java PSM type
Integer	int
Real	double
Boolean	boolean

Table 5.3: Mapping of UML types to Java

ping, and user-defined enumerated types map to corresponding constructions in Java. For example the enumeration *Direction* with values {*vertical, horizontal*} is represented as two constants:

```
public static final int vertical = 0;
public static final int horizontal = 1;
```

All such types could be placed in a single *SystemTypes* class, which is then accessed via interface inheritance (*implements* in Java) by any class that needs to refer to these values.

Figure 5.23 shows a Java PSM class diagram for the Scrabble system. Protected visibility is used for the features *squareLetter* and *playerRack*, since these belong to classes which have subclasses, so that these features may need to be directly referenced in these subclasses.

5.11   Exercises

1   Give a detailed design for *PairIterator* as described in Section 5.3.2 above.

2   Give a detailed design for *SublistIterator* as described in Section 5.3.2 above.

3   Give a module design for the *Board* module, supporting operations *placeMove*(*b* : *Board, m* : *Move*), *isOccupied*(*b* : *Board, i* : 1..15, *j* : 1..15) : *Boolean, getSquare*(*i* : 1..15, *j* : 1..15) : *Square*.

4   Apply model transformations to the class diagram of Figure 5.24 to improve its structure.

5   Design a GUI for a noughts-and-crosses (tic-tac-toe) game which has a display with nine buttons arranged in a three-by-three grid for the board, and a button to clear the board. There are two players who alternate moves: one with the symbol 'O' and the other with the symbol 'X'. When a player moves

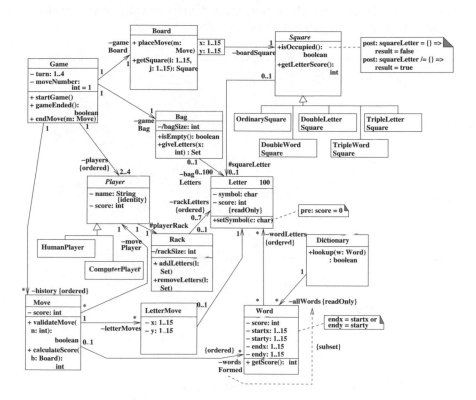

Figure 5.23: Scrabble Java PSM

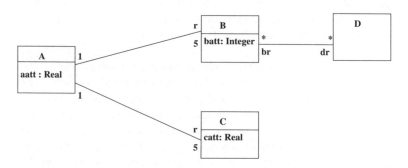

Figure 5.24: PIM class diagram

in their turn, they click on a vacant board button and their symbol appears on that button. If there are three buttons in a line vertically, horizontally or diagonally with the same symbol, then that player has won.

6 Apply the subclass amalgamation transformation to the model shown in Figure 5.25.

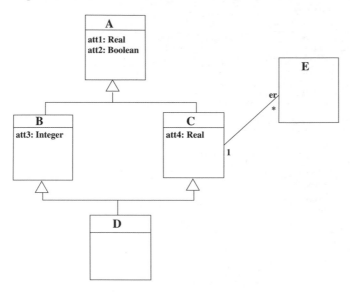

Figure 5.25: Subclass amalgamation exercise

7 Use a state machine to describe the intended behaviour of a face recognition system. The initial operation that a user performs is to load an image (identified by a file name) into the system, then to select at least ten points in the image (identified by x and y coordinates relative to its top left corner) to indicate the area of the image that is considered significant, then either to proceed directly to analysis (comparison against stored face data), or to translate the image (eg, to move it so the face is horizontally aligned) before analysis.

8 Apply the template method pattern to the following problem: the system should represent male and female persons, and model their weekly consumption of alcohol. A method *consume(units : Integer)* of either class models the consumption of the given number of alcohol units (a unit equates to half a pint of beer). This method should give a warning when the total amount consumed goes over the person's recommended weekly allowance (28 units for men, 21 for women). A method *reset()* resets the total to zero again on Monday morning.

9 Does the PIM class diagram of Figure 5.26 conform to the restrictions for Java? If not, explain where it fails to conform, and how these problems could be corrected.

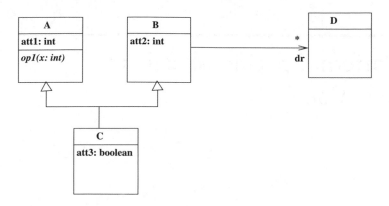

Figure 5.26: Proposed Java PSM

10 Identify what constraints would be used to define the state of the GUIs of a multi-view version of the Scrabble system, where each player sees a separate version of the interface, in which their own rack is always shown (other parts of the interface being the same for all players).

Chapter 6

From Platform-Specific Models to Executable Code

Once a platform-specific design has been produced, it can be used as the basis for an implementation in executable code. In this chapter we show the mapping from a Java PSM to Java code. The process is similar for other related languages such as C++ or C$^\#$.

6.1 Production of a Java implementation

Starting from the PSM diagrams and module descriptions, class definitions in Java can be produced, with some degree of automation. Each construct in the PSM class diagram needs to be mapped to a programming language construct. Table 6.1 lists the main correspondences for Java.

From this table it can be seen that most of the class diagram elements map quite directly to corresponding Java elements, merely with different keywords being used (*final* instead of *readOnly*, etc). However the last three cases are more difficult. An *identity* attribute has the constraint that no two objects of the class can have the same value for it. This means that the constructor must check if the value has already been used, and abort the construction if it has. Likewise for any operation that modifies the attribute.

An association directed from class A to class B can be implemented as an attribute of A, with the name of the B-end role, of an appropriate type. If the B end has multiplicity 0..1 or 1, the attribute simply has type B. For other multiplicities, the attribute will be of a collection type. Certain forms of such association and association end correspond very closely to Java data structures (Figure 6.1):

- An ordered association end of multiplicity $a..b$ corresponds to a Java array of size b.
- An ordered *-multiplicity association end corresponds to a Java List.
- An unordered *-multiplicity association end corresponds to a Java Set.

Class Diagram Element	Java Program Construct
class	class
abstract class	abstract class
interface	interface
guarded class	synchronised class
leaf class	final class
utility class	static class
inheritance	extends
interface inheritance	implements
static attribute	static (class) attribute
non-static attribute	instance attribute
readOnly attribute	final attribute
abstract operation	abstract method
static operation	static method
non-static operation	instance method
guarded operation	synchronised method
identity attribute	no direct translation
association	attribute of class/collection type
constraint	no direct translation

Table 6.1: Mapping of UML elements to Java

- A qualified association with 1 or 0..1 multiplicity at the unqualified end corresponds to a Java Map (or an array/multi-dimensional array if the qualification types are all ranges $a..b$).

Using these rules we obtain the following outline class declarations for the Scrabble system:

```
public class Game
{ private Board gameBoard;
  private Player[] players = new Player[4];
  private List history = new ArrayList();
  private Bag gameBag;
  private int turn;
  private int moveNumber = 1;

  public void startGame()

  public boolean gameEnded()

  public void endMove(Move m)
}

public class Board
{ private Square[][] boardSquare = new Square[15][15];

  public void placeMove(Move m)
```

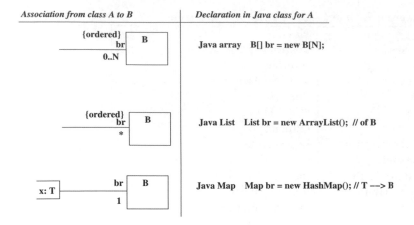

Figure 6.1: Correspondence of associations and program data

```
  public Square getSquare(int i, int j)
}

public abstract class Square
{ private Letter squareLetter;

  public boolean isOccupied()

  public int getLetterScore()
}
```

UML expressions map directly to Java expressions: most operators such as $+$, $*$ and $-$ on numbers are represented by the same symbols in Java, *div* is represented by $/$, and *mod* by %. Operations such as $\backslash/$ or $<:$ have direct equivalents in Java (eg, as *addAll* and *containsAll* on *Collection*).

The translation of constraints to executable code is the most complex step, and can only be partly automated. The decisions required are:

- Which class(es) are to be responsible for maintaining the truth of a particular constraint? If the constraint is a class invariant then it would normally be that class which is responsible for it, however a constraint attached to an association might be managed by either (or both) of the classes that it connects.
- What data structures to use to represent associations and attributes?
- What algorithms to use to implement query and update methods?

In some cases, constraints can only be ensured at the module (instead of class) level, or at the inter-module level. In the Scrabble system, for example, the constraint $C5$ that the occupied squares on the board are all connected, requires co-operation between the *Board* and *Move* modules. The former checks that either a new move is the first move (the board is empty before the move is placed), or at least one square covered in the new move is adjacent to an existing occupied square. The *Move* module checks that the new move itself is in a single connected line.

6.2 Synthesis of Java code

In the following we describe one automated program synthesis approach, which uses the following code generation strategies:

- Classes are responsible for maintaining their own *local* invariants only – that is, invariants which do not involve features of other classes. All other invariants are made the responsibility of a single *Controller* class, representing the entire system.
- Basic types are mapped to Java as in Table 5.3 above, and collection types as in Figure 6.1.
- Apart from algorithms already defined in the PSM, the algorithms in the generated code are simple 'brute force' iterations over all objects of a certain kind. They may be very inefficient in some cases.

Figure 6.2 shows the architecture translation which takes place from UML to Java, using this strategy. *ControllerInterface* lists the externally-available services of the generated executable. Typically the generated code is the functional core of a system, and this interface enables it to be used by a GUI for the system. The code may alternatively represent only one module within a system, in which case the *ControllerInterface* becomes the interface of this module, by which other modules use it.

Table 6.2 describes how particular kinds of feature in UML are translated into their Java counterparts.

Constraints $A \Rightarrow B$ attached to associations rs, relating attributes of the connected classes, have a systematic translation: iterate through all objects x_1, ..., x_n connected by rs, evaluating $A(x_1, \ldots, x_n)$ for each, and if this is true, perform an action to establish $B(x_1, \ldots, x_n)$.

For example, in the class diagram of Figure 3.7, the constraint

$$triggered = true \Rightarrow alarm = true$$

has the following translation to code:

```
public static void settriggered(Sensor sensorx, boolean triggeredx)
{ sensorx.settriggered(triggeredx);
  if (triggeredx == true)
  { for (int i0 = 0; i0 < systems.size(); i0++)
    { System systemx = (System) systems.get(i0);
      if (systemx.getallsensors() != null &&
          systemx.getallsensors().contains(sensorx))
      { systemx.setalarm(true); }
```

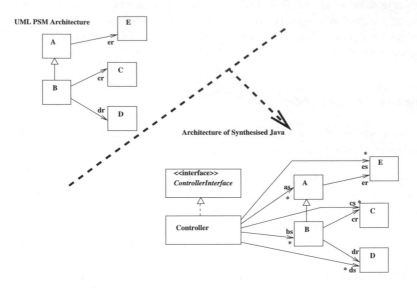

Figure 6.2: UML to Java architecture transformation

UML Element	Java Translation
identity attribute *att* : *T* of class *C*	Attribute *att* : *T'* of class *C*, plus map attribute *attCindex* of controller, mapping from *T'* to *C*. The controller checks *attCindex.get*(*newid*) is *null* before creating a new *C* object with *att* = *newid*, or allowing *setatt*(*cx*, *newid*) to execute to change *cx.att* to *newid*. *attCindex.put*(*val*, *obj*) is executed whenever *obj* : *C* is given *att* value *val*.
readOnly attribute *att* : *T* of class *C*	*final* attribute *att* : *T'* of class *C*, with no *setatt* operation in *C* or in the controller.
derived attribute *att* : *T* of class *C*	attribute *att* : *T'* of class *C*, with no *setatt* operation in controller interface.
0..1 association end *role* from class *C*	*List* attribute *role* of *C*, with checks on *setrole* and *addrole* that new value of *role* has *role.size*() < 2.
addOnly association end *role* from class *C*	*List* attribute *role* of *C*, with no *removerole* operation in *C* or controller.

Table 6.2: Synthesis strategy for UML elements

```
    }
  }
}
```

This is written in the *Controller* class, which has sets

```
private List systems = new ArrayList();
private List sensors = new ArrayList();
```

of all existing system and sensor objects.

Table 6.3 shows the translation of some LOCA expressions into Java. *varE*

LOCA	Java
Variable, constant, string or primitive value x	x
Attribute *att* of entity E	*varE.getatt*()
Role *role* of entity E	*varE.getrole*()
obj.f where *obj* is a single object	*obj'.gelf*()
objs.f where *objs* is a set	
of objects of type E.	$E.getAllf(objs')$
objs.f where *objs* is a sequence	
of objects of type E.	$E.getAllOrderedf(objs')$
$x : y$	$y'.contains(x')$
$x \ / : y$	$!(y'.contains(x'))$
$x = y$ for primitive x, y	$x' == y'$
$x = y$ for objects x, y	$x'.equals(y')$
$P \ \& \ Q$	$P' \ \&\& \ Q'$
$P \ or \ Q$	$P' \ || \ Q'$

Table 6.3: Query form of LOCA expressions

in cases two and three denotes the variable ranging over E in the context in which the expression occurs. For example, for *System*, *varSystem* is *systemx* in the *settriggered* implementation shown above.

The translation of Table 6.3 is typically applied to antecedent conditions, such as A above. e' denotes the translation of e.

There is a corresponding 'update form' which interprets a binary expression $e_1 \ op \ e_2$ as a command to modify e_1 or e_2 to make the expression true. Table 6.4 shows the basic cases. e' is the query form of e, and e'' its update form.

This translation is applied to postconditions or constraint conclusions, such as B above. Notice that x must denote an object in the first and second cases. For other forms of constraint conclusion, eg, involving $<$ or other operators, a precondition of the operations that may invalidate the constraint is generated instead of update code, the precondition ensures that the operation does not break the invariants.

As an example, the postcondition $x : guesses.value$ of *addGuess* in the lottery system is interpreted as the code

```
guesses.add(new Integer(x));
```

LOCA	Java
$x : obj.role$ *role* set-valued, single object *obj*.	if $(obj'.getrole().contains(x'))$ {} else $obj'.addrole(x')$;
Multiple objects *obj* of E	$E.addAllrole(obj', x')$;
$x\ /: obj.role$ *role* many-valued	$obj'.removerole(x')$; *obj* single-valued $E.removeAllrole(obj', x')$; *obj* set-valued, of type E
$obj.f = x$	$obj'.setf(x')$; *obj* single-valued $E.setAllf(obj', x')$; *obj* set-valued, of type E
$result = val$	$result = val'$;
$val : result$	$result.add(val')$;
$A \Rightarrow B$	if (A') { B'' }
$A\ \&\ B$	A'' B''

Table 6.4: Update form of LOCA expressions

in Java, where *guesses* is a Java *Set*.

There is also a systematic translation of statecharts to code, for operations specified algorithmically. If class C has a statechart describing the behaviour of its operations, then:

1. Define an enumerated type for the basic states of the statechart, and add a variable *stateC* of this type to the implementation of C.
2. For each event that corresponds to an update operation, collect together all transitions for that event. Each transition

$$s \longrightarrow_{op[G]/act} t$$

gives rise to a conditional statement

```
if (G' && stateC == s)
{ stateC = t;
  act';
  return;
}
```

in the code of *op*, where G' and act' are the translations of G and act, respectively.

6.3 Synthesis case study: railway signalling system

The synthesis process can be illustrated by a simple example of a reactive control system for managing the passage of trains through a railway network [13]. Figure 6.3 shows the class diagram of this system.

There are many constraints that can be defined for this system, but we will only consider three:

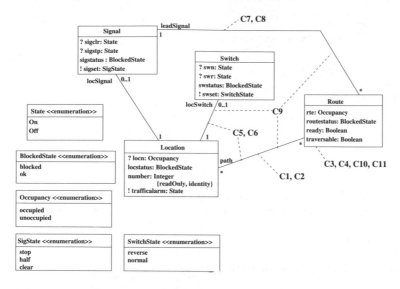

Figure 6.3: Class diagram of signalling system

1. $C1$ 'If any location in a route is occupied, the route is occupied':

$$locn = occupied \implies rte = occupied$$

2. $C3$ 'If a route is not ready (some switch is in neither the normal or reverse position) then it is not traversable':

$$ready = false \implies traversable = false$$

3. $C7$ 'If a route is occupied, its signal must be set to stop':

$$rte = occupied \implies sigset = stop$$

Of these, $C3$ is a local invariant of *Route* and the others are global (inter-class).

The generated code is as follows. A class *SystemTypes* is used to hold all the definitions of enumerated types in the system. It also contains classes such as *Set* to implement the OCL collection data types:

```
import java.util.List;
import java.util.Vector;

public interface SystemTypes
{ public static final int unoccupied = 0;
  public static final int occupied = 1;

  public static final int stop = 0;
  public static final int half = 1;
  public static final int clear = 2;
```

```
public class Set
{ private Vector elements = new Vector();

  public Set add(Object x)
  { elements.add(x);
    return this; }

  ....

}
}
```

Each class in the class diagram translates to a corresponding Java class with the same attributes, and with operations to modify and access these attributes:

```
public class Location implements SystemTypes
{ private int locn; // sensor
  private List locSignal = new Vector(); // of Signal

  public Location()
  { locn = unoccupied; }

  public void setlocn(int locnx) { locn = locnx;  }

  public static void setAlllocn(List locations,int val)
  { for (int i = 0; i < locations.size(); i++)
    { Location locationx = (Location) locations.get(i);
      Controller.setlocn(locationx,val); } }

  public void setlocSignal(List locSignalxx)
  { if (locSignalxx.size() > 1) { return; }
    locSignal = locSignalxx;
    }

  public void addlocSignal(Signal locSignalxx)
  { if (locSignal.size() > 0) { return; }
    locSignal.add(locSignalxx);
    }

  ....
}
```

The checks on *setlocSignal* and *addlocSignal* arise from the fact that this association end has multiplicity 0..1.

Local invariants of a class, such as *ready* = *false* $\Rightarrow$ *traversable* = *false* (of *Route*) can be ensured within the class itself:

```
public class Route implements SystemTypes
{ private int rte; // internal
  private boolean ready; // internal
  private boolean traversable; // internal
```

```
    private List path = new Vector(); // of Location
    private Signal leadSignal;

    public Route(Signal leadSignal)
    { rte = unoccupied;
      ready = false;
      traversable = false;
      this.leadSignal = leadSignal;
    }

    public void setrte(int rtex) { rte = rtex;  }

    public void setready(boolean readyx) { ready = readyx;
      if (readyx == false) { traversable = false; }
    }


    ....
}
```

Global constraints such as $C1$ and $C7$ are ensured instead by the controller class:

```
public class Controller
  implements SystemTypes, ControllerInterface
{ private Vector locations = new Vector();
  private Vector routes = new Vector();
  private Vector signals = new Vector();
  private static Controller uniqueInstance = null;

  private Controller() { }

  public static Controller inst()
  { if (uniqueInstance == null)
    { uniqueInstance = new Controller(); }
    return uniqueInstance;
  }

  public void addLocation(Location oo) { locations.add(oo); }

  public void addRoute(Route oo) { routes.add(oo); }

  public Location createLocation()
  { Location locationx = new Location();
    addLocation(locationx);
    setlocn(locationx,unoccupied);
    setlocSignal(locationx,new Vector());
    return locationx;
  }

  public Route createRoute(Signal leadSignalx)
  { Route routex = new Route(leadSignalx);
```

```
    addRoute(routex);
    setrte(routex,unoccupied);
    setready(routex,false);
    settraversable(routex,false);
    setpath(routex,new Vector());
    setleadSignal(routex,leadSignalx);
    return routex;
}

public void setlocn(Location locationx,
                    int locnx)
{ locationx.setlocn(locnx);
  if (locnx == occupied)
  { for (int i2 = 0; i2 < routes.size(); i2++)
    { Route routex = (Route) routes.get(i2);
      if (routex.getpath() != null &&
          routex.getpath().contains(locationx))
      { setrte(routex,occupied); }
    }
  }
}

public void setrte(Route routex, int rtex)
{ routex.setrte(rtex);
  Signal signalx = routex.getleadSignal();
  if (rtex == occupied) { setsigset(signalx,stop); }
}
  ....
}
```

The Singleton pattern is used to obtain a unique controller instance.

6.4   Synthesis case study: inheritance example

This example illustrates how inheritance and method pre- and postcondition
constraints are translated into Java. Figure 6.4 shows the class diagram of this
system. In Figure 6.4 the pre- and postconditions of *inc* are:

class A

```
    pre: true
    post: result = att * 2
```

class B

```
    pre: true
    post: result = att * 4
```

class C

```
pre: att < 100
post: result = att + 4
```

class D

```
pre: att > 3
post: result = att * 9
```

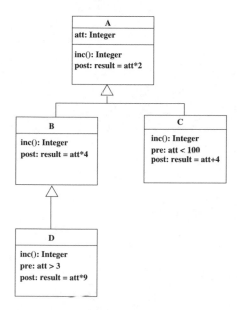

Figure 6.4: Operation example

This translates directly into the Java code:

```
class A implements SystemTypes
{ private int att; // internal

  public A()
  { att = 0; }

  public void setatt(int attx) { att = attx;  }

  public int getatt() { return att; }

  public int inc()
  { int result;
    result = att * 2;
```

```
    return result;
  }
}


class B implements SystemTypes
  extends A
{ public B() { }

  public int inc()
  { int result;
    result = att * 4;
    return result;
  }
}

class C implements SystemTypes
  extends A
{ public C() { }

  public int inc()
  { int result;
    if (att >= 100) { return result; }
    result = att + 4;
    return result;
  }
}


class D implements SystemTypes
  extends B
{ public D() { }

  public int inc()
  { int result;
    if (att <= 3) { return result; }
    result = att * 9;
    return result;
  }
}


public class Controller implements SystemTypes, ControllerInterface
{ private Vector as = new Vector();
  private Vector bs = new Vector();
  private Vector cs = new Vector();
  private Vector ds = new Vector();
  ...

  public void addA(A oo) { as.add(oo); }
```

```
   public void addB(B oo) { bs.add(oo); addA(oo); }

   public void addC(C oo) { cs.add(oo); addA(oo); }

   public void addD(D oo) { ds.add(oo); addB(oo); }

   ...
}
```

Preconditions of operations are expressed by testing the negation of the precondition at the start of the operation code, and exiting from the operation if this test is true.

The writer of the specification overlooked the necessity of using *protected* visibility for *att*. As a result an error message will be produced when the generated code is compiled, and the specification will need to be revised.

6.5 Synthesis case study: derived attributes example

This example illustrates the generation of code to maintain the values of derived attributes in order to satisfy their defining properties. Figure 6.5 shows the class diagram of this system.

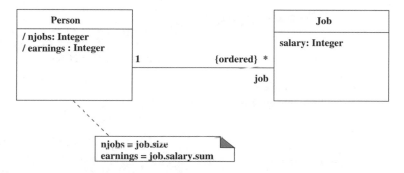

Figure 6.5: Derived attributes example

The generated code for this system is as follows:

```
class Person implements SystemTypes
{ private int njobs; // internal
  private int earnings; // derived
  private List job = new Vector(); // of Job

  public Person()
  { this.njobs = 0;
    this.earnings = 0;
  }
```

```
  public void setnjobs(int njobsx) { njobs = njobsx; }

  public void setearnings(int earningsx) { earnings = earningsx; }

  public void setjob(List jobxx) { job = jobxx; }

  public void addjob(Job jobxx) { job.add(jobxx); }

  public void removejob(Job jobxx) { job.remove(jobxx); }

  public int getnjobs() { return njobs; }

  public int getearnings() { return earnings; }
}


class Job implements SystemTypes
{ private int salary; // internal

  public Job()
  { salary = 0; }

  public void setsalary(int salaryx) { salary = salaryx;  }

  ...
}


public class Controller implements SystemTypes, ControllerInterface
{ private Vector persons = new Vector();
  private Vector jobs = new Vector();
  private static Controller uniqueInstance;

  private Controller() { }

  public static Controller inst()
  { if (uniqueInstance == null)
    { uniqueInstance = new Controller(); }
    return uniqueInstance; }

  public void addPerson(Person oo) { persons.add(oo); }

  public void addJob(Job oo) { jobs.add(oo); }

  public Person createPerson()
  { Person personx = new Person();
    addPerson(personx);
    setnjobs(personx,0);
    setearnings(personx,0);
    setjob(personx,new Vector());
```

```
      return personx;
  }

  public Job createJob()
  { Job jobx = new Job();
    addJob(jobx);
    setsalary(jobx,0);
    return jobx;
  }


  ...


  public void setjob(Person personx, List jobxx)
  { personx.setjob(jobxx);
    setnjobs(personx,personx.getjob().size());
    setearnings(personx,
      Set.sumint(Job.getAllOrderedsalary(personx.getjob())));
  }

  public void addjob(Person personx, Job jobxx)
  { if (personx.getjob().contains(jobxx)) { return; }
    personx.addjob(jobxx);
    setnjobs(personx,personx.getjob().size());
    setearnings(personx,
      Set.sumint(Job.getAllOrderedsalary(personx.getjob())));
  }

  public void removejob(Person personx, Job jobxx)
  { personx.removejob(jobxx);
    setnjobs(personx,personx.getjob().size());
    setearnings(personx,
      Set.sumint(Job.getAllOrderedsalary(personx.getjob())));
  }

  public void setsalary(Job jobx, int salaryx)
  { jobx.setsalary(salaryx);
    for (int i2 = 0; i2 < persons.size(); i2++)
    { Person personx = (Person) persons.get(i2);
      if (personx.getjob() != null &&
          personx.getjob().contains(jobx))
      { setearnings(personx,
          Set.sumint(Job.getAllOrderedsalary(
                          personx.getjob())));
      }
    }
  }
}
```

The definition of *setjob*, *setsalary*, *addjob* and *removejob* is due to the need to preserve the truth of the invariants

$$njobs = job.size$$
$$earnings = job.salary.sum$$

defining the derived attributes of *Person*.

Because *job* is an ordered association, the method

```
static List getAllOrderedsalary(List jobs)
```

is used to obtain the list of salary values *jb.salary* for *jb* in *jobs*, so that duplicate salary values will be retained and summed.

In the case of *setsalary(jobx, salaryx)*, the change to the salary of *jobx* may require recalculation of the earnings of each person object whose set of jobs includes *jobx*.

6.6　Data repository implementation: choosing a database

A large number of database systems exist, of which Microsoft Access, MySQL, PostgreSQL and Oracle are some of the most widely used. Table 6.5 summarises the properties and differences of these.

Property	MS Access	MySQL	PostgreSQL	Oracle
Data Capacity	Medium	High	High	High
Concurrency	Low	High	High	High
SQL Support	Medium	Medium	High	High
Referential Integrity	√	×	√	√
Operating Systems	Win	Win Unix Linux	Unix Linux	Win Unix Linux

Table 6.5: Comparison of databases

Referential integrity refers to the ability of the database to enforce the integrity constraint that if a table row with primary key value x is deleted, then any row in any table that has x as a foreign key value to the first table must also be deleted. Also foreign keys can also only be set to a value if there is an existing row in the referenced table with that key value.

MySQL does not support referential integrity or stored procedures (although support for stored procedures is to be introduced). However it is generally considered to be the fastest of the databases listed here.

6.7　Production of an XML data repository

Suppose that XML [53] has been chosen as the implementation medium for storing the history of moves in the Scrabble system, instead of a relational database. This has the advantage of independence of any commercial database system, but means that data on moves and scores will be stored as (possibly very large) text files, structured in a way that corresponds to the PSM class diagram information.

The data to be stored must be structured as a directed acyclic graph (DAG) with regard to navigation from one entity (the 'master') to another ('subordinate'). In the Scrabble game this is possible, with *Move* being the top-level entity, with subordinates *Player* and *LetterMove*, and *LetterMove* having subordinate class *Letter*. An example XML file representing the move 'c', 'a', 'p' starting on the centre square, could be:

```
<history>
<move>
  <score>10</score>
  <player>
    <name>P1</name>
    <score>10</score>
    <playerFlag value="HumanPlayer"/>
  </player>
  <lettermove>
    <x>8</x>
    <y>8</y>
    <letter>
      <symbol>c</symbol>
      <score>3</score>
    </letter>
  </lettermove>

  <lettermove>
    <x>9</x>
    <y>8</y>
    <letter>
      <symbol>a</symbol>
      <score>1</score>
    </letter>
  </lettermove>

  <lettermove>
    <x>10</x>
    <y>8</y>
    <letter>
      <symbol>p</symbol>
      <score>1</score>
    </letter>
  </lettermove>
</move>
</history>
```

The structure of an XML file is defined by a *Data Type Definition* (*DTD*) file, which lists all the tags that can occur in the XML file and specifies their

attributes and how they can be structured in terms of subordinate tags. The
DTD for the above file is:

```
<!ELEMENT history (move*)>
<!ELEMENT move (score, player, lettermove*)>
<!ELEMENT score (#PCDATA)>
<!ELEMENT player (name,score,playerFlag)>
<!ELEMENT name (#PCDATA)>
<!ELEMENT playerFlag EMPTY>
<!ATTLIST playerFlag value
   (HumanPlayer | ComputerPlayer)  HumanPlayer>
<!ELEMENT letterMove (x,y,letter)>
<!ELEMENT x (#PCDATA)>
<!ELEMENT y (#PCDATA)>
<!ELEMENT letter (symbol,score)>
<!ELEMENT symbol (#PCDATA)>
```

This DTD means that a history is composed of a sequence of moves, a move
consists of a score, followed by a player and then by a sequence of lettermove
elements. In turn, a lettermove consists of x, y and letter elements in that order,
a player consists of name, score and playerFlag elements, and a letter consists
of symbol and score elements. The x, y, symbol and score elements contain
just string data, whilst the playerFlag can have either the value HumanPlayer,
or the value ComputerPlayer, with HumanPlayer being the default.

The mapping from a PSM class diagram to an XML DTD is:

- The data must be organised into a strict hierarchy (a tree or directed
  acyclic graph of entities). The root of the XML schema is the master
  entity.
- If an entity e has attributes $att_1, \ldots, att_n$ and roles $role_1, \ldots, role_m$, then
  its DTD specification is:

  ```
  <!ELEMENT e (att1, ..., attn, role1, ..., rolem)>
  ```

  An attribute is normally represented as 'printable character data', if it is
  a number or string:

  ```
  <!ELEMENT att (#PCDATA)>
  ```

  A boolean or element of an enumerated type can instead be represented
  as an empty element, as with playerFlag above.
  A role is represented as a list or single item of the entity f it is attached
  to, depending on its multiplicity. For a $*$ role we would have:

  ```
  <!ELEMENT role (f*)>
  ```

  for example. For a 0..1 role ? is used, and for a 1..* role + is used. The
  default (no annotation) means 1 multiplicity.

The effect of this mapping is:

- For each entity instance its attributes are listed as subordinate tags with the attribute name, enclosing the value of the attribute for that instance. Attributes of an enumerated or Boolean type can be written in an abbreviated form with the value as the value of an XML attribute of the tag.
- A link to a subordinate object is represented by including the subordinate object within the elements of its master. If there are different associations to the same class the subordinate objects would be listed as elements of a tag named after the rolename of the subordinate entity in that association. The rolename tag would be listed at the same level as the attributes of the master entity.

Notice that attributes or roles with the same name belonging to different entities must have the same DTD translation – an example is *score*.

An alternative way to specify the allowed structure of an XML document is via an XML *Schema* (http://www.w3.org/XML/Schema).

Writing XML for a class is a simple matter of printing out the attribute data enclosed by their tags. For example, the methods which do this for the move histories are:

```
In Move::
  public String toXml()
  { String res = "<move>\n  <score>" + score + "</score>\n";
    String playerXml = p.toXml();
    res = res + playerXml;
    for (int i = 0; i < letterMoves.size(); i++)
    { LetterMove lm = (LetterMove) letterMoves.get(i);
      res = res + lm.toXml();
    }
    return res + "</move>\n";
  }
```

```
In Player::
  public String toXml()
  { String res = "  <player>\n" +
      "    <name>" + name + "</name>\n" +
      "    <score>" + score + "</score>\n" +
      playerKind() +
      "  </player>\n";
    return res;
  }
```

```
In LetterMove::
  public String toXml()
  { String res = "  <lettermove>\n" +
      "    <x>" + x + "</x>\n" +
      "    <y>" + y + "</y>\n" +
      letter.toXml() +
      "  </lettermove>\n";
    return res;
```

```
     }

In Letter:
  public String toXml()
  { return "     <letter>\n" +
      "        <symbol>" + symbol + "</symbol>\n" +
      "        <score>" + score + "</score>\n" +
      "      </letter>\n";
  }
```

However, parsing XML files and recreating object data is much more complex. There are two general strategies for parsing XML:

1. *SAX (Simple API for XML):* These parsers traverse the XML document, generating events when the parser encounters XML tags or other content.
2. *DOM (Document Object Model):* These parsers build a complete tree structure containing the XML document data. Their use of memory may therefore be much greater than a SAX parser, but they provide a more convenient programming interface if large parts of the XML data are required, or if the data is to be modified by the program.

Since in the Scrabble example we need to obtain all the information stored in the XML parse tree, DOM parsing is more appropriate in this case (if only selected items were needed SAX processing could be used instead).

Java 1.5 contains SAX parsing classes in the *org.xml.sax* package, and DOM parsing classes in the *org.w3c.dom* package. The DOM methods we will use are:

- `Element root = doc.getDocumentElement();` This obtains the root node of the XML data tree.
- `NodeList children = e.getChildNodes();` Get the immediate descendents (in the data tree) of *Element e*. Navigation along the *children* list is typically via an iteration of the form:

```
      for (int i = 0; i < children.getLength(); i++)
      { Node cn = children.item(i);
        if (cn instanceof Element) // skip white space
        { Element ce = (Element) cn;
          ... do something with child element ce ...
        }
      }
```

- `e.getTagName();` Get the tag name, a String, of element *e*.
- `ce.getFirstChild();` Get first child node of *ce*. If *ce* represents a tag that contains only basic data, such as *score*, this obtains the data associated with *ce*.

The following code applies these DOM navigation methods to extract move data from an XML file.

```
import java.io.*;
import javax.swing.JFileChooser;
import java.util.List;
import java.util.Vector;
import javax.xml.parsers.*;
import org.w3c.dom.*;
import org.xml.sax.SAXException;

public class HistoryParser
{ private DocumentBuilder builder;

  public HistoryParser()
  throws ParserConfigurationException
  { DocumentBuilderFactory factory =
      DocumentBuilderFactory.newInstance();
    builder = factory.newDocumentBuilder();
  }

  public List parse(String file)
  throws SAXException, IOException
  { File ff = new File(file);
    Document doc = builder.parse(ff);
    Element root = doc.getDocumentElement();
    return getHistory(root);
  }

  private static List getHistory(Element e)
  { Vector moves = new Vector();
    NodeList children = e.getChildNodes();
    for (int i = 0; i < children.getLength(); i++)
    { Node cn = children.item(i);
      if (cn instanceof Element) // skip white space
      { Element ce = (Element) cn;
        if (ce.getTagName().equals("move"))
        { Move mv = getMove(ce);
          moves.add(mv);
        }
      }
    }
    return moves;
  }

  private static Move getMove(Element e)
  { NodeList children = e.getChildNodes();
    Player player = null;
    String score = null;
    Vector letterMoves = new Vector();
    for (int i = 0; i < children.getLength(); i++)
    { Node cn = children.item(i);
      if (cn instanceof Element)
```

```
    { Element ce = (Element) cn;
      String tag = ce.getTagName();
      if (tag.equals("player"))
      { player = getPlayer(ce); }
      else if (tag.equals("score"))
      { Text tn = (Text) ce.getFirstChild();
        score = tn.getData();
      }
      else if (tag.equals("lettermove"))
      { letterMoves.add(getLetterMove(ce)); }
    }
  }
  return new Move(player,letterMoves);
}

private static Player getPlayer(Element e)
{ NodeList children = e.getChildNodes();
  String att = e.getAttribute("playerFlag");

  String name = "";
  int score = 0;
  for (int i = 0; i < children.getLength(); i++)
  { Node cn = children.item(i);
    if (cn instanceof Element)
    { Element ce = (Element) cn;
      String tag = ce.getTagName();
      Text tn = (Text) ce.getFirstChild();
      String data = tn.getData();
      if (tag.equals("score"))
      { score = Integer.parseInt(data); }
      else if (tag.equals("name"))
      { name = data; }
    }
  }
  if (att != null && att.equals("HumanPlayer"))
  { return new HumanPlayer(name); }
  else
  { return new ComputerPlayer(name); }
}

private static LetterMove getLetterMove(Element e)
{ NodeList children = e.getChildNodes();
  int x = 0;
  int y = 0;
  Letter letter = null;
  for (int i = 0; i < children.getLength(); i++)
  { Node cn = children.item(i);
    if (cn instanceof Element)
    { Element ce = (Element) cn;
      String tag = ce.getTagName();
```

```
        Text tn = (Text) ce.getFirstChild();
        String data = tn.getData();
        if (tag.equals("x"))
        { x = Integer.parseInt(data); }
        else if (tag.equals("y"))
        { y = Integer.parseInt(data); }
        else if (tag.equals("letter"))
        { letter = getLetter(ce); }
      }
    }
    return new LetterMove(x,y,letter);
  }

  private static Letter getLetter(Element e)
  { NodeList children = e.getChildNodes();
    String symbol = " ";
    int score = 0;
    for (int i = 0; i < children.getLength(); i++)
    { Node cn = children.item(i);
      if (cn instanceof Element)
      { Element ce = (Element) cn;
        String tag = ce.getTagName();
        Text tn = (Text) ce.getFirstChild();
        String data = tn.getData();
        if (tag.equals("symbol"))
        { symbol = data; }
        else if (tag.equals("score"))
        { score = Integer.parseInt(data); }
      }
    }
    return new Letter(symbol.charAt(0),score);
  }
}
```

6.8 Summary

We have shown how it is possible to construct platform-independent designs and transform these systematically into platform-specific models, and finally, to executable code. The methodology proposed here is similar in intention to that of Agile MDA/Executable UML [29], although we recommend starting from a more abstract CIM/PIM consisting of a data model and invariants, in place of the explicit message passing of Agile MDA models.

6.9 Exercises

1 Translate the PSM diagram of Figure 6.6 to outline Java classes.

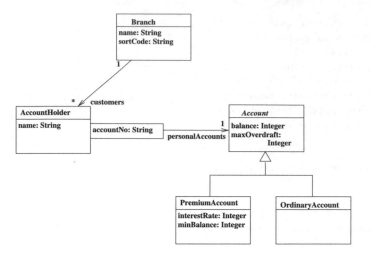

Figure 6.6: Java PSM 1

2 Translate the PSM diagram of Figure 6.7 to outline Java classes, including the code needed to maintain the constraint.

3 Complete the implementation of the lottery system, using the Java collection class *Set*.

4 Translate the Person-Company system of Figure 3.4 to Java, including code to maintain the invariant when a person changes job from one company to another.

5 Convert the diagram of Figure 6.8 to a relational database schema.

6 Convert the PSM of Figure 6.8 into a form suitable for direct translation into Java, using the assumption that navigation from *D* to *B* is not required.

7 Give the XML DTD for the class diagram in Figure 6.9, and show how an example *Order* object would be represented in XML using this DTD.

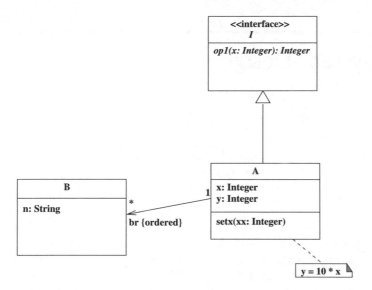

Figure 6.7: Java PSM 2

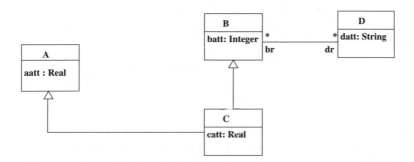

Figure 6.8: PSM class diagram

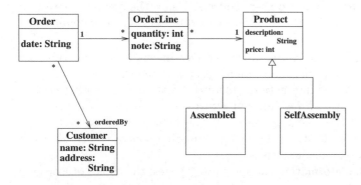

Figure 6.9: Class diagram for DTD

Chapter 7

Internet System Design

This chapter describes the structure and components of internet systems, and the technologies and languages involved in internet system design, including XHTML, Javascript, JSP, Servlets and Flash. We describe an MDA-based design process for such systems, using UML and OCL for PIMs and PSMs of internet systems, and synthesis of implementation components from UML models. We discuss issues of usability, portability across browsers, and how to ensure that the W3C standards for accessibility are met.

An example of an online property search system is used as a running case study.

7.1   Fundamentals of internet systems

Many software systems today operate across the internet, allowing users to access the system from any internet-connected computer with a browser, anywhere in the world. Examples include online banking, travel agents, online shopping, even online voting[1]. These systems are more than just software, their visual presentation and information content aspects are often just as important as their capabilities to respond to user requests. Hence the development of an internet system must involve the integration of three forms of development:

1. Development of the software which receives information from the user (the *client* in the internet interaction), processes information (usually on the *server* side of the interaction, where the databases and other critical resources of the system reside), and returns information to the client.
2. Development of the visual appearances and behaviour of the web pages interfacing to the client, eg, by using animation software such as Flash (http://www.macromedia.com).
3. Deciding on the information content of web pages, the choice of words to use, what information to emphasise, etc.

---

[1]Internet voting was proposed for the 2004 US presidential election primaries.

Different systems require different combinations of these aspects. Development of a university website will mostly involve work on the second and third aspects, for example, focusing on informing readers about the university, in a visually appealing and interesting manner, whereas an online banking system will need to support accountholder operations such as fund transfers and electronic payments, etc.

The three aspects are nevertheless interrelated. Bad programming impacts on the visual/behavioural design of a system, and vice-versa. For example, it is still unfortunately possible to come across online registration forms which span five separate pages, yet only inform the user of mistakes in entry when they press 'submit' after labouriously completing all the pages, and which then wipe clean all the form fields, just to be extra helpful!

Figure 7.1 shows a typical internet system architecture.

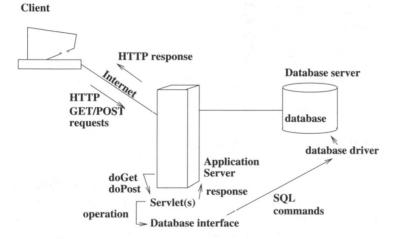

Figure 7.1: Typical structure of internet application

When a user points their browser at a web address, for example http://www.propertysearch.co.uk, the content of an initial page (usually *index.html*) is transferred from the server for this site to the user's computer, and then displayed by the browser. In this example, the initial page directs a new user to a registration form (Figure 7.2) to find out details from the user about what kind of property they are looking for. Assuming the user fills this in correctly, then presses *Register*, their information will then be sent across the internet to the server.

There are two main ways in which the client side of an internet application sends information to the server side using the *Hypertext transfer protocol (HTTP)*:

- GET is mainly used to extract information from the server (eg, to perform a search). GET requests send information to the server as part of the request URL. These data values appear after a ? sign in the URL, for example: http://www.serv.org?param1=val1&param2=val2.

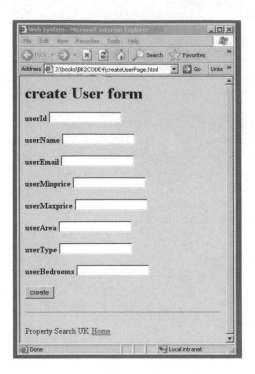

Figure 7.2: Register web page of property search system

- POST requests send information to the server in a separate message body (not the URL). They are therefore more secure because the data being transmitted is not visible in the browser URL display. POST requests are used for updating server data, eg, entering details from a form into a database.

An advantage of GET is that browsers can cache the results of GET queries, so making redisplay of the same results faster. However a disadvantage of GET is that some browsers may place a limit on the length of a URL, thus restricting the amount of data that can be appended as part of the GET request. This limit may be as low as 255 bytes (characters).

The choice of which method to use is specified in the *form* tag in HTML. For example, the web page shown in Figure 7.2 uses GET to submit user information:

```
<html>
<body>
<form name = "registerform"
 method = "GET"
 action =
 "http://www.propertysearch.co.uk:8080/servlet/RegisterUserServlet">
....
</form>
```

```
</body>
</html>
```

In this case the data is sent using GET to the server-side program, a Java servlet, specified in the action clause. 8080 is the default *port number* for web servers.

The servlet will receive this data, and add the new user and their preferences to the database of users. It will send back to the client browser a web page including an acknowledgement that the registration was successful, and giving further options, eg, to search the property database using the requirements.

7.1.1 Internet system technologies

A large number of software technologies and languages exist to support the construction of all elements of internet systems, which may be conveniently divided into client-side (executing under the control of the client browser) and server-side technologies. On the client side, there are:

JavaScript This is a Java-like scripting language (a simplified programming language) which executes on the client when the client browser views web pages containing embedded JavaScript. There are a number of similar languages such as Microsoft's *JScript*, and *VBScript*, based on Visual Basic instead of Java.

Flash An animation language for web pages, which allows movie-like visual effects to be embedded in pages.

JavaScript can be used to check that forms are valid before the form information is sent to the server via an HTTP GET or POST message. It can also be used to animate web pages, by responding to events such as the mouse cursor moving over a page element, etc.

Flash can be used to make pages look more visually appealing and distinctive, and therefore to increase the number of users of a web site.

On the server side there are:

JSP JavaServer Pages. These embed Java statements in HTML, these statements are executed on the server when the page receives a request from a client browser. The results of processing are returned as web pages.

ASP Active Server Pages. Server-side scripting for Windows servers, using Visual Basic as the scripting language. Scripts to be executed on the server are embedded in the web pages that trigger them, and can access and update server data directly. The results of processing are presented by generating a web page and returning this to the client browser.

PHP An open-source, platform-independent server-side scripting language, with powerful facilities for string matching and manipulation using regular expressions. As with ASP and JSP, database query and update mechanisms are provided, and output to the client is via web pages generated by the script.

Servlets A pure Java server-side technology: methods of servlet classes respond to HTTP GET and POST requests and generate web pages which
are returned to the client for display on the client browser.

JSPs are recommended for use when the web pages to be generated are mainly
fixed XHTML text, with only a small element of dynamic content (content that
varies depending on the input request data), whereas servlets are suitable for
situations where the response pages are mainly dynamic content. JSPs also
have the advantage of being HTML-like in their syntax, and, so, in principle,
easier to develop than servlets, which use full Java. In this chapter however,
we use a servlet-based approach and show how to use servlets and auxiliary
page-generation classes to separate fixed from dynamic XHTML content.

7.1.2 Online databases

The essential form of many simple internet systems is an 'online database', by
which data stored on the server can be queried, augmented or modified via a
web page interface. For example, an online sports centre would allow users to
register, to make, alter and cancel bookings for themselves, and to query the
availability of facilities or staff at particular times.

There are the following characteristic actions which a client of such a system
may do:

- *create* – add a new instance of an entity to the database, ie, add a new
  row to a table in the case of a relational database;
- *delete* – remove an existing instance of an entity/a row from a table;
- *edit* – modify one or more attributes of an instance/row in the database;
- *check* – compare values entered in a form to database values (for example
  when checking a user's password at login);
- *list* – display all rows of a table/instances of an entity which satisfy certain
  properties;
- *add* – add an instance to a role set, by creating a foreign key link from a
  table row at the role end to a table row at the other end of the association;
- *remove* – remove an instance from a role set.

The *submit* action on a web page displayed to a client may initiate one of these
operations, the processing of which will mainly take place on the server, since
all essentially involve the database of the system.

We will therefore use the above classifications of operations as stereotypes
of the *submit* operations of classes representing the corresponding web pages.

7.2 Design of internet systems

The following steps are needed when a system is to be developed as an online
application:

- Transform the PIM of the system into a PSM oriented to online implementation by determining which entities and associations are to be *persistent*, ie, stored in a database or some other permanent data storage, and, if a relational database is to be used, transforming the classes and associations to produce a relational database schema.
- Identify new entities (often derived directly from the persistent entities) which represent data groups to be entered or presented on web pages. In the case of input data, the entities will have an operation corresponding to the *submit* action on the web page, this operation should be stereotyped with one of the above standard actions, *create*, *delete*, *list*, etc, if possible. Other operations, such as *reset* (clear all the text fields to the empty string) may also be present for an entity representing an input form.
- Identify invariants of the system: (i) invariants of entities representing web forms express validity criteria for the data input into the form; (ii) invariants of entities representing persistent data correspond to integrity constraints on the database; (iii) invariants linking view and repository data express the functionality of the system, ie, how it responds to submit actions or other client-side actions.

As discussed above, consideration of the interaction between users and the system, and the presentation of information, is particularly critical in the case of internet systems. We have therefore to also consider what information to present on each web page, how to explain what data is to be entered, or how to display the output of an operation. The visual design of the system should be consistent across all the web pages of the system, should enhance rather than interfere with the users' use of the system, and should take account of accessibility standards (eg, for blind users, significant images should always contain an *alt = text* attribute which explains what the image is; this attribute can be used by screen-reading software).

7.2.1 Example: online property-search system

As an example of the development process for internet systems, we will construct a system which enables housebuyers to register their requirements on a website, and then view properties which match their requirements. Figure 7.3 shows the PIM use cases for customers, and Figure 7.4 shows the PIM class diagram of this system.

Some example constraints of this system in LOCA are:

1. $C1$ 'A user's minimum price must be at least 0, and less than or equal to their maximum price choice':

   $0 \leq userMinprice$ &
   $userMinprice \leq userMaxprice$

   as a class invariant of *User*.

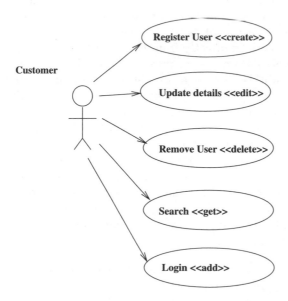

Figure 7.3: PIM use cases of property search system

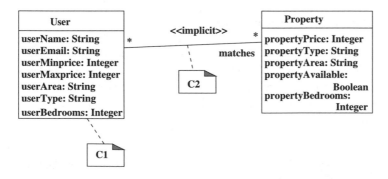

Figure 7.4: PIM class diagram of property search system

2. *C2* 'A property matches a user's requirements if its price is in their range, it is available, has at least as many bedrooms as they require, and is of the same type and in the same area as required':

$$userMinprice \leq propertyPrice \ \&$$
$$userMaxprice \geq propertyPrice \ \&$$
$$userArea = propertyArea \ \&$$
$$userType = propertyType \ \&$$
$$userBedrooms \leq propertyBedrooms \ \&$$
$$propertyAvailable = true$$

The relationship of matching between users and properties is many-many, so it needs to be refined to a new class and two new associations if it is to be implemented in a relational database. Alternatively, it may be stereotyped as *implicit* to indicate that it will be calculated as required, using SQL queries for example, not stored in the database. Both *User* and *Property* can be stereotyped as *persistent*. For *User* we invent a new primary key, *userId*, and likewise we construct a key *propertyId* for properties.

Forms will be needed to enter user and property data and to modify this data. Figure 7.5 shows the resulting PSM class diagram, omitting forms for staff operations of adding, removing and editing property details.

Key invariants are:

User class: That $0 \leq userMinprice \leq userMaxprice$

Property class: That $0 \leq propertyPrice$ and $0 \leq propertyBedrooms$

User_Property association: $userMinprice \leq propertyPrice \leq userMaxprice$ and $userArea = propertyArea$ and $userType = propertyType$ and $userBedrooms \leq propertyBedrooms$ and $propertyAvailable = true$

Register user form: $0 \leq minprice \leq maxprice$, since these items will be used to set the corresponding attributes of *User*

Add property form: $price \geq 0$ and $bedrooms \geq 0$.

An invariant linking the web pages and database is the postcondition

$$User[NEWID] \neq \{\} \ \&$$
$$NEWID \notin User.userId@pre \ \&$$
$$User[NEWID].userName = name \ \&$$
$$User[NEWID].userArea = area \ \&$$
$$User[NEWID].userMinprice = minprice \ \&$$
$$User[NEWID].userMaxprice = maxprice \ \&$$
$$User[NEWID].userBedrooms = bedrooms \ \&$$
$$User[NEWID].userType = type \ \&$$
$$User[NEWID].userEmail = email$$

of the *register* operation. *NEWID* is a constant representing the new id of the *User* object. This expresses that submission of the register user form adds the form data to the database as a new row in the *User* table (even if a user with the same name and email already exists – allowing users to have multiple

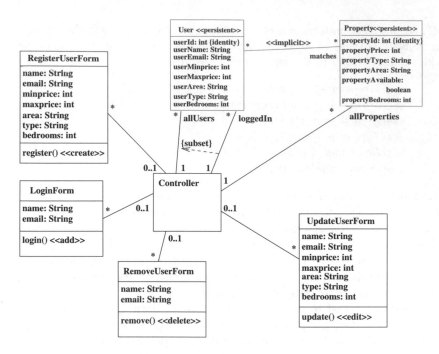

Figure 7.5: PSM of property search system

preferences/profiles. More usually a warning should be issued if such an update is attempted).

Detailed design of the interface, functional core and data repository of the system can then take place.

As an example of a complete implementation of one of the use cases of this system, consider the *Register* function. The customer initiates this use case via the registration form of Figure 7.2. The purpose of this page is to extract sufficient information from the user so that useful searches can be carried out on the property database. This database could be very large, so the form has to prompt the user for the property features that they consider essential if they are to be interested in a property, to cut down the search results to a manageable number. Price range and area attributes are particularly useful in this respect.

Forms should however be no larger than necessary – since the system does not need any information about its customers other than their name and email address (to communicate with them and uniquely identify them), it should not try to collect other information (such as their postal address, for example).

To design web pages, we can sketch diagrams of their intended structure and appearance, and review these for usability, visual consistency, etc. Figure 7.6 shows an outline design for the user registration form of the property system.

The complete registration form for the property search system could therefore be:

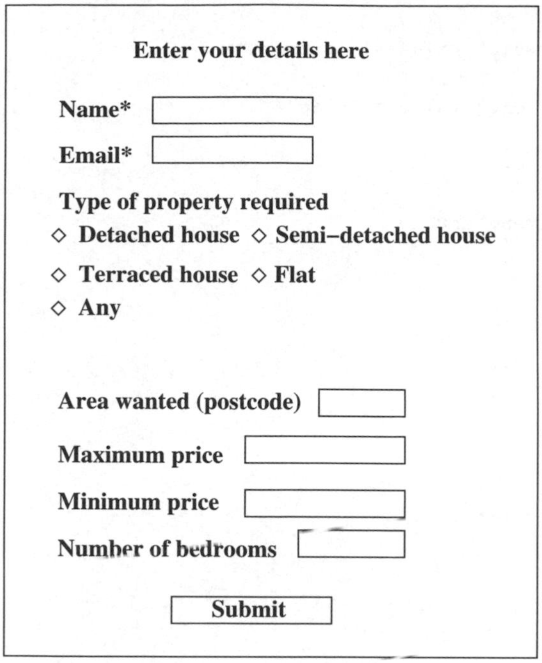

Enter your details here

Name* [   ]

Email* [   ]

Type of property required
◇ **Detached house** ◇ **Semi–detached house**

◇ **Terraced house** ◇ **Flat**

◇ **Any**

Area wanted (postcode) [   ]

Maximum price [   ]

Minimum price [   ]

Number of bedrooms [   ]

[**Submit**]

Figure 7.6: Sketch of registration form


```
<html>
<head><title>User Registration</title></head>

<form name = "registerform"  method = "GET"
 action =

"http://www.propertysearch.co.uk:8080/servlet/RegisterUserServlet">

<p>
<strong>Your name</strong>
<input name = "name" type = "text"></p>

<p>
<strong>Email address</strong>
<input name = "email" type = "text"></p>

<p>
<strong>What type of property are you
looking for?</strong><br>
Detached
<input name = "type" type = "radio"
value = "detached">
Semi-detached
<input name = "type" type = "radio" value = "semi" checked>
```

```
Terraced
<input name = "type" type = "radio" value = "terraced">
Flat
<input name = "type" type = "radio" value = "flat">
</p>

<p>
<strong>How many bedrooms?</strong><br>
<input name = "bedrooms"
 type = "text" size = "1"></p>

<p>
<strong>Maximum price?</strong><br>
<input name = "maxprice" type = "text"></p>

<p>
<strong>Minimum price?</strong><br>
<input name = "minprice" type = "text"></p>

<p>
<strong>What area (postcode)?</strong><br>
<input name = "area" type = "text" size = "4">
</p>

<input type = "submit" value = "Register">
</form>
</body>
</html>
```

This produces the web page of Figure 7.2.

To make the form less prone to data entry errors, selection boxes with pre-fixed selections could be used for options such as property type, number of bedrooms (eg, with options 1, 2, 3, 4 and 5+), and max and min price. The disadvantage of selection boxes is that they make the interface less flexible: a user cannot specify a min or max price different to those in the preset lists, for example.

Alternatively, JavaScript can be used to check the validity of fields, eg, to ensure that an email address has a valid *text@text.text* format and that max and min price are numbers with max price larger than min price.

The above page could send registration information to the following registration servlet for user information:

```
import java.io.*;
import java.util.*;
import javax.servlet.http.*;
import javax.servlet.*;

public class RegisterUserServlet extends HttpServlet
{ private DBI dbi; // Interface to database
```

```
public RegisterUserServlet() {}

public void init(ServletConfig cfg)
throws ServletException
{ super.init(cfg);
  dbi = new DBI();
}

public void doGet(HttpServletRequest req,
                  HttpServletResponse res)
  throws ServletException, IOException
{ res.setContentType("text/html");
  PrintWriter pw = res.getWriter();
  String name = req.getParameter("name");
  String email = req.getParameter("email");
  String type = req.getParameter("type");
  String bedrooms = req.getParameter("bedrooms");
  String maxPrice = req.getParameter("maxprice");
  String minPrice = req.getParameter("minprice");
  String area = req.getParameter("area");

  pw.println("<html><head>");
  pw.println();
  pw.println("<title>Registration Details</title>");
  pw.println("</head>");
  pw.println();
  pw.println("<body bgcolor=#FF69CC>");
  pw.println();
  pw.println("<h1>Thank you, " + name +
             " for registering. </h1>");
  pw.println();
  pw.println("<hr>");
  if (dbi != null)
  { dbi.createUser(name,email,minPrice,maxPrice,
                   type,bedrooms,area);
    pw.println("<h2>Your details have " +
               "been recorded.</h2>");
  }
  else
  { pw.println("<h2>Error: details not " +
               "recorded.</h2>"); }
  pw.println("</body></html>");
  pw.close();
}

public void doPost(HttpServletRequest req,
                   HttpServletResponse res)
throws ServletException, IOException
{ doGet(req,res); }
```

```
    public void destroy()
    { dbi.logoff(); }
}
```

The *init* method establishes the database connection, whilst *destroy* closes it down. In intensively-used applications where there may be hundreds of client sessions running concurrently, database connections would need to be acquired from a connection *pool* when needed by a client and released once a database operation was complete.

When the servlet receives an HTTP GET message from the registration web page, it executes the method *doGet*. The parameter *req* holds all the completed form data of the submitted page. The statements

```
    res.setContentType("text/html");
    PrintWriter pw = res.getWriter();
```

set up the response data *res*, which will simply be a stream of HTML as a text file.

The statements

```
    String name = req.getParameter("name");
    String email = req.getParameter("email");
    String type = req.getParameter("type");
    String bedrooms = req.getParameter("bedrooms");
    String maxPrice = req.getParameter("maxprice");
    String minPrice = req.getParameter("minprice");
    String area = req.getParameter("area");
```

obtain each of the form field values that have been transmitted in the HTTP GET message, and store them in corresponding local variables.

The next statements construct the output of the servlet, which is a web page that will be displayed on the browser that initiated the request, replacing the registration form page:

```
    pw.println("<html><head>");
    pw.println();
    pw.println("<title>Registration Details</title>");
    pw.println("</head>")
    pw.println();
    pw.println("<body bgcolor=#FF69CC>");
    pw.println();
    pw.println("<h1>Thank you, " + name +
               " for registering. </h1>");
    pw.println();
    pw.println("<hr>");
    if (dbi != null)
    { dbi.createUser(name,email,minPrice,maxPrice,
                     type,bedrooms,area);
      pw.println("<h2>Your details have " +
                 "been recorded.</h2>");
```

```
  }
  else
  { pw.println("<h2>Error: details not " +
               "recorded.</h2>"); }
  pw.println("</body></html>");
  pw.close();
}
```

In the case that the database interface *dbi* does not exist, an error message is sent back to the user, otherwise the details are recorded using the *createUser* method, and a confirmation displayed.

The database interface uses the PostgreSQL object/relational database [32] to store tables for the users and for properties. Management of connections is deferred to the database manager itself in this case, situations where there are too many open connections may therefore arise, and can lead to exceptions.

```
import java.io.*;
import java.sql.*;

public class DBI
{ private Connection conn;
  private Statement stat;

  /** Construct a database connection and
      statement for "propertydb" with username "kcl" */
  public DBI()
  { try
    { // get postgres database driver:
      Class.forName("org.postgresql.Driver");
      // create a connection to property database:
      conn =
          DriverManager.getConnection(
              "jdbc:postgresql:propertydb", "kcl", "");
      stat = conn.createStatement();
    }
    catch (Exception e)
    { e.printStackTrace(); }
  }

  /** Add a new user to the database. */
  public synchronized void createUser(String name,
          String email, String minpr, String maxpr,
          String type, String bedrooms, String area)
  { int maxId = getMaxUserId();
    maxId++;

    try
    { stat.executeUpdate("INSERT INTO User " +
        "VALUES (" + maxId + ",'" + name + "','" +
                email + "','" + minpr + "','" +
                maxpr + "','" + type + "','" +
```

```
                    bedrooms + "','" + area +
                    "')");
    conn.commit();
  }
  catch (Exception e)
  { e.printStackTrace(); }
}

private int getMaxUserId()   // Returns max primary key
{ int maxId = 0;             // value used in database.
  try
  { String sQuery = "SELECT MAX(userId) " +
                    "AS MaxId FROM User";
    ResultSet res = stat.executeQuery(sQuery);
    while (res.next())
    { maxId = res.getInt("MaxId"); }
  }
  catch(SQLException e)
  { System.err.println("Error in getting max id");
    e.printStackTrace();
  }
  return maxId;
}

/** Close connection to database. */
public synchronized void logoff()
{ try
  { stat.close();
    conn.close();
  }
  catch (Exception e)
  { e.printStackTrace(); }
}
}
```

In a professional application, the name of the database, the table and database driver should not be hard-coded into the database interface class, but instead defined in a separate *configuration file*.

> **Coding Rules:**
> Instance variables of a servlet, such as *dbi*, are shared between all requests that are currently being responded to by the servlet. To ensure that data is private to a particular request, define it as a local variable of *doGet* or *doPost*.
> A database interface must define its operations as *synchronized* to prevent multiple concurrent executions of them, if the database being used cannot support such concurrent access.

7.2.2   Client-side design: web page design issues

Design of the visual and information content of web pages involves consideration of the following issues:

- Aesthetics – that the pages project a positive image of the organisation that they are designed for.
- Usability – that users can effectively use and navigate through the web site to find information or services that they require.
- Portability – that the web pages or equivalent versions of them should be viewable under a number of different browsers.
- Accessibility – that users with different abilities, such as older or disabled users, should be able to use the web pages.

To design web pages, we should first sketch diagrams of their intended structure and appearance, and review these for their usability and the other criteria described above. For example, including too many input fields on a form makes it hard to fit on one page without forcing the user to scroll down. A large form should be shortened if possible, or split into several pages, each page grouping fields that form a coherent set of data, eg, all personal data on one page, all details of the required service on another.

Aesthetics   Page design may use a wide variety of styles and structuring approaches. These range from styles borrowed from other media, such as the newspaper format of *msn* or *amazon* front pages, to very individual and idiosyncratic formats based on one or two striking images/multimedia elements and sparse textual content. The intended audience of a site is probably the most important factor in deciding the appearance of a website. For a commercial organisation, such as an estate agent or stock broker, a sedate and professional appearance without flashy visual/audio tricks or strident colours is probably appropriate. On the other hand, for a site designed for schoolchildren, a more cartoon-like appearance using bright colours, sound and animation is more likely to retain the interest of users. The book [9] gives many examples of current websites and discusses their design choices.

Usability   The same principles of usability that apply to conventional software systems [15] also apply to web systems: the users should be able to achieve each of the functions that the system is supposed to support, without excessive effort. This means that information should be presented in a clear manner, that command buttons should be instantly recognisable as such, and that they have meaningful names that identify their function, etc. Aesthetic issues may conflict with usability – for example black backgrounds seem to be favoured by some web designers, and do serve to make web pages look distinctive and stylish – unfortunately they can also make the page content almost unreadable. Ease of navigation is a key principle to observe – users should not have to scroll down a long page or follow convoluted chains of links to access the functions or other pages that they need. To achieve this, some of the top commercial

sites such as Amazon, or java.sun.com, devote a large part of their initial web
pages to navigation. Navigation links should have text which clearly identifies
what the link does, and a graphic which makes clear that the item is a link and
not a stray title or other text. It should always be easy to return to a central
navigation point, such as the homepage, within a site.

Clear and simple labels should be used for fields. Make clear which fields are
mandatory, by putting a * next to them. In general you should avoid exposing
internal id's, unless these are generally used in the domain: property id's, NI
numbers for adults (which are de facto national identity numbers in the UK),
ISBNs for books, etc. In the property system, the name and email together are
used as a compound key to uniquely identify users.

Portability   Because a user may try to access the system using any existing
browser, including archaic versions of browsers, the system developer must
take care to ensure that their web pages will render reasonably well on as
many browsers as possible, and certainly include the current versions of the
most popular browsers: Internet Explorer (IE), Netscape (NN) and Mozilla.

Portability problems with web pages include:

- Scripting languages such as JavaScript executing correctly in one browser
  but not in another.
- Colours and positioning of page elements may display differently on different browsers.
- The XHTML features supported may vary between browsers, for example
  blinking text does not work under IE, and some browsers still do not
  support frames (for these, the *noframes* tag can be used to provide an
  alternative presentation or web page).
- The tags needed to achieve a particular effect are different in different
  browsers. For example, to embed a Flash movie into a web page to
  display under NN, we need to use the *embed* tag, whilst the *object* tag is
  used for IE.
- Pages intended for users in different countries should ensure that data
  such as lengths, weights and dates are expressed in internationally comprehensible terms: the date 3.5.1999 will probably mean different things
  to a resident of the USA and a resident of the UK, for example. An
  unambiguous version could be '5th of March, 1999'. Likewise weight,
  volume and distance measurements should always include units (metric
  or imperial) to make clear what is intended.

One general solution to these problems is to provide alternative versions
of a website for different browsers, and switch to the appropriate page when
the browser being used has been detected, using the *navigator* attribute of
a browser. This however multiplies the development and maintenance work
needed.

To avoid the need for separate versions of pages, a developer can try to
restrict the features used in their pages to a subset that will display correctly
whatever browser is used. An example is colours: only 216 colours (those

whose red, green and blue components have values in the set of hexadecimal numbers 00, 33, 66, 99, CC and FF) will display in a consistent way across platforms and in the main browsers. These are called the 'web-safe' colours (http://www.lynda.com).

Web pages can be checked for conformance to the W3C XHTML standard via the W3C validation service at `http://www.w3c.org/`. The pages of a system should also be tested for the widest collection of browsers that can be obtained.

Accessibility Another issue which should be taken into consideration is accessibility: users of the system may have differing abilities, may be partially sighted, colour blind, or have hearing impairments. The number of such users is significant: around ten million American men have red-green colour-blindness, for example, and there are more than two million people in the UK with vision problems.

To achieve accessibility by such users a web page developer should:

- Ensure there is good contrast between the colours used on their page, eg, between the background colour/image and the colours used for unvisited and visited links, etc. Ideally a monochrome version of the page should still be clear and usable. Preview the pages using a tool which shows how they would appear to colour-blind people.
- Ensure the minimum font size is reasonably large: 12 point, for example, and avoid absolute specification of fonts, instead define them as a percentage of the default font size.
- Ensure that images and other visual elements such as animations have an alternative text description, so that screen readers can still communicate information about them to visually-impaired readers. The *alt* attribute can have value "*" for bullet graphics, a dashed line for horizontal rules, and for button graphics, place the command/option text inside square brackets: "[Submit]".
- Similarly, explanatory text can be added to audio elements of a web page, which enables captions to be displayed explaining the elements, for users who are deaf or hard of hearing.
- Ensure that XHTML structural elements such as headings are used appropriately to break up a document into meaningful chunks, similarly, ensure that other tags are used where possible to convey information. For example, the *th* tag should be used for header cells of a table, instead of *td*, so that screen readers can interpret the table as intended.

Improving a website to make it accessible for disabled users can also improve its usability for all users. It may also be a legal requirement in some circumstances, or help to avoid legal action. A disabled user sued the organisers of the 2000 Olympics, for example, over the lack of accessibility of the website for this event [20]. In the UK the Disability Discrimination Act makes it unlawful for a service provider (in the general sense) to discriminate against a disabled person by refusing to provide a service which it provides to the general public.

The W3 consortium has a set of guidelines and standards for accessibility of websites, at: www.w3c.org/WAI/.

7.2.3   Client-side design: JavaScript

There are two primary uses of JavaScript in an internet application:

1. To provide interactive features on a web page, such as messages which pop up when the mouse cursor moves over a command button on the page, to explain the purpose of the command.
2. To carry out some of the application processing on the client side, in order to reduce the load on the server. Typically this involves a series of checks on form data to prevent the form being submitted with incomplete or clearly invalid data.

JavaScript is written in the 'head' section of a web page, between $< script >$ and $< /script >$ tags. Its syntax is similar to, but generally simpler than, Java.

An elementary example of a JavaScript program, which displays a table of the first ten integers and the sums of numbers up to the integer, is:

```
<html> <head>
<title>Sums of numbers in 1..10</title>

<script language = "JavaScript">
  document.writeln("<table border = '1' width = '60%'>");
  document.writeln("<tr><th width = '30%'>Number</th> " +
    "<th width = '30%'>Sum</th></tr>");
  var sum = 0;
  for (var i = 1; i <= 10; i++)
  { sum = sum + i;
    document.writeln("<tr><td> " + i +
              " </td><td> " + sum + " </td></tr>");
  }
  document.writeln("</table>");
  // end of main function
</script>
</head>  <body>  </body>
</html>
```

Figure 7.7 shows the web page produced by this program. This example illustrates the typical mix of HTML and JavaScript which is involved in client-side scripting.

Variables in JavaScript are declared by the syntax

```
  var sum = 0;
```

A type for the variable is not explicitly given, instead any data may be stored in the variable. In this example the integer value 0 is stored in *sum*. As in

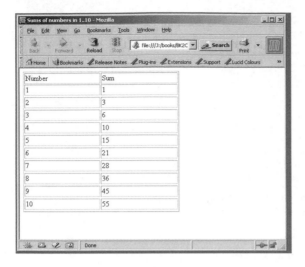

Figure 7.7: Output of sums script

Java, variables may be read and updated by using their name to refer to the value they hold.

The same control structures: *if*, *while*, *do*, *for*, *return*, may be used in JavaScript as in Java. The syntax of these constructs is the same as in Java, except that the index variable of a *for* loop is declared using *var*. A simpler version

```
for (var index in collection)
{ ... collection[index] ... }
```

of the for loop can be used to iterate over all members of an array or other collection.

JavaScript programs can manipulate elements of the web page in which they reside. The statement

```
document.writeln("<table border = '1' width = '60%'>");
```

writes the table declaration to the current *document*, ie, it inserts this information into the currently displayed web page.

JavaScript programs can also read data from the web page, in particular, the values of fields in an HTML form. The following page contains a form with one field, intended to contain an integer. The script consists of a function *cube*, which displays the cube of the value of the field, when the button *Cube* is pressed:

```
<html> <head>
<title>Cube form</title>
<script language = "JavaScript">
```

```
function cube()
{ var x =
    parseInt(document.form1.field1.value);
  document.writeln("<h1>The cube is: " + x*x*x + "</h1>");
}
</script>
</head>

<body>
<form name = "form1" action = "">

<p>
<strong>Enter integer to be cubed:</strong>
<input name = "field1" type = "text"></p>

<p><input type = "button"
 value = "Cube" onclick = "cube()"></p>
</form>
</body>
</html>
```

Figure 7.8 shows an example of the execution of this page.

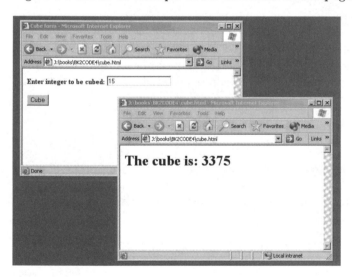

Figure 7.8: Output of cube script

Data in a text field such as *field*1 is considered to be a string, so must be converted to an integer using the function *parseInt* before numeric processing can be applied to it.

This program also demonstrates two key features of JavaScript:

1. Programs can be divided into separate *functions*, which carry out a spe-

cific task. These can be used to structure the program in the same way that methods of a Java class modularise the definition of the class.

2. Functions can be invoked by *events*, such as buttons being pressed, the content of fields changing, or mouse actions. This enables immediate responses to user actions, such as opening a help message for a form field when a user moves the mouse into the field.

Functions can be given parameters, as input data. In the following example the function *isNumber* checks if its input string *str* represents a number (real number or integer) by trying to convert the string to a number and then checking if the result is not a number (*isNaN*):

```
function isNumber(str)
{ if (isNaN(parseFloat(str)))
  { return false; }
  return true;
}
```

This might be called when a form is submitted, to check that a value in a field of the form represents a numeric quantity:

```
<html> <head>
<title>Number check form</title>
<script language = "JavaScript">
function check()
{ if (isNumber(document.form1.field1.value))
  { window.alert("Ok, it is a number"); }
  else
  { window.alert("ERROR: not a number!"); }
}

function isNumber(str)
{ if (isNaN(parseFloat(str)))
  { return false; }
  return true;
}
</script>
</head>

<body>
<form name = "form1" action = "">

<p>
<strong>Enter integer to be checked:</strong>
<input name = "field1" type = "text"></p>

<p><input type = "button"
 value = "Check" onclick = "check()"></p>
</form>
</body>
</html>
```

Figure 7.9 shows an execution of this page.

Figure 7.9: Output of number check script

A natural way to represent a form-based page together with its JavaScript functions is as a class in a UML class diagram, where the fields of the form become attributes of the class, and the functions become its methods. The different copies of the page displayed in different browsers correspond to instances of the class. Figure 7.10 shows the class for the cube example.

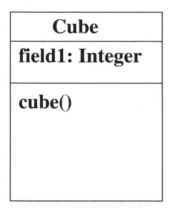

Figure 7.10: Class of cube form

JavaScript functions can be triggered by a large number of browser and document events. Table 7.1 lists some of the most frequently used events, and gives the location of the *event = function* attribute setting. *onmouseover* and *onmouseout* are particularly useful for *rollover* effects on the elements they are attached to, ie, actions that change the appearance of the element when the mouse passes over it, or that carry out other actions triggered by this event.

For example, the *area* field in the property search registration form could trigger a helpful message when the mouse goes over it:

Event	Occurs	Location
onload	page first loaded into browser	body tag
onclick	mouse clicked over element	element tag
onmousemove	mouse moved	body tag
onmouseover	mouse enters element	element tag
onmouseout	mouse leaves element	element tag
onfocus	form element selected by click/tab	element tag
onblur	a different form element selected by click/tab	element tag
onsubmit	form submit button pressed	form tag
onreset	form reset button pressed	form tag
onabort	image download cancelled	img tag
onhelp	help key F1 pressed	body tag
onkeydown	a key is pressed	body tag
onkeyup	a key is released	body tag
ondblclick	mouse is double clicked	body tag
onchange	form element data changed	element tag
onresize	when window or frame resized	body or frame tag

Table 7.1: JavaScript event handling

```
<p>
<strong>What area (postcode)?</strong><br>
<input name = "area"
 type = "text"
 onmouseover = "areaMessage()"
 size = "4">
</p>
```

where *areaMessage*() is defined as:

```
function areaMessage()
{ window.alert("Enter a postcode, eg:\n" +
            "SW19 or EC1R");
}
```

Functions may also be invoked at timed intervals or after a set delay from an event. This can be used to achieve animation or other dynamic effects, such as a movie-like tour of a property for sale. The following web page loops through five photographs named 0.jpg, 1.jpg, 2.jpg, 3.jpg and 4.jpg, showing each for two seconds:

```
<html>
<head>
  <title>Image Loop</title>
  <script type = "text/javascript">
  var count = 0;

  function startTimer()
  { window.setInterval("tick()",2000); }

  function tick()
  { count = (count + 1) % 5;
    document.photos.src = count + ".jpg";
  }
</script></head>
<body onload = "startTimer()">
<img name = "photos" src = "0.jpg">
</body>
</html>
```

The representation of forms as classes suggested above leads to the question of what invariants of the class represent on the form. Such constraints can be regarded as properties that the form fields should satisfy in order for the form to be valid. In particular, a field that corresponds to an attribute with a numeric type needs a JavaScript check on the web page to ensure that it really is numeric, before the form data is submitted. Table 7.2 lists the JavaScript checks derived from attribute typings. Other type-related invariants and checks could include, for string attributes stereotyped as ≪ email ≫, that the '@' symbol occurs in the string, and not as the first or last character:

```
function isEmail(str)
```

Attribute type	JavaScript check
Real	*isNumber*
Integer	*isNumber* and '.' does not occur in the value
Boolean	value equals "true" or "false"

Table 7.2: JavaScript checks derived from attribute types

```
{ var ind = str.indexOf("@");
  return ind > 0 && ind < str.length - 1;
}
```

More complex constraints on attributes of the form class can be translated directly into properties of the corresponding form data fields. For example, the OCL/LOCA constraint that a form *name* field is non-empty:

$$name.size > 0$$

becomes the check

```
name.length > 0
```

in JavaScript.

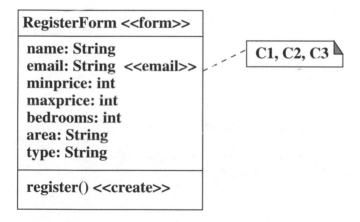

Figure 7.11: Class of registration form

For the property search system, the class description of the user registration form is given in Figure 7.11. The constraints are:

1. $C1$: $0 \leq minprice$ and $minprice \leq maxprice$
2. $C2$: $name.size > 0$
3. $C3$: $bedrooms > 0$

in addition to the typing constraints and stereotype of *email*.

Properties involving information about other objects of the class, such as the *identity* property of an attribute, can normally only be feasibly checked on the server, since only it will have access to the set of existing instances of entities (created from web pages such as the user registration form).

The complete JavaScript code for validating the user registration page is:

```
<html>
<head> <title>User</title>
<script type = "text/javascript">
  function isNumber(str)
  { if (isNaN(parseFloat(str)))
    { return false; }
    return true;
  }

  function isInteger(str)
  { return isNumber(str) &&
          str.indexOf(".") == -1;
  }

  function isEmail(str)
  { var ind = str.indexOf("@");
    return (ind > 0 && ind < str.length - 1);
  }

  function checkName()
  { if (document.User.name.value.length > 0) { }
    else
    { window.alert("Name cannot be empty!"); }
  }

  function checkEmail()
  { if (isEmail(document.User.email.value)) { }
    else
    { window.alert("Not an email address: " +
                  document.User.email.value);
    }
  }

  function checkMinprice()
  { if (isInteger(document.User.minprice.value))
    { document.User.minprice.value =
        parseInt(document.User.minprice.value);
    }
    else
    { window.alert("Not an integer: " +
                  document.User.minprice.value);
    }
  }
```

```
    function checkMaxprice()
    { if (isInteger(document.User.maxprice.value))
      { document.User.maxprice.value =
          parseInt(document.User.maxprice.value);
      }
      else
      { window.alert("Not an integer: " +
                     document.User.maxprice.value);
      }
    }


    function checkBedrooms()
    { if (isInteger(document.User.bedrooms.value))
      { document.User.bedrooms.value =
          parseInt(document.User.bedrooms.value);
        var bedroomsx =
          parseInt(document.User.bedrooms.value);
        if (bedroomsx <= 0)
        { window.alert("Bedrooms must be > 0"); }
      }
      else
      { window.alert("Not an integer: " +
                     document.User.bedrooms.value);
      }
    }


    function formSubmit()
    { var maxp = parseInt(document.User.maxprice.value);
      var minp = parseInt(document.User.minprice.value);
      if (minp >= 0 && maxp >= minp) { }
      else
      { window.alert("Prices not valid!");
        return false;
      }
      return true;
    }
</script>
</head>

<body>
<form name = "User"
 action =
   "http://www.propertysearch.co.uk:8080/servlet/RegisterUserServlet"
 method = "POST">

<p>
<strong>Your name</strong>
<input name = "name" type = "text"
  onchange = "checkName()"></p>
```

```
<p>
<strong>Email address</strong>
<input name = "email" type = "text"
  onchange = "checkEmail()"></p>


<p>
<strong>What type of property are you
looking for?</strong><br>
Detached
<input name = "type" type = "radio" value = "detached">
Semi-detached
<input name = "type" type = "radio"
 value = "semi" checked>
Terraced
<input name = "type" type = "radio"
 value = "terraced">
Flat
<input name = "type" type = "radio"
 value = "flat">
</p>


<p>
<strong>How many bedrooms?</strong><br>
<input name = "bedrooms" type = "text" size = "1"
  onchange = "checkBedrooms()"></p>


<p>
<strong>Maximum price?</strong><br>
<input name = "maxprice" type = "text"
  onchange = "checkMaxprice()"></p>


<p>
<strong>Minimum price?</strong><br>
<input name = "minprice" type = "text"
  onchange = "checkMinprice()"></p>


<p>
<strong>What area (postcode)?</strong><br>
<input name = "area"
 type = "text" size = "4">
</p>


<input type = "submit" value = "Register"
  onclick = "return formSubmit()">
</form>
</body>
</html>
```

When *formSubmit* returns a *false* value, it cancels the default action of the *onclick* event – the submission of the form. So if data on the form is erroneous, the form will not be submitted.

Invariants connecting the form and database data become specifications of the functionality of the server side components responding to form submissions, as discussed in Section 7.2.8 below.

JavaScript code can be debugged by typing *javascript* : into the location bar of a Netscape Navigator browser displaying the page. The line numbers and descriptions of any errors are identified.

7.2.4 Client-side design: image maps

An *image map* designates areas within an image as links, these can be normal HTML links either to other parts of the same document or to different documents. When a point within a designated area of the image is clicked on, the link is activated and the browser displays the linked-to document.

An example of a web page with an image map could be a page giving information on three football players in a photograph:

```
<html>
<head><title>Image Map Example</title></head>
<body>

<map name = "mymap">
<area shape = "rect" coords = "2,2,50,100"
 href = "player1.html"
 alt = "Player 1 information" />
<area shape = "rect" coords = "52,2,100,100"
 href = "player2.html"
 alt = "Player 2 information" />
<area shape = "rect" coords = "102,2,150,100"
 href = "player3.html"
 alt = "Player 3 information" />
</map>

<img src= "players.gif" width= "200" height = "120"
 alt = "Image of three players" usemap = "mymap"/>
</body>
</html>
```

The *usemap* attribute in the *img* element indicates that the image map *mymap* is to be used for this image. Figure 7.12 shows the structure of this map.

Several kinds of shape can be specified as link areas:

1. Rectangular areas, specified by their top left and bottom right corner coordinates:

   ```
   <area shape = "rect" coords = "x1,y1,x2,y2"
    href = "link.html"
    alt = "Explanatory text" />
   ```

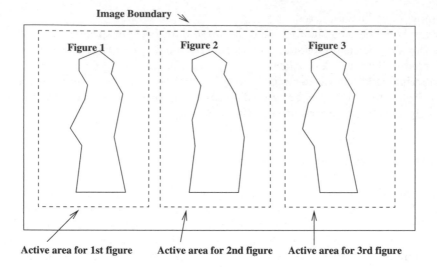

Figure 7.12: Image map example

2. Circular areas, specified by their centre point and radius:

```
<area shape = "circle" coords = "x,y,radius"
 href = "link.html"
 alt = "Explanatory text" />
```

3. Polygonal areas, specified by a series of coordinates for the vertices:

```
<area shape = "poly" coords = "x1,y1,x2,y2,x3,y3"
 href = "link.html"
 alt = "Explanatory text" />
```

It is important to include the *ALT* tag with each area, so that screen readers can give useful information to visually-impaired users.

7.2.5   Client-side design: Macromedia Flash

Macromedia Flash is a commercial application for the construction of visual and multi-media effects for display on web pages. It is based around a paradigm of *movies*, whereby the developer defines, frame by frame, what images or sound effects should be played to the user. The Flash development tool can interpolate between frames to automatically create intermediate frames (a process called *tweening*), so the developer does not need to specify every frame themselves.

We will illustrate the use of Flash by constructing a 'virtual tour' of a property, showing a floor plan of the property with a moving blob indicating the location of the viewer, and a slideshow of photos of each location. A viewer

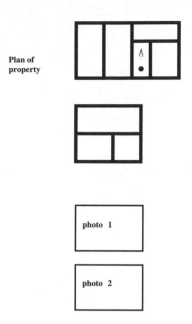

Plan of property

Figure 7.13: Virtual tour display

can click on a location to move to it (restarting the movie from that point). Figure 7.13 shows how this is intended to appear.

Design using Flash consists of specifying a set of *layers* of the movie to be produced, each layer is a separate sequence of images, or *frames*. The combination of the separate layers produces the final movie. Frames in separate layers occur simultaneously, and there are typically between five to fifteen frames per second. The rapid succession of similar frames is used to create the illusion of motion. For the property system we will use ten frames per second.

For the property search 'virtual tour' we can identify three layers:

1. A mainly static schematic plan of the floors of the property. Each room is a separate button, and turns from black to red when the viewer (represented by a blob) enters it. Any of the buttons can be pressed at any time to restart the movie from that room.
2. A moving blob, with motion tweening used to animate it, with 10 frames (1 second) spent in each room.
3. Photos of the room the viewer is in, changing when they move to a different room.

Figure 7.14 shows the frame sequences involved. If we have a property with n rooms, the tour starts in room one at frame one and enters room i at frame $10 * i + 1$.

To create this movie using the Flash development tool, we define each layer separately. For the first layer, we draw the floor plan and identify each of the rooms as buttons. Only the first frame needs to be specified in each group of

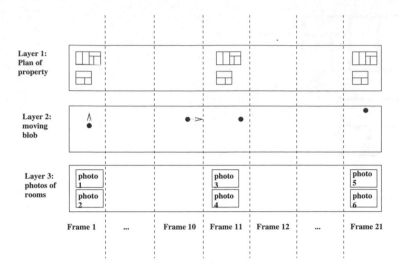

Figure 7.14: Virtual tour design

ten frames $10 * i + 1$ upto $10 * (i + 1)$, this frame has room i coloured red and the rest black. As with JavaScript, we can set actions for each button event. In this case, we attach the action:

```
on(press)
{ gotoAndPlay(10*i + 1); }
```

to the button representing room i. This instructs the Flash movie to restart from frame $10 * i + 1$ when the button is pressed.

The next layer is the animation of the blob representing the viewer. Only certain frames need to be explicitly created (those where the blob changes direction), the others can be created by *motion tweening*, interpolating the blob's position for intermediate frames. The final layer contains the photos to be displayed.

7.2.6   Interaction design using statecharts

As described in Section 7.2.3 above, class diagrams can be used to document the data of internet systems: the contents of forms and database tables. The other core UML notation, statecharts, also have an important role to play, in describing the interaction behaviour of an internet system in terms of what sequence of pages are displayed to a user, and the effect of user commands. Figure 7.15 shows an example for the property search system. States correspond to web pages that are displayed to the user (whether these are fixed hard-coded pages or dynamically generated): the name of the page is given, together with a summary of its content. Transitions are labelled with events that correspond to user commands or links that can be selected in the source state (page). The effect of commands is described, and the target state is the next web page shown to the user. In this example, various design choices have

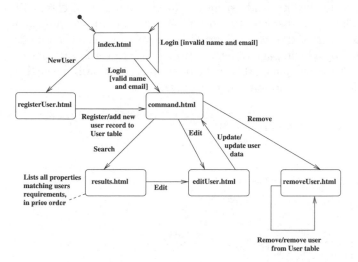

Figure 7.15: User interaction state machine of property system

been made, and are shown explicitly on this diagram:

- The initial page includes a login form, rather than requiring an additional step in interaction and a separate *login.html* page: in general the interaction should be simplified as much as possible to reduce the effort/time needed by users to interact with the system.
- After registering as a new user, or logging on as an existing user, the next page shown contains three buttons for the options *Search*, *Remove* and *Edit Preferences*. The name and email is remembered by the system from the previous page, using a *session*, so the customer does not have to re-enter this data.
- Having searched, the results page shows a list of the matching properties, and includes the *Edit Preferences* button again so the customer can directly modify their choices, instead of needing to press the 'back' button in the browser and choose the edit option from *command.html*.
- Having updated their preferences, the customer is taken back to *command.html*.

This design would be derived by analysis of the required use cases and scenarios of use of the system. When reviewing the design, we must check that it supports all the requirements, whilst minimising the effort and number of steps needed for the customer to achieve the desired functionality. We should also check that information presented in each page is appropriate and necessary.

In the property system, the administrators/staff of the system have a separate set of operations, to modify the property data.

The default user interaction statechart of a web system involving stored entities E_1, ..., E_n and roles $role_1$, ..., $role_m$ has a single command page, giving an introduction to the site, and listing all the commands to create, edit and delete each of the E_i, to list all elements of the E_i and to list, add and remove elements from each of the $role_j$. Figure 7.16 shows this. The commands page may be preceded by a login page which requires a user to verify themselves before reaching the command page: this layer of security is usually needed if data is to be modified, or if secure data is to be read.

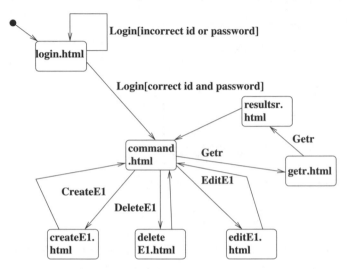

Figure 7.16: Default web statechart

7.2.7 Design review

At this point in a development, where the client-side components and behaviours have been defined, at least on paper, we can carry out a review of the design and identify aspects that can be improved.

- The pages need more information, particularly the initial page, which should explain what the site offers: 'We hold details of over 100,000 properties for sale in London and the South East', for example. Some images, such as photos of selected properties, would also improve the attractiveness of this and other pages.
- Forcing the customer to enter their name and email before they can proceed is rather user-hostile. It discourages customers from browsing through other pages of the site to see if it offers what they want.
- Rather than relying on (possibly non-portable) scripts, select boxes could be used for prices and number of bedrooms, to enforce that these items are entered as integers. This restricts the customers slightly, however. Likewise, areas could be chosen from select lists or an image map.

- Forms should indicate which fields are mandatory and which are optional: the convention is to put a ∗ beside the mandatory fields.
- Contact details for the estate agent or vendor (if a private sale) of the property need to be included in the property details, so that customers can make further enquiries about properties they are interested in.

7.2.8 Server-side design: Java servlets

Servlets are Java classes which respond to HTTP requests and carry out actions on the server such as modifying data in the repository of a system, or generating response pages as XHTML text files, which are then returned to the client for display on the client browser.

Within the server-side components, the code that actually generates web pages from code should be separated from code that manages the flow of control. The code that directly manages the database should be separated from both of these as well.

Table 7.3 compares Servlets to JSP (Java Server Pages), an alternative Java technology for server-side web programming.

	Servlets	*JSP*
Advantages	Conceptually simple.	Easy to integrate content and visual appearance with programming.
Disadvantages	Requires Java programming skills.	Hard to debug, delay on first access to page due to compilation.

Table 7.3: Servlets versus JSP

In Section 7.2 we summarised typical internet system functionalities as *create*, *delete*, *edit*, etc. For each kind of operation a standard form of pre/post condition specification of the operation can be given, which leads in turn to a standard structure of servlet code.

createEntity: all attribute values need to be supplied (normally, unless there are defaults that can be used for missing attributes). The postcondition is

$$Entity[keyatt] \: /= \: \{\} \: \&$$
$$Entity[keyatt].att_1 = formatt_1 \: \&$$
$$\ldots \: \&$$
$$Entity[keyatt].att_n = formatt_n$$

where *keyatt* is the primary key attribute of *Entity* and the att_i are all the other attributes of *Entity*. The $formatt_i$ are the corresponding attributes of the input form.

$Entity[keyatt] = \{\}$ is a precondition, and such a key attribute value may be selected automatically by the system, as an alternative to the user supplying one.

deleteEntity: only a key attribute needs to be provided in the web page form. The postcondition is

$$Entity[keyatt] = \{\}$$

That is, all instances of *Entity* with the supplied key value have been deleted.

Alternatively, some non-key attributes may be supplied, in which case all rows with these attribute values are deleted:

$$Entity \mid (att_1 = formatt_1 \ \& \ \ldots \ \& \ att_m = formatt_m) \ = \ \{\}$$

editEntity: The key attribute and all attribute values to be changed need to be supplied. The precondition is

$$Entity[keyatt] \ / = \ \{\}$$

The postcondition is

$$Entity[keyatt].att_1 = formatt_1 \ \&$$
$$\ldots \ \&$$
$$Entity[keyatt].att_n = formatt_n$$

where the att_i are all the updated attributes of *Entity* and the $formatt_i$ the corresponding attributes of the update form.

checkEntity: The key attribute and one or more others need to be supplied. If there is an instance in the database with this key value, and the values of the form attributes match the attribute values in the database, return *true*, otherwise return *false*:

$$(Entity[keyatt] \ / = \ \{\} \ \&$$
$$Entity[keyatt].att_1 = formatt_1 \ \&$$
$$\ldots \ \&$$
$$Entity[keyatt].att_m = formatt_m) \ \Rightarrow \ result = true$$

listEntity: The form contains information to be used in matching, the result page has a list of items which are exactly those stored *Entity* instances that match the specified properties P. The postcondition is:

$$items.asSet = Entity \mid (P(formatt_1, \ldots, formatt_n))$$

Notice that a collection such as *Entity* | *P* corresponds directly to an SQL *SELECT * FROM Entity WHERE P* query, and it will be implemented using this query in a relational database interface. Whatever ordering of results is required must be carried out programmatically, or by using the ORDERED BY *field* option of SQL SELECT.

getrole: The form contains the value *akeyval* of the primary key of the entity
that owns *role*, the result is the set of instances of the entity at the other
end of the association, which have their foreign key *akey* value equal to
akeyval:

$$items \ = \ Entity2 \mid (akey = akeyval)$$

in the case of an explicit association, or which satisfy the defining predicate *Prop* of the association, in the case of an implicit association:

$$items \ = \ Entity2 \mid (Prop)$$

7.2.9   Server-side design: web-page definitions

The generated web pages returned by a server to a client can be constructed
as objects of suitable Java classes, classes whose features represent elements of
web pages, such as forms and form fields. Appendix B gives a set of possible
definitions of classes *HtmlComponent*, *HtmlPage*, etc, which can be used as the
basis of generated pages.

Within a single application, such as the property search system, the pages
generated by the system usually have common features such as images, layout,
text or buttons, and these common features can be placed in a superclass, which
is inherited by all the classes representing pages of the system. When two or
more pages are very similar in their construction, a superclass representing
their commonalities can also be defined, and is inherited by the classes for
the particular pages (eg, the *registerUser.html* and *editUser.html* pages in the
property search system). If two pages are *identical* in structure and differ only
in the values of features such as their titles, then only one class may be needed
for the two pages, and the setting of those features that differ can be achieved
by providing the feature values as parameters of the constructor of this class.

For the property system, we can define a general *PSPage* class, based on
HtmlPage, which holds all the common elements of pages in the system, such
as a standard page footer image giving the contact details of the company.
Inheriting from this (Figure 7.17) are the classes for the commands page, the
search results page, and a class *NameEmailPage*, which describes a page with
a form containing two fields for name and email data. *RemoveUserPage* and
LoginPage inherit directly from *NameEmailPage*, since they both consist of
such a form, but differ: the name field being non-editable in the *RemoveUserPage*
case, and the names of the submit buttons on the pages being different.

Inheriting from *NameEmailPage* is *PSUserPage*, which adds the remaining
fields for price, bedrooms, area and type of property to the form. Subclasses
RegisterUserPage and *EditUserPage* describe the corresponding web pages,
which differ only in their titles and the name of their submit buttons (so could
be merged into a single class with these two string properties provided in the
constructor).

The general *PSPage* is created by the following class:

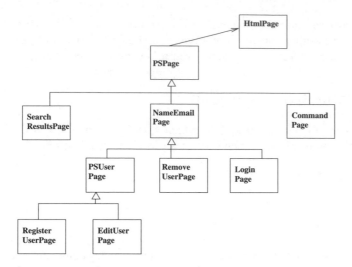

Figure 7.17: Classes for web-page generation

```
public class PSPage
{ protected HtmlPage page = new HtmlPage();
  protected HtmlHead psHead =
      new HtmlHead("Property Search UK");
  protected HtmlBody psBody = new HtmlBody();

  public PSPage()
  { psBody.setAttribute("bgcolor","#FF69CC");
    psBody.setFooter("Property Search UK: 0888 999222");
    page.setHead(psHead);
    page.setBody(psBody);
  }

  public String toString()
  { return page.getHtml(); }
}
```

This defines common style elements for all the pages of the system: an attractive (although perhaps inappropriate!) background colour, a title and a footer for the page.

The *NameEmailPage* has a form with these two fields, and is constructed by the following class:

```
public class NameEmailPage extends PSPage
{ protected HtmlForm form = new HtmlForm();
  protected HtmlInput button = new HtmlInput();

  public NameEmailPage()
  { super();
```

```
      form.setAttribute("method","GET");
      HtmlText nameLabel =
        new HtmlText("Your name:","strong");
          // label for name field
      form.add(nameLabel);
      HtmlInput nameField = new HtmlInput();
          // input field for name
      nameField.setAttribute("type","text");
      nameField.setAttribute("name","name");
      form.add(nameField);

      HtmlItem para = new HtmlItem("p");
      form.add(para);

      HtmlText emailLabel =
        new HtmlText("Email address:","strong");
      form.add(emailLabel);
      HtmlInput emailField = new HtmlInput();
      emailField.setAttribute("type","text");
      emailField.setAttribute("name","email");
      form.add(emailField);
      form.add(para);

      button.setAttribute("type","submit");

      psBody.add(form);
    }

  public void setName(String nme)
  { form.setField("name","value",nme); }

  public void setEmail(String eml)
  { form.setField("email","value",eml); }
}
```

The *form* and *button* details will be modified in specific subclasses such as *LoginPage*, so they are provided as instance variables of *NameEmailPage*.

```
public class PSUserPage extends NameEmailPage
{ public PSUserPage()
  { super();
    HtmlText propertyLabel =
      new HtmlText("What type of property?:","strong");
    form.add(propertyLabel);
    HtmlRadioGroup propertyField =
      new HtmlRadioGroup("type");
    propertyField.addOption("detached",false);
    propertyField.addOption("semi",true);
    propertyField.addOption("terraced",false);
    propertyField.addOption("flat",false);
    form.add(propertyField);
```

```
    HtmlItem para = new HtmlItem("p");
    form.add(para);

    HtmlText bedLabel =
      new HtmlText("How many bedrooms?:","strong");
    form.add(bedLabel);
    HtmlInput bedField = new HtmlInput();
    bedField.setAttribute("type","text");
    bedField.setAttribute("name","bedrooms");
    bedField.setAttribute("size","1");
    form.add(bedField);
    form.add(para);

    HtmlText maxLabel =
      new HtmlText("Maximum price?:","strong");
    form.add(maxLabel);
    HtmlInput maxField = new HtmlInput();
    maxField.setAttribute("type","text");
    maxField.setAttribute("name","maxprice");
    maxField.setAttribute("size","8");
    form.add(maxField);
    form.add(para);

    HtmlText minLabel =
      new HtmlText("Minimum price?:","strong");
    form.add(minLabel);
    HtmlInput minField = new HtmlInput();
    minField.setAttribute("type","text");
    minField.setAttribute("name","minprice");
    minField.setAttribute("size","8");
    form.add(minField);
    form.add(para);

    HtmlText areaLabel =
      new HtmlText("What area (postcode)?:","strong");
    form.add(areaLabel);
    HtmlInput areaField = new HtmlInput();
    areaField.setAttribute("type","text");
    areaField.setAttribute("name","area");
    areaField.setAttribute("size","4");
    form.add(areaField);
    form.add(para);
  }

  public void setBedrooms(String b)
  { form.setField("bedrooms","value",b); }


    ...
}
```

The *registerUser* and *editUser* pages differ only in their titles, actions and buttons:

```
public class RegisterUserPage extends PSUserPage
{ public RegisterUserPage()
  { super();

    HtmlText heading =
      new HtmlText("Enter your details to register",
                   "h1");
    psBody.add(0,heading);
    form.setAttribute("action",
 "http://www.propertysearch.co.uk:8080/servlet/RegisterUserServlet");
    button.setAttribute("value","Register");
    form.add(button);
  }
}
```

The edit page is very similar:

```
public class EditUserPage extends PSUserPage
{ public EditUserPage()
  { super();

    HtmlText heading =
      new HtmlText("Enter your new details",
                   "h1");
    psBody.add(0,heading);
    form.setAttribute("action",
 "http://www.propertysearch.co.uk:8080/servlet/EditUserServlet");
    button.setAttribute("value","Update");
    form.add(button);
  }
}
```

Figure 7.18 shows the web page created by this class.

Scripts can be added to a page by creating *HtmlScript* objects:

```
HtmlScript hs = new HtmlScript("text/javascript");
hs.add(HtmlScript.NUMBER_CHECK_FUNCTION);
hs.add(HtmlScript.INT_CHECK_FUNCTION);
hs.add(HtmlScript.EMAIL_CHECK_FUNCTION);
....
psHead.add(hs);
```

The constants *HtmlScript.NUMBER_CHECK_FUNCTION*, etc, are strings giving the standard definitions of JavaScript check functions.

The *RegisterUserPage* class is used by the servlet *InitialServlet* that responds to the initial page. To detect which command *New User*, or *Login*, was selected from this page, the servlet tests the value of corresponding variables. The non-null variable corresponds to the selected command:

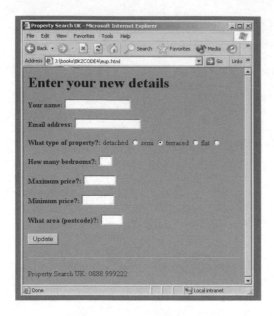

Figure 7.18: Output of EditUserPage

```java
import java.io.*;
import java.util.*;
import javax.servlet.http.*;
import javax.servlet.*;

public class InitialServlet extends HttpServlet
{ private DBI dbi; // Interface to database

  public InitialServlet() {}

  public void init(ServletConfig cfg)
  throws ServletException
  { super.init(cfg);
    dbi = new DBI();
  }

  public void doGet(HttpServletRequest req,
                    HttpServletResponse res)
    throws ServletException, IOException
  { res.setContentType("text/html");
    PrintWriter pw = res.getWriter();
    String name = req.getParameter("name");
    String email = req.getParameter("email");

    String registerC = req.getParameter("NewUser");
```

```
   String loginC = req.getParameter("Login");

   if (registerC != null)
   { RegisterUserPage rup = new RegisterUserPage();
     rup.setName(name);
     rup.setEmail(email);
     pw.println(rup);
   }
   else // login
   { // check it is a valid user:
     boolean valid = dbi.checkUser(name,email);
     if (valid)  // show command page, create session
     { CommandPage cp = new CommandPage();
       pw.println(cp);
       HttpSession session = req.getSession(true);
       session.setAttribute("name",name);
       session.setAttribute("email",email);
     }
     else
     { LoginPage lp = new LoginPage();
       pw.println(lp);
     }
   }
   pw.close();
}

public void doPost(HttpServletRequest req,
                   HttpServletResponse res)
throws ServletException, IOException
{ doGet(req,res); }

public void destroy()
{ dbi.logoff(); }
}
```

By using helper classes such as *LoginPage*, it should be possible to avoid writing any HTML code in a servlet at all, thus improving the separation of the GUI and business logic of a system.

An *HttpSession* object records information about a particular client and a particular interaction session of that client with the system. In the above code, we record someone's name from the opening login prompt of a website:

```
HttpSession session = req.getSession(true);
session.setAttribute("name",name);
```

The parameter *true* in *getSession* indicates that a session object should be created for the client if one does not already exist for this client. If a session already exists, it is returned, otherwise a new session is created and returned.

The session can be referred to in another method, and its values extracted:

```
HttpSession session = req.getSession(false);
if (session != null)
{ String username = (String) session.getAttribute("name");
  ...
}
```

If this code is called within the same browsing session, for example, by the client submitting data from another form, then the session object will exist and the name value stored by the initial request will be returned. This can be used to check authorisation for taking an action or giving information.

There is effectively a qualified association *value* from *HttpSession* to *Object*, qualified by *parameter* : *String*, the name of the item being stored (Figure 7.19).

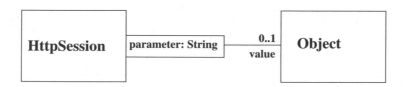

Figure 7.19: HttpSession data

In this system, a user is logged in if there exists an *HttpSession* with their name and email:

$$loggedIn \;=\; User \;|\;$$
$$(HttpSession \;|\; (userName : value["name"] \; \& $$
$$userEmail : value["email"]) \; / = \{\})$$

7.2.10 Server-side design: using JSPs to generate web pages

Instead of web page generation classes such as *HtmlPage*, JSP files can be used as templates of the required web pages, with additional embedded Java statements to provide dynamic page functionality (eg, if page content has to vary depending on database data).

Database update code is separated out into 'entity beans' invoked from JSPs, representing the data (eg, instances of entities) being processed. Figure 7.20 shows the architecture for this version.

In such architecture diagrams a solid arrow from component A to component B indicates that A invokes some functionality of B, possibly via the internet (if A is a web page component). A dashed line from A to (a web page) B indicates that A generates B or that there is an HTML link from A to B. Following the dashed and solid lines between web pages should give the same interaction sequence as the statechart of the system.

JSPs that modify the database use a bean to convert and check the data, and then to invoke the database interface:

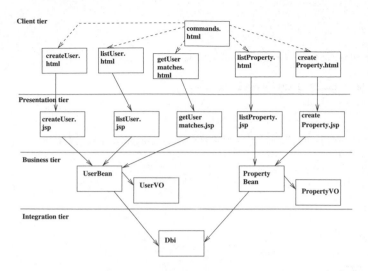

Figure 7.20: JSP architecture of property search system

```
<jsp:useBean id="user" scope="session"
 class="beans.UserBean"/>
<jsp:setProperty name="user"
  property="name" param="name"/>
<jsp:setProperty name="user"
  property="email" param="email"/>
... and store the other fields in user ...

<html>
<body>
<% if (user.isError())
{ %> <h2>Error in data: press Back to re-enter</h2> <% }
else { user.createUser(); %>
<h2>User added to database</h2>
<% } %>

<hr>

<a href="commands.html">Command options</a>
</body>
</html>
```

The *useBean* statement links the page to the object *user* of the class *UserBean* (this object is created if it does not already exist). *user* is valid for the remainder of the current browsing session. The *setProperty* statements copy request parameters to the corresponding fields of *user*.

Java statements are written within < % and % > brackets. Here, the methods *isError*() and *createUser*() are invoked on *user* to check if the submitted data was correct, and store it in the database if correct.

commands.html lists links to the create user, list users, etc, web pages:

```
<html>
<body>
<p><a href="createUser.html">Create User</a></p>

<p><a href="listUser.html">List Users</a></p>
</body>
</html>
```

Or these links could be given directly in the response page of *createUser.jsp*.
   UserBean could be:

```
package beans;

import java.sql.*;

public class UserBean
{ private String name;
  private String email;
  // ... other fields ...

  public UserBean() {}

  public void setName(String nm)
  { name = nm; }

  public void setEmail(String eml)
  { email = eml; }


  ...

  public String getName()
  { return name; }

  public String getEmail()
  { return email; }

  public boolean isError()
  { // checks if name, email, prices are sensible data
    return (name == null || name.length() == 0);
  }

  public void createUser()
  { // get database connection,
    // call createUser on it with
    // current name, email, etc data
  }
}
```

   listUsers.jsp could have the form:

```
<%@ page import = "java.util.*" %>
<%@ page import = "beans.*" %>
```

```
<jsp:useBean id="user"
 scope="session" class="beans.UserBean"/>
<html>
<head><title>List of all users</title></head>
<body>
<h1>List of all users</h1>

<% Iterator users = user.getUsers(); %>
<table border="1">
<tr><th>Name</th> <th>Email</th> .... </tr>
<% while (users.hasNext())
   { User ur = (User) users.next(); %>
   <tr><td> <%= ur.getName() %> </td>
       <td> <%= ur.getEmail() %> </td>
       ...
   </tr>
<% } %>
</table>

<hr>

<a href="commands.html">Command options</a>
</body>
</html>
```

Where *getUsers* is a method of the user bean class which uses the SQL statement SELECT * FROM User to extract all rows from the user table, and converts these rows into objects.

The JSPs are purely concerned with view construction, the beans with other processing.

7.2.11 Server-side design: defining SQL statements

Whatever database is chosen for the persistent data store of a system, it will usually support the use of SQL for reading and writing data. SQL provides a simple programming language using statements such as *UPDATE*, *SELECT*, etc, to modify and access database data.

Consider the case where there are two persistent entities A and B, linked by an association which is either implicit (not stored, but computed on demand) or explicitly represented via a foreign key from B to A in the database (Figure 7.21).

Then Table 7.4 shows the SQL implementations of standard object and association operations on this class diagram.

Each stereotype of an operation also leads to a characteristic form of SQL statement, which is used in the database interface for the system to carry out the data repository actions of that operation, and will be invoked by the

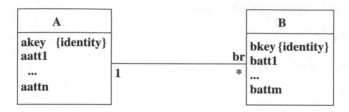

Figure 7.21: Persistent entities A and B

Class Diagram Operation	SQL
$ax.setatt(val)$	UPDATE A SET att = val WHERE A.akey = ax.getakey()
$ax.addbr(bx)$ (br explicit)	UPDATE B SET B.akey = ax.getakey() WHERE bkey = bx.getbkey()
$ax.removebr(bx)$ (br explicit)	DELETE FROM B WHERE bkey = bx.getbkey() AND B.akey = ax.getakey()
$ax.getatt()$	SELECT att FROM A WHERE A.akey = ax.getakey()
$ax.getbr()$	SELECT * FROM B WHERE B.akey = ax.getakey() (br implemented as foreign key) SELECT $bkey, batt_1, \ldots, batt_m$ FROM A, B WHERE P AND A.akey = ax.getakey() (br an implicit association defined by P)
$createA(id, val1, \ldots, valn)$	INSERT INTO A VALUES $(id, val1, \ldots, valn)$
$deleteA(ax)$	DELETE FROM A WHERE A.akey = ax.getakey()

Table 7.4: SQL implementation of class diagram operations

servlet handling the operation in response to an HTTP request from the web page whose submit action is associated to the operation.

For example, in the property system, we have the SQL operations given in Table 7.5. The matches association is a virtual (implicit) association, so the

Entity Operation	SQL
editUser(nme, eml, minp, maxp, typ, bed, ar)	UPDATE User SET userMaxprice = maxp, userMinprice = minp, userType = typ, userBedrooms = bed, userArea = ar WHERE userName = nme AND userEmail = eml
deleteUser(nme, eml)	DELETE FROM User WHERE userName = nme AND userEmail = eml
checkUser(nme, eml)	SELECT * FROM User WHERE userName = nme AND userEmail = eml If result set non-empty, check is true
getUserMatches(nme, eml)	SELECT propertyId, propertyPrice, propertyType, propertyArea, propertyAvailable, propertyBedrooms FROM User, Property WHERE userName = nme AND userEmail = eml AND userMinprice ≤ propertyPrice AND userMaxprice ≥ propertyPrice AND userArea = propertyArea AND userType = propertyType AND propertyAvailable = 'true' AND userBedrooms ≤ propertyBedrooms
createUser(nme, eml, minp, maxp, typ, bed, ar)	INSERT INTO User VALUES (nme, eml, minp, maxp, typ, bed, ar)

Table 7.5: SQL implementation of property system operations

properties matching a given user's requirements are computed using a search over the set of users and properties. The predicate of the SQL statement is essentially the constraint $C2$ defining the association in Figure 7.4.

7.2.12 Completing the case study

Figure 7.22 shows the final architecture of the property search system, comprising web page, servlet, web page construction and database interface components.

Alternative structures are also possible, for example, using a single servlet in the *action* clause of each web page, where this servlet subsequently forwards or directs the requests to appropriate Java objects that deal with the particular operation involved. This is the *Front Controller* pattern of [12].

Given a particular internet server, the components of the case study have to be placed in particular directories in the server machine, and suitable deployment files written to tell the server where to look for (in this case) servlets

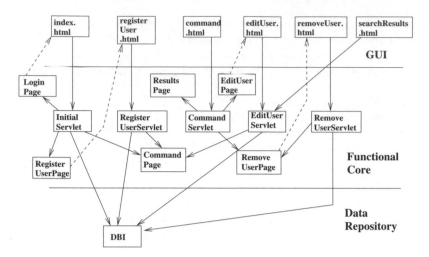

Figure 7.22: Complete servlet architecture of property search system

to respond to requests directed at them.

- For the *resin* server: place the *java* files of the servlet in the *resin-ver/doc/WEB-INF/classes* directory.
- For the *tomcat* server: in the *jakarta-tomcat-ver/conf* directory, edit the *server.xml* file and create a $<$ *Context ...* $>$ element under the *admin* context element:

```
<Context path = "/propsearch" docBase = "webapps/propsearch"
  reloadable = "true"> </Context>
```

A deployment descriptor *web.xml* must also be created for the application, and placed in a *WEB-INF* subdirectory of *propsearch*, which is a subdirectory of *jakarta-tomcat-ver/webapps*. The compiled class files of servlets are also placed in *WEB-INF*, in a subdirectory *classes*. The *.java* files are however placed in *propsearch/servlets*. *web.xml* lists all the servlets of the system:

```
<web-app>

    <display-name>Property search</display-name>
    <description>
      Property search system
    </description>

    <servlet>
        <servlet-name>RegisterUserServlet</servlet-name>
        <servlet-class>RegisterUserServlet</servlet-class>
    </servlet>
```

```
      <servlet>
          <servlet-name>EditUserServlet</servlet-name>
          <servlet-class>EditUserServlet</servlet-class>
      </servlet>
      ...

      <servlet-mapping>
          <servlet-name>RegisterUserServlet</servlet-name>
          <url-pattern>/RegisterUserServlet</url-pattern>
      </servlet-mapping>

      <servlet-mapping>
          <servlet-name>EditUserServlet</servlet-name>
          <url-pattern>/EditUserServlet</url-pattern>
      </servlet-mapping>
      ...


   </web-app>
```

7.3 Design process for internet systems

The complete design process for internet systems, using all the techniques described in the previous sections, consists of the following steps:

1. Define PIM abstract data model of entities involved.
2. Define PIM use cases describing the operations required from the system.
3. Transform data model into PSM appropriate for data storage approach to be adopted.
4. Define entities representing web pages, based on what operations are to be provided (step 2): an input page should only require users to enter the minimal information necessary to support the operation it is involved in. Define page invariants and any client-side scripts to check/enforce these.
5. Define the user interaction sequence of pages, using statecharts.
6. Define the visual design and information content of pages, this should usually be consistent in style across an application.
7. A complete prototype of the client side of the system can be produced at this point and reviewed, this should include checks that accessibility and portability requirements have been met, and evaluation involving usability trials with typical users.
8. Define which pages are to be hard-coded in XHTML, and which are to be generated.
9. For generated pages, define an inheritance hierarchy of the classes representing the pages, so that pages with common subparts can be expressed as subclasses of a class with these subparts as its features. Each generated page should have a class which can be used as a template by the server side of the system for constructing instances of the page, eg, by using *new XPage()*; in Java.

10. Define server-side response pseudocode (or full code) for each operation: extraction of parameters from request; checking constraints on parameters; processing of operation, usually involving database interaction; and construction of the result/next web page.
11. Define SQL queries/updates, for virtual associations these can be based on the constraints defining the association, as for *matches* in the property search example.
12. Define database interface(s) to support operations required from the server-side functional core components.

Step 9 could alternatively use JSPs instead of Java classes to generate the web pages.

Figure 7.23 shows the process steps, dashed arrows indicate manual processes, solid lines automated or semi-automated processes.

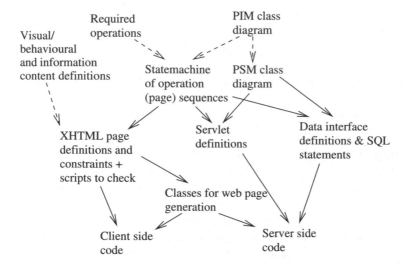

Figure 7.23: Internet system development process

Many of these steps can be performed in parallel or in alternative orders to that listed here. In particular, once the system operations have been specified, client- and server-side design can proceed mostly independently.

Tools to support development of internet systems from PIMs include *WebObjects* (http://www.apple.com/webobjects/), and our own *UML2Web*, included on the supporting website for this book.

7.4 Summary

We have described one set of techniques for systematically constructing an online version of a system, from a PIM, and a process model for applying these techniques. Other approaches, such as the use of JSPs to separate HTML from server-side code, could also be used instead of or together with this approach. Guidelines for improving the usability and portability of web interfaces have also been given.

7.5 Exercises

1 (Project) Draw the use case diagram for the administrator/staff operations of adding, removing and editing property details in the property search system. Define the web pages, user interaction statechart, the servlets, web-page construction classes, and SQL queries for these operations.

2 What are the problems of the following web page (for a petstore website) with regard to accessibility?

```
<html>
<head><title>Furry Friends Pet Store</title></head>
<body>
<strong>All our pets in stock</strong><br>

<img src="fido.jpg"><p>

<table>
<tr><td>Name</td><td>Breed</td><td>Age</td><td>Price</td></tr>
<tr><td>Fido</td><td>daschund</td><td>4 months</td><td>$30</td></tr>
<tr><td>Loca</td><td>siamese</td><td>6 months</td><td>$50</td></tr>
<tr><td>Manuel</td><td>rat</td><td>3 months</td><td>$20</td></tr>
<tr><td>Felix</td><td>collie</td><td>1 year</td><td>$35</td></tr>
</table>
</body>
</html>
```

Write an improved version of the page which corrects these problems.

3 Design a page construction class for a magazine distribution company web page that consists of three text fields, for surname, first name and phone number, followed by a text area for their address, then six independent checkboxes labelled with the name of a different magazine (eg: *Airgun World, Viz, Granta, Reader's Digest, Time*, etc ...) that the customer wants to subscribe to, followed by textboxes for their email address and fax number.

4 Design a suitable user interaction statechart diagram for the following system:

- The system is an on-line dating agency. Users can register their details, on payment of a fee of ten dollars by credit card, which keeps their details on the system for a year, or until they explicitly remove them.
- Existing members can log in with a username and password.

- The operations that a registered user can do are: search for matching members; remove themselves from the database; go to an internal messaging tool to send/receive mail from other members.

5 Write a web page that calculates and displays the factorial of an integer typed in by the user.

6 Write a JavaScript function to check that a string is a valid postcode: ie, that its first character is a letter, and the second is a letter or digit.

7 Design the user interaction statechart and system architecture for a student accommodation system. This allows students of a college to book accommodation for the coming year, specifying preferences for particular halls and accommodation features. The system also sends emails to students once they have been allocated a room and allows a student to check on-line what their allocation is. The data input involves a large number of fields, so should be split into three forms: one for personal details (name, address, student number, etc), one for course details (course title, year, etc) and one for preferences (three top preferences for accommodation, smoking/non-smoking, etc).

8 Write a JavaScript function to check that a form data item is in the correct format of a British National Insurance number: two letters, followed by six numbers and then a letter. Write the server side checks for the same test.

9 What are the advantages and disadvantages of using a single 16-character length text field for the entry of credit card numbers, versus the use of four separate 4-character fields for the number groups of the credit card number?

10 Design image maps based on images of South-East England with three areas: (i) London; (ii) Kent region; (iii) Surrey/Sussex/Hampshire region, to allow a customer of the property search system to specify their desired area interactively.

11 Identify suitable constraints for an on-line hotel room booking system, which uses the data model of Figure 7.24.

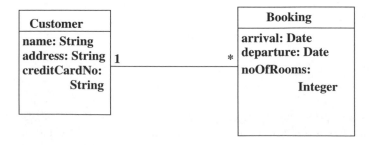

Figure 7.24: Hotel booking system

12 An on-line property agency is to be developed, from the analysis model of Figure 7.25, which shows entities of *Property*, *House* and *Flat*. Define a design

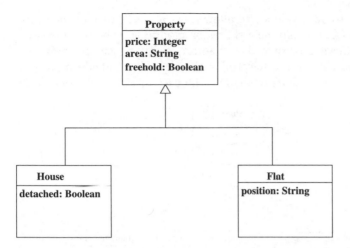

Figure 7.25: Estate Agency Analysis Model

data model of the system, suitable for implementation in a relational database.

Give form descriptions (as classes) for forms to create a new property, list all properties, and remove a property.

Give a user interaction statechart of this system, assuming that no login is needed for access.

13 A web system is to be developed to allow a library to keep track of the books that have been borrowed. Figure 7.26 shows the analysis class diagram of this system. Draw a design class diagram for this system, including forms

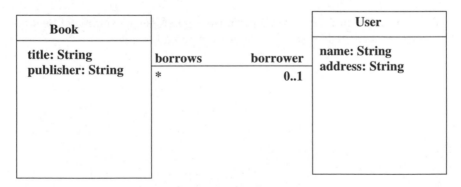

Figure 7.26: Library Analysis Model

for creating a book and listing all borrowers of a given book.

Draw a design architecture for this system, showing all components (web pages, servlets, page generation classes and database interface) and dependencies between them.

14   A web system is to be developed to allow users to keep track of the shares they have purchased, and to buy new shares or modify the details of existing shares. Figure 7.27 shows the design class diagram of this system, including the forms for creating new share data, selecting a share to edit, and editing it, plus the login form. Draw a statechart describing the user interactions possible for

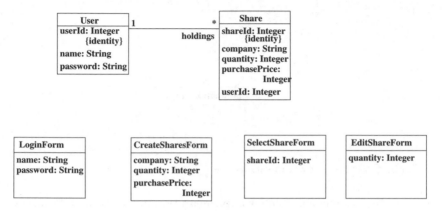

Figure 7.27: Share System Design Model

this system, where a user must login before accessing a commands page, with commands *NewShares* and *EditShares*, and the commands page is redisplayed to the user once an edit or creation operation is complete.

Draw a Servlet-based design architecture for this system, showing all components (web pages, servlets, page generation classes and database interface) and dependencies between them.

15   What usability problem is there with the *areaMessage* example of Section 7.2.3? Write a corrected version of this web page and script.

Chapter 8

Web Services

Web services are a further step on the path to using the internet to carry out distributed processing. In contrast to the simple internet systems described in the previous chapter, web services need not be browser based, and the distributed components of a web service may initiate interaction with each other autonomously of human clients (for example, a share management system which automatically starts selling shares for a customer when the price of the share passes a pre-set limit). Web services support integration of applications at different network locations, enabling these applications to function as if they were part of a single large software system.

In this chapter we will give definitions and examples of web services, and describe how they can be implemented using frameworks such as J2EE.

8.1 Definitions of web services

The ICT companies working on the promotion and implementation of web services provide different definitions of what a web service is:

IBM: Web services are self-contained, modular applications that can be described, published, located and invoked over a network, generally the web, to create innovative products, processes and value chains. Web services can be local, distributed or web-based. They interact with and/or invoke each other, fulfilling specific tasks and requests that, in turn, carry out specific parts of complex transactions or workflows.

A web service has its public interfaces and bindings defined and described using WSDL; can be discovered by other components (at build time or run time), and can communicate using XML messages across industry-standard protocols (HTTP, JMS, HTTPS, etc) [19].

Microsoft: A web service is a unit of application logic providing data and services to other applications. Web services combine the best aspects of component-based development and the web [33].

Sun: 'Services on Demand' denotes how enterprises use ICT to transact and report business operations and to communicate with others anywhere, anytime, on any device. This concept is the foundation for a modular, flexible and automated access to digital assets, including computing resources, from virtually anywhere. A 'smart web service' is a web service that can understand situational context and share that context with other services. It produces dynamic results based on who, what, when, where and why it was called [48].

Hewlett-Packard: E-services are assets – information, business processes, computing resources, and applications – made available via the internet. In the emerging technology landscape, any object, device, infrastructure, or 'thing' with an embedded chip can be tracked electronically, called on to perform a task, or serve as a link to services.

Some examples of web services in common use are:

- Payment services such as *PayPal* [38], which enable applications to handle online credit card payments, with PayPal providing the card verification and cash transfer processes.
- Merchant support services, allowing organisations to directly update product information on a third-party retailing website, such as Amazon.
- Search services, such as that provided by http://www.technorati.com to search weblogs and links.

To be useful, the web services provided by a site are usually listed in some publically-accessible directory, so that potential clients of the service can identify if a service that meets their requirements is available (Figure 8.1).

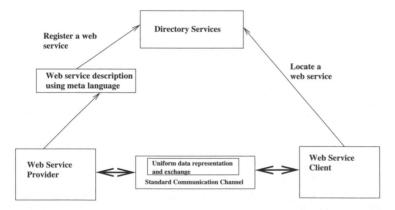

Figure 8.1: Web service architecture

In the following sections we will examine examples of web services and how they can be implemented, in the two leading environments for web systems, J2EE from Sun Microsystems, and .Net from Microsoft.

8.2   J2EE

The Java 2 Platform, Enterprise Edition (J2EE) is a collection of Java technologies, such as Servlets and JSP, which provides a framework for developing
distributed enterprise systems. It includes:

- Servlets and JSP.
- Enterprise Java Beans (EJB) – representing distributed business com-
  ponents, possibly with persistent data.
- JDBC.
- Java Message Service (JMS) – an API to communicate with message-
  oriented middleware (MOM) to provide messaging services between sys-
  tems.
- Java Naming and Directory Interface (JNDI) – an interface to support
  naming and directory services, such as the Java RMI registry for locating
  remote methods.
- JavaMail – an API for platform-independent mailing and messaging in
  Java.

Figure 8.2 shows the typical structure of a J2EE system.

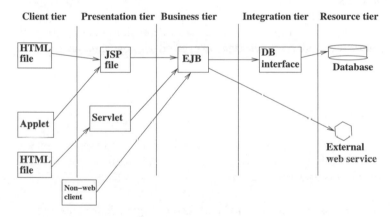

Figure 8.2: Typical J2EE system structure

This five tier architecture is used by [12] to describe J2EE systems:

Client tier: This has the responsibility to display information to the user and
receive information from the user and transmit this to the presentation
tier. It may be either a *thin client* with minimal processing apart from its
visual interface functionality, or a *fat client* doing more substantial computation. The overall trend is towards thin clients, typically using web
browsers to achieve maximum portability: any machine with a browser
and an internet connection can provide an interface to the application.
Such clients are called *web clients*.

Typical components of this tier are HTML pages or applets.

Presentation tier: This has the responsibility of managing the presentation of information to the client: which pages to send to the client, for example, an error report page versus a confirmation page for a new user registering with a system, and what sequence of interaction to follow. It also relays user requests to the business tier.

Typical components of this tier are servlets and JSPs.

Business tier: This tier contains the business rules of the application. For example, rules concerning what customers can be accepted for an online bank system, what their credit limit will be, etc.

Typical components in this layer are EJBs.

Integration tier: This tier mediates between the business tier and the resource tier. It manages the detail of data retrieval, using interfaces such as JDBC. It insulates the business tier and higher tiers from direct knowledge of how the data is stored and retrieved. An example could be a method to add a new customer details into a database table, using a JDBC connection to a database, and SQL statements.

Resource tier: This includes persistent data storage and external resources such as credit card authorisation services or business-to-business services. It usually involves an external commercial piece of software such as a relational database.

In the J2EE architecture description [21] the presentation tier is called the *web tier*, and the integration and resource tiers are bundled together as the *EIS tier*.

8.2.1 Enterprise Java Beans

EJBs are the core mechanism for carrying out the business logic on the server side of a J2EE-based system. Two forms of EJB that feature in most J2EE systems are *session beans* and *entity beans*:

Session bean A business component: dedicated to a single client or user; that lives only for the duration of the client's session; that is not persistent; that can be used to model statefull or stateless interactions between the client and the business tier components.

Entity bean A course-grained business component which: provides an object view of persistent data; is multiuser and long-lived.

Session beans can either store some (client-specific) state: *statefull* session beans, or be stateless: *stateless* session beans. Statefull session beans are a more general version of the HttpSession objects we used in the previous chapter, and can be used in the same way to record client information through a session, to control access to resources, etc. But their general role is much wider and can encompass any client session-specific business process that needs more than a single method call to perform. A shopping cart is a typical example.

On the other hand, stateless session beans provide a service by a single method call. These include utility functions or logging services, or invocation of remote web services. Sending an email confirming that a client request has been received could be an example of a task carried out by this type of component. Stateless session beans can be pooled by the server, since as soon as one client has finished using the bean, it can be used by another client. Statefull session beans cannot be reused in this way.

Some uses of entity beans include:

- Encapsulating checks and business rules on data which require access to persistent data or external services, such as credit checks on a new customer application to a bank.
- Providing an object-oriented interface to one or more relational database tables.
- As components in business tier patterns, such as observer (Section 8.8).

Every method call made to an EJB is potentially *remote* and may therefore involve some network processing overhead. This is a consequence of the desire to have a uniform method of using both local and remote resources, and has the advantage that if the location of the resource wrapped by the EJB changes, then users of the EJB do not need to modify their code. The cost of this flexibility is a possible loss of efficiency, which can be moderated by avoiding multiple unnecessary method calls on an EJB and transferring data in groups where possible (cf, the *Value Object* pattern of [12]). For similar reasons, entity beans should not be created for each persistent class in a PSM, but instead for groups of closely related classes, ie, classes where a data access/update to one is likely to also involve access/update to another in the group.

A common situation is where one entity in a group is the 'master' entity of the others, which are termed 'subordinate' or 'auxiliary' entities: they represent parts of the data and behaviour modelled by the master entity, and can only be accessed via it. An example would be an *OrderItem* as a subordinate entity of an *Order* in a restaurant management system. The master entity and its subordinate entities can be managed by the same EJB, with the interface of the EJB based on that of the master entity.

The persistence of entity bean data can either be achieved by the programmer of the bean explicitly providing suitable logic, such as saving data to a database using JDBC, or by the J2EE environment itself. The first option is termed *bean-managed persistence* (BMP), the second is termed *container-managed persistence* (CMP). CMP provides potentially greater portability, avoiding the use of platform-specific code within the bean classes.

Associated with any enterprise bean are several interfaces (Figure 8.3):

- A *remote interface*, which lists the business operations specific to the bean. For example, in the property search system, an operation to determine the matching properties for a user would be listed in the remote interface of the *User* EJB.

- A *home interface*, which lists lifecycle operations (creation, deletion) and methods (such as *findByPrimaryKey*) to return particular bean objects.
- A *local interface*, listing business operations that can be accessed by local clients, ie, those executing in the same JVM as the EJB.
- A *local home interface*, listing life-cycle and finder methods for local clients.

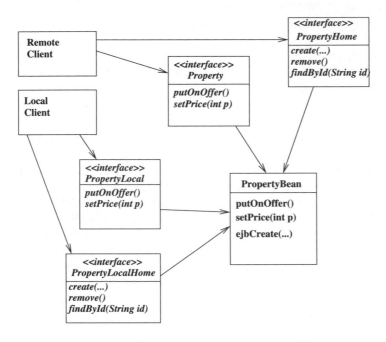

Figure 8.3: Bean interfaces

If two different EJBs are related by an (explicit) association in the class diagram of the system, then the bean that is the destination of navigation along this association must have a local interface (since the persistent data accessed by the two beans resides on the same machine). Remote interfaces however give greater flexibility and extensibility.

8.2.2   Example: property system

The property system can be implemented in the J2EE framework by creating entity beans for *Property* and *User*, which mediate between the presentation tier servlets and helper classes, and the integration tier DBI (Figure 8.4). *Property* is responsible for maintaining all the data constraints of this entity, in particular, the server-side checks for *createProperty* and *editProperty* operations are carried out in this class, and not in *CreatePropertyServlet* or *EditPropertyServlet*. Similarly for *User*. The *...Page* generation classes are used as in the previous version of the system, in Figure 7.22.

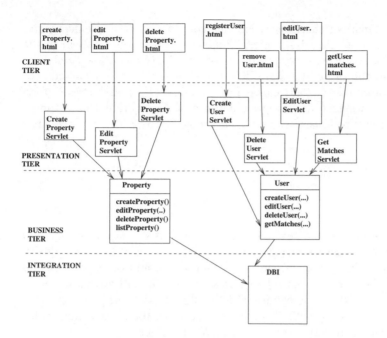

Figure 8.4: Property system enhanced for J2EE architecture

8.2.3 Development process for J2EE applications

The steps given in the previous chapter for development of general internet systems can be extended for the J2EE framework, on the server side:

- *Business Tier*: Group classes into modules which are suitable for implementation as EJBs, where there are strong connections between the classes within the module (eg, several invariants relating them) and weaker connections between classes in different modules. Each module is responsible for maintaining the constraints which involve its contained entities. The module normally has a 'master' or interface class, through which all updates to data of the module pass. Individual classes in the module enforce their own local invariants, and may invoke operations of the database interface.
- *Presentation Tier*: The servlet and web-page generation classes are defined as before, however the servlets now only check the correct typing of parameters received from web pages, and pass on the request data to the business tier for checking of other constraints.
- The database interface in the integration tier has the same form as before, although now it is invoked from the EJBs in the business logic tier, rather than directly from servlets.

Ideally, no database interface code should appear in the business tier (ie, no SQL statements, JDBC calls or references to *ResultSet*, in the case of a JDBC implementation), instead the integration tier should deliver implementation-neutral sets of objects. Likewise, no HTTP-specific code should appear in the business tier. This structure accords more closely to the Model-View-Controller architecture than the original system did: the servlets act as controllers, co-ordinating the views (the ...*Page* classes) and models (*User* and *Property*) to ensure that the views accurately represent the models, eg, that the instances displayed in response to a *listUser* request are exactly the *User* instances that currently exist.

8.2.4 Summary

J2EE provides a sophisticated environment for distributed and internet system construction, and for the definition of web services. However its complexity can lead to poor design practices, and a substantial amount of experience and familiarity with the environment seems necessary to take full advantage of its features. Solutions to this problem are to define design patterns [12] to provide reusable design structures for J2EE applications, or to encode expert knowledge of J2EE into a code generation tool for J2EE applications.

8.3   .Net

.Net is a framework for multi-language programming, and in particular, for web system and web service programming. Typical languages used in .Net are Visual Basic, C# and ASP. It can be considered as a successor to the Microsoft Windows API, providing services which programmers can access from a wide range of different programming languages. This is an important contrast to J2EE, which is oriented to a 'use Java for everything' approach.

.Net acts as a layer between applications and the operating system (Figure 8.5). It provides a set of class libraries, the .Net Framework classes, analogous to Java or C++ foundation class libraries, and the ADO.Net database access API. It provides specific support for web service construction, using the SOAP message exchange mechanism via HTTP.

8.3.1 Summary

.Net has the advantage of supporting multiple languages on an equal basis, and it should have a performance advantage over J2EE for Windows deployment, since it is optimised for the Windows OS. The main disadvantage is that it is specific to one family of operating systems, and is a product available only from a single vendor.

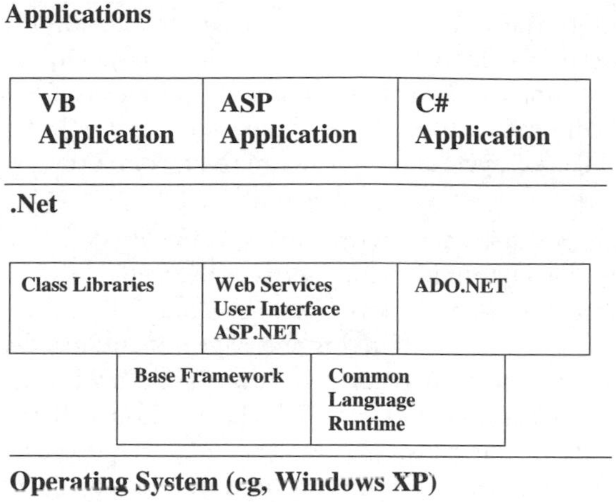

Applications

VB Application	ASP Application	C# Application

.Net

Class Libraries	Web Services User Interface ASP.NET	ADO.NET
	Base Framework	Common Language Runtime

Operating System (cg, Windows XP)

Figure 8.5: .Net architecture

8.4 Communicating with web services

There are several ways in which one application can make its data and services available to other applications over the internet:

Raw HTML The most basic way that a client program can extract data from a server website is by downloading its pages and then parsing them, using a parser such as the *HTMLEditorKit* class in the *java.swing.text.html* package in Java 2. This approach has the advantage that it does not depend on any communication software being available at the server end, beyond support of HTTP. However, analysis of the results depends very much on the format of the web pages, which obviously can be changed at any time, beyond the control of the client, possibly requiring continual changes from the client program.

CSV A server may make its data available as *comma-separated value* files, which are a text format for database tables. An example, of house data, could be:

```
Type, Price, Bedrooms, Area
Flat, 208000, 2, SW11
Detached house, 415000, 7, CR4
Terraced house, 450000, 3, SW19
Flat, 550000, 4, SE1
```

The yahoo.co.uk finance site adopts this approach, providing CSV files of the FTSE 100 and other table data for download by clients.

FTP The *file transfer protocol* provides a means to access files stored on a remote computer connected to the internet. It is used to download files from servers to a client, but can also be used to upload and modify files.

To respond to FTP requests the remote computer needs to be running an FTP server, such as Cerberus (http://www.cerberusftp.com). On the client side, the Java package *org.apache.commons.net.ftp* provides a Java API for creating an FTP connection to a specified host and sending FTP requests to it. Eg, in the jukebox system, playlists are read from a remote server and new playlists are uploaded to it using FTP.

SOAP A more sophisticated approach is to use a protocol specifically designed for application-to-application communication across the web, such as SOAP (Simple Object Access Protocol) http://www.w3.org/TR/SOAP, which is an XML-based protocol for exchanging messages, including descriptions of remote procedure calls. A SOAP message is an XML document, consisting of an *envelope*, which describes the method call the message concerns. The body of the message can either be a request or a response: a request specifies the method to be executed by the receiver of the message, and any parameters needed. SOAP defines XML encodings for most data types that may be used for parameter data. A response message contains results or other information sent back from the remotely executed method to its initiator. HTTP POST is typically used to transmit SOAP messages. J2EE provides support for SOAP messaging in the JAX-RPC package.

WSDL The Web Services Definition Language is also XML-based (http://www.w3.org/TR/wsdl). It supports the description of network services operating on messages with document or procedural content. The operations and messages are described abstractly, then bound to a concrete network protocol and message format to define an endpoint. WSDL files are XML files with tags <wsdl:portType> to describe an interface offered by a web service, as a list of <wsdl:operation>s, <wsdl:binding> to describe the way the service is invoked under different protocols (eg, HTTP versus JMS), and <wsdl:port> to identify a physical location of the service.

The concept of *discovery* is likely to become more important as part of web service communication in the future. Discovery means:

- Dynamically (at runtime) locating a service required by a program, via some remote registry of services
- dynamically identifying the number and type of arguments needed by that service.

At present, discovery is not widely used, although some standards and mechanisms for discovery services have been produced. In particular, UDDI (Universal Description, Discovery and Integration protocol) acts as a registry of web services, and provides the WSDL needed to invoke these services.

8.5 Examples of web services

We describe three case studies of web services: a system for calculating bid prices on the electronic auction site eBay, a system for analysing financial data extracted from a website, and the internet jukebox introduced in Chapter 1.

8.5.1 EBay auction analysis

EBay is one of a number of websites which provide electronic auction services. Customers can place items for auction and make bids for items. The main auction type on eBay is the 'English' auction, with one seller and multiple buyers, each buyer can put in multiple bids and the buyer who has bid the highest amount over the time the auction is open wins. Because eBay auctions may last for several days, a range of software exists to support bidders in checking on the progress of an auction (*auction watcher* programs) and in making last-minute bids just before the auction closes (*auction snipers*).

Another useful function that could be considered is a system which evaluates previous auctions for a particular item, in order to give advice on a reasonable bid price for future auctions of the same merchandise. Such a system would need to:

- Extract information such as the final purchase price from previous auctions on eBay for a specific type of item.
- Calculate functions of the auction data, such as the average purchase price, an average weighted in favour of busier auctions (more bids) and a linear regression estimate of the price in a new auction.

Figure 8.6 shows the use cases, and Figure 8.7 the class diagram of this system.

Figure 8.6: Auction monitor use cases

Figure 8.8 shows a possible design structure of this system.

The *eBay data lookup* module is responsible for the 'get bid data' use case. It is passed a list of search strings as input, and assembles a URL from these and the eBay address http://www.ebay.co.uk. This query is then sent to eBay, and the response page is then received as raw HTML text. The *eBay data lookup* module passes this to the *HTML filter* module by invoking a *filter* function with

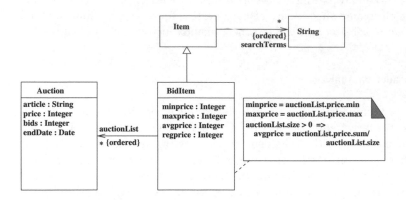

Figure 8.7: Auction monitor class diagram

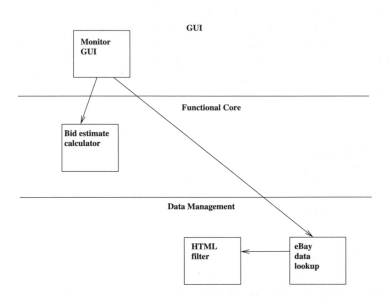

Figure 8.8: Auction monitor system structure

this string as its argument. The *HTML filter* module extracts the particular table data items that are needed from this text: the name of the item being auctioned, the final price, the number of bidders, and the closing date. It returns a list of *Auction* objects. The user can then invoke functions of the *Bid estimate calculator* module with this data to calculate the price data.

Figure 8.9 shows the interface of this system.

Figure 8.9: Auction monitor GUI

8.5.2 Financial analysis system

This system makes use of the yahoo.uk financial website, downloading data for the FTSE 100 from this site and performing simple analyses on this data. The FTSE 100 data on yahoo.uk is free, however it is twenty minutes out of date. Extraction of this data consists of two steps:

1. Downloading the CSV data for the FTSE 100 from the yahoo.uk website and storing it as a local file.
2. Reading this file and converting its data into Java data structures: essentially a list of lists, where each row of the CSV table is converted to a Java list of strings, and the table itself is a Java list of these lists.

The *DownloadURL* program opens a connection to the designated URL (in this case the address of the CSV download location for the FTSE 100), and

uses a file stream to transfer the data of this location to a target file, in this
case *out.csv*:

```java
import java.net.URL;
import java.net.MalformedURLException;
import java.io.*;

public class DownloadURL
{ public static void main(String args[])
  {  download("http://uk.finance.yahoo.com/" +
       "d/quotes.csv?" +
       "s=^FTSE+@UKX.L&f=sl1d1t1c1ohgv&e=.csv",
           "out.csv");
  }

  public static void download(String urlName,String outFile)
  { URL theURL = null;
    try { theURL = new URL(urlName); }
    catch(MalformedURLException e)
    { System.out.println(e.toString());
      System.exit(1);
    }

    try
    { byte buf[] = new byte[1000];
      InputStream is = theURL.openStream();
      FileOutputStream fout =
        new FileOutputStream(outFile);
      int count = 0;
      while (true)
      { int ch = is.read(buf,0,1000);
        if (ch == -1) break;    // end of input
        fout.write(buf,0,ch);
        count += ch;
        System.out.print(".");
        System.out.flush();
      }
      fout.close();
      is.close();
    }
    catch(IOException e)
    { e.printStackTrace();
      System.exit(1);
    }
  }
}
```

The output file is a database table of values in CSV format. For example:

```
"^FTSE",4376.60,"7/7/2004","8:18",+5.90,4370.70,4381.90,4370.70,54819004
"AAL.L",1090.00,"7/7/2004","7:20",0.00,N/A,N/A,N/A,0
```

```
"ABF.L",612.50,"7/6/2004","16:52",0.00,N/A,N/A,N/A,0
"AHM.L",825.00,"4/7/2004","17:14",0.00,N/A,N/A,N/A,43179376
"AL.L",813.50,"7/7/2004","7:18",0.00,N/A,N/A,N/A,0
"ALLD.L",456.25,"7/6/2004","16:57",0.00,N/A,N/A,N/A,0
"ANL.L",485.50,"7/7/2004","7:20",0.00,N/A,N/A,N/A,0
"AUN.L",654.50,"7/7/2004","7:21",0.00,N/A,N/A,N/A,0
"AV.L",555.00,"7/7/2004","7:23",0.00,N/A,N/A,N/A,0
"AVZ.L",349.75,"7/7/2004","7:22",0.00,N/A,N/A,N/A,0
"AZN.L",2434.00,"7/7/2004","7:21",0.00,N/A,N/A,N/A,0
"BA.L",212.50,"7/7/2004","7:22",0.00,N/A,N/A,N/A,0
"BAA.L",556.00,"7/7/2004","7:23",0.00,N/A,N/A,N/A,0
"BARC.L",458.75,"7/7/2004","7:21",0.00,N/A,N/A,N/A,0
"BATS.L",849.00,"7/7/2004","7:22",0.00,N/A,N/A,N/A,0
"BAY.L",263.00,"7/7/2004","7:22",0.00,N/A,N/A,N/A,0
"BB.L",264.75,"7/7/2004","7:20",0.00,N/A,N/A,N/A,0
"BG.L",340.25,"7/7/2004","7:23",0.00,N/A,N/A,N/A,0
"BLND.L",700.00,"7/7/2004","7:23",0.00,N/A,N/A,N/A,0
"BLT.L",479.00,"7/7/2004","7:23",0.00,N/A,N/A,N/A,0
"BNZL.L",451.25,"7/7/2004","7:22",0.00,N/A,N/A,N/A,0
"BOC.L",922.50,"7/7/2004","7:22",0.00,N/A,N/A,N/A,0
"BOOT.L",667.00,"7/7/2004","7:21",0.00,N/A,N/A,N/A,0
"BP.L",486.00,"7/7/2004","7:23",0.00,N/A,N/A,N/A,0
"BSY.L",608.00,"7/7/2004","7:22",0.00,N/A,N/A,N/A,0
"BT.L",193.75,"7/7/2004","7:21",0.00,N/A,N/A,N/A,0
"CBRY.L",462.50,"7/7/2004","7:22",0.00,N/A,N/A,N/A,0
"CCL.L",2683.00,"7/7/2004","7:21",0.00,N/A,N/A,N/A,0
```

The program *RawCSV* reads data from such a file and stores it in a list of lists, for further manipulation by a Java program:

```
import java.io.*;
import java.util.*;

public class RawCSV
{ private ArrayList rows = new ArrayList();

  public RawCSV(File f)
  { BufferedReader br;
    try
    { br = new BufferedReader(new FileReader(f)); }
    catch (Exception e) { return; }

    String line = "";
    while (line != null)
    { try
      { line = br.readLine();
        if (line == null) { break; }  // end of data
        StringTokenizer st =
          new StringTokenizer(line,", ");
        ArrayList row = new ArrayList();
        while (st.hasMoreTokens())
```

```
        { row.add(st.nextToken()); }
        rows.add(row);
    } catch (Exception e) { line = null; }
  }
}

public void removeRow(int i)
{ if (i < 0 || i >= rows.size()) { }
  rows.remove(i);
}

public List getAll(int n)
{ // returns list of all values in column n
  List res = new ArrayList();
  for (int i = 0; i < rows.size(); i++)
  { List row = (ArrayList) rows.get(i);
    if (n < row.size())
    { res.add(row.get(n)); }
  }
  return res;
}

public double getDoubleMax(List r)
{ double res = 0;
  for (int i = 0; i < r.size(); i++)
  { double val = 0;
    try
    { val = Double.parseDouble((String) r.get(i)); }
    catch (Exception e) { }
    if (val > res)
    { res = val; }
  }
  return res;
}

public static void main(String[] args)
{ RawCSV db = new RawCSV(new File("out.csv"));
  db.removeRow(0); // the header
  List r = db.getAll(1);
  System.out.println(r);
  System.out.println(db.getDoubleMax(r));
}
}
```

In this case the processing is to determine the maximum share price of any of the FTSE 100 companies, which is 2683.00 of CCL.

8.5.3 Internet jukebox

The aim of this system is to provide a home entertainment system, using data *streaming* from a server holding a repository of music tracks, organised into playlists. Users can modify the playlists, add and remove tracks, and play tracks.

Streaming of multimedia data (video, audio, etc) means that this data is transferred from the server to the client in a continuous stream of packets, and these packets can be used by the client immediately they are received. This is in contrast to older approaches in which the data needed to be transferred in its entirety before it could be viewed/played.

Audio files can be stored in several different formats such as .wav or .mp3. These may be very large (eg, 40MB per track for .wav, 4MB per track for .mp3), so streaming is relevant as a means of transferring audio data.

There are several streaming technologies, such as RealMedia (http://www.real.com), QuickTime and Windows Media. Each technology consists of:

- Servers and media files
- Media players or plug-ins
- Encoding and creation tools

Each technology has its own proprietary versions of these components, and the components of one brand of streaming are generally not compatible with those provided by a different technology.

Streaming servers may be able to provide thousands of simultaneous media streams at a time. Such servers are an example of a web service which may be used by many clients: instead of setting up their own media server, a developer may outsource this task to an external hosting service, selecting a server which can provide files in the format needed for the technology chosen by the developer (eg, RealMedia, QuickTime, Windows Media, etc). The external host may enable a customer to upload and modify files in the customers data area on the host, using a mechanism such as FTP, the file transfer protocol.

For the Jukebox, the RealMedia streaming technology was selected, and a wireless link used to enable a remote control to be used, on a PDA. The PDA controls the Jukebox by accessing its website in a web browser. Figure 8.10 shows the physical layout of the complete Jukebox system. The RealMedia streaming server, Helix, runs on computer 1 together with the Cerberus ftp server. This is the location of the actual audio files that comprise the playlists.

A normal web server, the Tomcat Servlet Container, runs on computer 2, and hosts the Jukebox software and the database for managing user access, song repository and playlists. The RealPlayer, Real Media's media player, also runs on this machine. The PDA only needs to run a web browser to access and control the system.

There are two functions of the system which illustrate web service techniques:

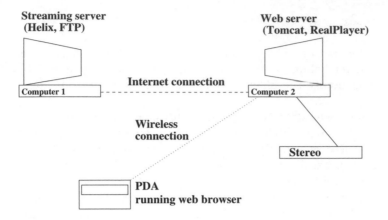

Figure 8.10: Jukebox components

1. The request to play a track or a playlist, which is initiated by the remote control and results in the media player requesting that a particular track is streamed to it from the streaming server;
2. The interaction via FTP between the web server and the streaming server, whereby the web server updates the jukebox database to match the actual set of tracks available on the streaming server.

The first function is initiated when a user clicks on a link

```
<a href = /jukebox/PlaySong?song=title.rmj>title</a>
```

embedded in the jukebox's display of song titles. This invokes the *PlaySong* servlet, passing to it the string "title.rmj", which is the name of the song with the RealMedia extension *rmj*. *PlaySong* in turn creates an instance of *InvokePlayer*, passing it the complete URL of the track to be requested, including the host address and port of the streaming server:

```
public class PlaySong extends HttpServlet
{ ....
  protected void doGet(HttpServletRequest req, ...)
  { ...
    String song = req.getParameter("song");
    InvokePlayer ip = new InvokePlayer();
    ip.playSong("http://host.isp.co.uk:80/ramgen/" + song);
    ...
  }
}
```

The *ramgen* directory on the server holds the tracks, in *.ram* format (Real Audio Metafile).

InvokePlayer makes a system call (in Windows) to the RealMedia player, asking it to download the song at the specified URL:

```
import java.lang.*;

public class InvokePlayer
{ public void playSong(String songurl)
  { try
    { Runtime.getRuntime().exec(
        "C:\\Program Files\\Real\\RealOne Player\\realplay.exe "
                              + songurl);
    } catch (Exception e) { ... }
  }
}
```

In order to update playlists to keep them consistent with the streaming server filestore, an FTP connection to the server needs to be created, and the list of tracks on the server obtained:

```
private String[] getSongsOnServer()
{ String[] res = null;
  FTPClient ftp = new FTPClient();
  int reply;

  try
  { ftp.connect("host.isp.co.uk");
    reply = ftp.getReplyCode();
    ftp.login("User","jukebox");
    String fileName = "Content";
    if (!FTPReply.isPositiveCompletion(reply))
    { // error in connecting
      ftp.disconnect();
      System.exit(1);
    }
    else
    { ftp.changeWorkingDirectory(fileName);
      res = ftp.listNames();
    }
  } catch (Exception e) { ... }
  return res;
}
```

The commands to upload data in *file* to the streaming server are:

```
FTPClient ftp = new FTPClient();
FileInputStream fis = new FileInputStream(file);
ftp.connect("host.isp.co.uk");
int reply = ftp.getReplyCode();
ftp.login("User","jukebox");
String fileName = "Content";
if (!FTPReply.isPositiveCompletion(reply))
{ // error in connecting
```

```
   ftp.disconnect();
   System.exit(1);
}
else
{ ftp.changeWorkingDirectory(fileName);
  // send data to streaming server:
  ftp.storeFile(newfile,fis);
}
...
```

where *newfile* is the name of the new file to be created in directory *fileName* to hold content *fis*.

8.6 Web service design guidelines

It is important to use web services in an appropriate way and for tasks for which they are a suitable solution. A task may be a candidate for a web service if:

- It necessarily involves access to remote data, or other business-to-business (B2B) interaction.
- It represents a common subtask in several business processes.
- If it does not require fine-grain interchange of data.
- If it is not performance-critical.

Because invocation of a web service is typically much more time-consuming than invocation of a local operation (data for the service has to be packaged into an XML message, for example, then sent across the internet, and unpackaged at the remote host, etc), it should not be used for operations that are frequently invoked within a process. For the same reason, data should be passed between the client and server in one group in a single call per web service request, not passed piece by piece.

In the property system, for example, it would be wrong to implement separate web services *getPropertyPrice(propertyId : Integer)*, *getPropertyArea(propertyId : Integer)*, etc. Instead the property data for a given key value should be returned by a single *getProperty(propertyId : Integer)* invocation.

It also makes little sense to use web services to implement the client-server relationship between the business and data tiers of an application, again because of the delays that are caused in such message-passing, even when the client and server are on the same machine.

8.7 Implementing web services using J2EE

J2EE provides an API, JAX-RPC, for programming web services that communicate using an XML-based protocol such as SOAP. This API hides the details of SOAP message formats and construction, and is similar to the Java RMI

(Remote Method Invocation) interface in its programming style. Unlike RMI, web clients and services do not have to be running on a Java platform, since standardised technologies such as HTTP, SOAP and WSDL are used to support client-server communication, and these are independent of any particular programming language.

Figure 8.11 shows the architecture of components used in JAX-RPC, and Figure 8.11 shows the steps undertaken when using JAX-RPC.

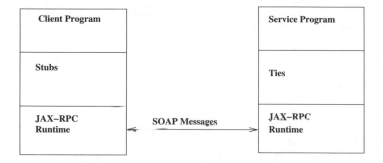

Figure 8.11: JAX-RPC architecture

The development steps are:

1. Specify a *service endpoint interface* (SEI): this is a Java interface which declares the methods that will constitute the services that a client can use.
2. Define the implementation of this interface: the actual code which will carry out the service on the server.
3. Compile the SEI and implementation, using *javac* or other Java compiler.
4. Write a configuration file (in XML format) which specifies the name of the service and the name of the SEI class. Run the *wscompile* compiler to create the WSDL and mapping files for the service, from the configuration file. The service will also be generated, as a servlet.
5. On the client side, use *wscompile* again to generate a *client stub*, which the client of the web service will use as a local proxy for the service.
6. Compile and run the client.

We will show these steps for a web service operation *getProperty(propertyId :*
Integer) : Property of the property system, which returns the details of a property, given its id.

A service endpoint must have the following properties:

1. It should extend the `java.rmi.Remote` interface
2. It should not define constants (these will be unusable by clients because their symbolic names are local to the server computer).
3. Each service method should include `java.rmi.RemoteException` in its declared exceptions.

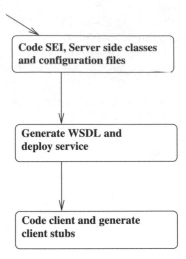

Figure 8.12: JAX-RPC process

4. Method parameters and return types should be supported JAX-RPC
   types (ie, primitive types, wrapper classes for primitive types, Strings
   or classes built directly out of such types).

   The property endpoint interface can be defined as follows:

```
import java.rmi.Remote;
import java.rmi.RemoteException;

public interface PropertyWSInterface extends Remote
{ public Property getProperty(int propertyId) throws RemoteException;
}
```

This obeys the above conditions, since *Property* is a *value type* in J2EE terminology, that is, a class with the properties:

1. All its attributes are of JAX-RPC types.
2. It has a public default constructor.
3. It does not implement `java.rmi.Remote`.
4. Every private attribute *att* has *getAtt* and *setAtt* methods.
5. It has no *final* public attributes.

   The implementation of this service will have the form:

```
import java.sql.*;

public class PropertyWS implements PropertyWSInterface
{ public Property getProperty(int propertyId)
  { ... extract data for propertyId from database
    ... and return it
  }
}
```

This class and its interface are then compiled using a normal Java compiler. A *configuration file* describing the service in XML also needs to be written, which could be:

```
<?xml version="1.0" encoding="UTF-8"?>
<configuration
  xmlns="http://java.sun.com/xml/ns/jax-rpc/ri/config">
  <service
    name = "PropertyService"
    targetNamespace = "http://propertysearch.co.uk"
    typeNamespace = "http://propertysearch.co.uk">
    <interface name = "PropertyWSInterface"/>
  </service>
</configuration>
```

The *wscompile* program of J2EE is run on this to produce a WSDL file and mapping file.

A JAX-RPC web service is actually implemented as a servlet, so can be deployed on a server in much the same way as a normal web system component, except that it needs to be recorded as an endpoint of a web service. If *propserv* is the server alias for the generated property service servlet, then clients will be able to access the servlet via the URL

```
http://www.propertysearch.co.uk:8080/jaxrpc/propserv
```

The WSDL of the service can be viewed by the request

```
http://www.propertysearch.co.uk:8080/jaxrpc/propserv?WSDL
```

A client of the service must create a stub object, a proxy for the remote service, set the endpoint address, and cast the stub object to *PropertyWSInterface*. The code could be:

```
import javax.xml.rpc.Stub;

public class PropertyClient
{ private static String endpoint;

  public static void main(String[] args)
  { try
    { endpoint = args[0];
      Stub stub = createProxy();
      stub._setProperty(
        javax.xml.rpc.Stub.ENDPOINT_ADDRESS_PROPERTY,
        endpoint);
      PropertyWSInterface prop =
                    (PropertyWSInterface) stub;
      // Property pr = prop.getProperty("23345");
    } catch (Exception e) { e.printStackTrace(); }
  }

  private static Stub createProxy()
```

```
{ return
    (Stub)
        (new PropertyService_Impl()).getPropertyWSInterfacePort();
}
}
```

wscompile is used to create the stubs for the client, using the WSDL of the service. The location of the WSDL needs to be informed to *wscompile* via a client-side configuration file:

```
<configuration
 xmlns = "http://java.sun.com/xml/ns/jax-rpc/ri/config">
 <wsdl
  location =
 "http://www.propertysearch.co.uk:8080/jaxrpc/propserv?WSDL"/>
</configuration>
```

The client can then be compiled using a normal Java compiler.

This form of client is a *static stub client*, meaning that the proxy class *PropertyService_Impl* is created before the client is run and is referred to explicitly in the client code. It is also possible to define *dynamic proxy clients*, which create a proxy object using factory objects that refer to the WSDL of the service. In this case the client stubs generated by *wscompile* are not used.

A further progression in client flexibility is the *dynamic invocation interface client* (DII client), which directly sets up the details of the service name and parameters (so that these can be identified at runtime) in a *javax.xml.rpc.Call* object. *wscompile* is not needed for such clients.

J2EE also provides a means to directly construct SOAP messages and interact with web services by sending such messages. The SAAJ (SOAP with Attachments API for Java) API supports construction of SOAP messages using DOM interface operations such as *addChildElement* and *addTextNode*, and the transmission of these messages over a *SOAPConnection*.

Code which uses SOAP messages to send a request to the property service could be:

```
// Create a message:
MessageFactory factory = MessageFactory.newInstance();
SOAPMessage mess = factory.createMessage();

// Add content to the message:
SOAPBody body = mess.getSOAPBody();
SOAPFactory sfact = SOAPFactory.newInstance();
// The tag for the request:
Name bname =
    sfact.createName("getProperty","m",
        "http://www.propertysearch.co.uk");
SOAPBodyElement belem = body.addBodyElement(bname);
// The tag and value of parameter:
Name param = sfact.createName("propertyId");
SOAPElement pid = belem.addChildElement(param);
```

```
pid.addTextNode("223398");

// Open SOAP connection and send message:
SOAPConnectionFactory scfact =
  SOAPConnectionFactory.newInstance();
SOAPConnection conn = scfact.createConnection();
java.net.URL pserv =
  new URL("http://www.propertysearch.co.uk/ws/getprop");
SOAPMessage response = conn.call(mess,pserv);
... process response ...
```

The message constructed in this code has the form:

```
<SOAP-ENV:Envelope
  xmlns:SOAP-ENV = "http://schemas.xmlsoap.org/soap/envelope/">
  <SOAP-ENV:Body>
    <m:getProperty xmlns:m = "http://www.propertysearch.co.uk">
    <propertyId>223398</propertyId>
    </m:getProperty>
  </SOAP-ENV:Body>
</SOAP-ENV:Envelope>
```

8.8 Mailing and Push technologies

Simple internet applications are client-driven: the server simply carries out functions and provides web pages in response to requests from the client. More sophisticated functionality is possible if the server is able to take the initiative and autonomously send information to the client when relevant events occur. Examples include news services to which a user can subscribe, and which then update themselves on arrival of new news items, modifying the display of information for each subscribed client. Systems which email customers with information are also simple examples of such a server-driven style of interaction, which is known as 'push technology'.

J2EE provides the JavaMail API to perform server-side composition and sending of email messages to customers. An example where this could be used is the property search system: whenever a new property is added to the database, or an existing property details are changed, then all users for whom the new details are a (new) match should be emailed with a message informing them of the details. This is in order to implement the informal CIM invariant

'The system always keeps users informed of all the properties which match their specifications.'

The observer pattern is the natural design structure to use in this case: each *createProperty* and *editProperty* operation committed to the database will also need to involve a notification of all observers – those users matching the new details – that some significant change has occurred in the data, the *Property* table in the database.

The email address of each user is stored in the User table, so it will be possible, in principle, to send all relevant users a short message describing the property that was created/changed. The JavaMail API enables the creation of such messages. These can either be text or HTML – text is probably preferable as it cannot be assumed that users will have an HTML-enabled mail reader.

The JavaMail API is contained in the *jar* file *j2ee.jar* with J2EE, or in the *mail.jar* file if downloaded separately. These files therefore need to be in the *CLASSPATH* to run JavaMail. The *activation.jar* file should also be included unless J2EE is being used.

The key JavaMail classes are:

Session Represents a mail session. It uses a property file to access information such as the current SMTP (mail) server:

```
import javax.mail.*;


...


Properties prop = System.getProperties();
prop.put("mail.smtp.host","mail.propertysearch.co.uk");
Session sess = Session.getDefaultInstance(prop,null);
```

getDefaultInstance gets a session that may be shared, to get a unique session use *getInstance*(). The *null* parameter can be replaced by an *authenticator* for the session – for example a popup dialog prompting the user for their login information, if the mail server requires such authentication.

Message An abstract class representing messages, the subclass *MimeMessage* is used for standard internet email messages. The statements

```
MimeMessage mess = new MimeMessage(sess);
mess.setSubject("New property details match");
mess.setText(text);
```

create a plain text MIME message with the given subject and a message body given by the string *text*.

Address This class represents addresses, for senders and receivers of messages:

```
Address from = new InternetAddress("admin@propertysearch.co.uk");
Address to = new InternetAddress(eml,nme);
mess.setFrom(from);
mess.addRecipient(Message.RecipientType.TO,to);
```

mess.setRecipient(*int*, *Address*[]) can be used to set an array of addresses as the recipients of the message in a single statement. The recipient types *CC* and *BCC* are alternatives to *TO*, for copying a message visibly and invisibly, respectively, to an additional recipient.

An address can have an optional name as well as the email specification. The *from* address can be set to anything – so JavaMail could be used for 'spamming' and other irresponsible uses of automated email.

Authenticator Represents a mechanism for authenticating an action, typically logging onto a mail server. A *PasswordAuthenticator* must provide a method *getPasswordAuthentication*() : *PasswordAuthentication* which returns login and password information, typically obtained from a dialog:

```
import javax.mail.*;
import javax.swing.*;
import java.util.*;

public class PropSysAuthenticator extends Authenticator
{ public PasswordAuthentication getPasswordAuthentication()
  { String user = JOptionPane.showInputDialog("Enter username:");
    String pass = JOptionPane.showInputDialog("Enter password:");
    return new PasswordAuthentication(user,pass);
  }
}
```

The session will then open this dialog when authentication is required, if an instance of *PropSysAuthenticator* is set as the authenticator for the session.

Transport Represents the actual mailing mechanism, such as SMTP. The simplest way to use this is to call

```
Transport.send(mess);
```

which uses the default transport mechanism. This approach closes the mail server connection after each message is sent. To avoid this, we can use a transport instance:

```
Transport transport = sess.getTransport("smtp");
transport.connect(mailhost,username,passwd);
transport.sendMessage(mess,tolist);
transport.close();
```

The new architecture of the system will be based on the observer pattern (Figure 8.13). The servlets for creating and editing property details will invoke *createProperty* and *editProperty* methods of the *Property* class. *Property* forwards these requests to the *DBI* (along with *listProperty* and *deleteProperty*), and invokes the *notify* method of *Observable*, with the data of the modified/new property. *notify* invokes *update* with these parameters, on the *User* class, which determines which users match this property and then sends an email to each of them:

```
public static void update(String propType, int propPrice,
                          int propBedrooms, String propArea,
                          String propAvailable)
{ String mailhost = "mail.propertysearch.co.uk";
  Properties prop = System.getProperties();
  prop.put("mail.smtp.host",mailhost);
  PropSysAuthenticator auth = new PropSysAuthenticator();
  Session sess =
```

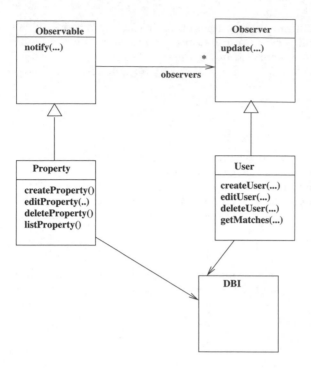

Figure 8.13: Extended property system class diagram

```
    Session.getDefaultInstance(prop,auth);
  String text = "The following property has just " +
    "been registered or has changed its details:\n" +
    "Property type: " + propType + "\n" +
    "Price:        " + propPrice + "\n" +
    "Bedrooms:     " + propBedrooms + "\n" +
    "Area:         " + propArea + "\n" +
    "Available:    " + propAvailable + "\n";
  MimeMessage mess = new MimeMessage(sess);
  try
  { mess.setSubject("New property details match");
    mess.setText(text);
    // Or: mess.setContent(text,"text/plain");
    Address from =
      new InternetAddress("admin@propertysearch.co.uk");
    mess.setFrom(from);
    ResultSet res = dbi.getMatched(propType,
                          propPrice,propArea,
                          propBedrooms,
                          propAvailability);
    while (res.next())
    { String nme = res.getString("userName");
      String eml = res.getString("userEmail");
```

```
         Address to = new InternetAddress(eml,nme);
         mess.addRecipient(Message.RecipientType.TO,to);
         mess.saveChanges();
      }
      Transport.send(mess);
      res.close();
   }
   catch(Exception e)
   { handleException(e); }
}
```

8.9   The Semantic Web

The 'Semantic Web' is the use of the web to represent data in a semantically meaningful manner, so that it can be used effectively by different applications for many different tasks, including e-commerce.

Originally the web was used simply for the visual presentation of information. The use of XML enabled the storage and transfer of non-visual data in a standard form, but XML does not supply any mechanism for defining relationships between data or for defining the meaning of data in terms of domain concepts. The DTD notation only allows the determination of what are valid and invalid XML documents according to the DTD. To support more complex tasks and representation, eg, such as logical reasoning, a more sophisticated language is required. W3C is developing the Resource Description Framework (RDF) in order to provide the necessary representation and data interchange language.

RDF describes resources and their properties using graphs, where the nodes are (references to) resources, or values, and the arcs are relations defining properties of resources. RDF specifications can be given as graphs, as sets of

```
node   relation   node
```

triples, or in an XML syntax.

An *ontology* is a language used to describe a domain or set of concepts (eg, 'parent' and 'child'). Ontology languages such as OWL [37] can specify many properties of a data set, for example that certain relationships are transitive and to specify cardinality constraints on particular classes or on the ranges of relationships. OWL uses RDF as a base language.

For example, to define that a person, Felix, is a parent of Katya and Alex, we could write RDF corresponding to the triples

```
Felix parentOf Katya
Felix parentOf Alex
```

In an actual RDF document, the names 'Felix', etc would be replaced by *Uniform Resource Identifiers* (URIs) for the people concerned, such as

`http://www.prop.org.uk/Staff/Felix/contact#me`, and the relations by URIs
describing the meaning of the relationships.

An XML version of this data could be:

```
<?xml version="1.0"?>
<rdf:RDF xmlns:rdf="http://www.w3.org/1999/02/22-rdf-syntax-ns#"
  xmlns:myterms="http://www.prop.org.uk/kcl/terms/">
  <rdf:Description
   rdf:about =
     "http://www.prop.org.uk/Staff/Felix/contact#me">
    <myterms:parentOf
     rdf:resource =
       "http://www.prop.org.uk/Staff/Felix/contact#Katya"/>
    <myterms:parentOf
     rdf:resource =
       "http://www.prop.org.uk/Staff/Felix/contact#Alex"/>

  </rdf:Description>
</rdf:RDF>
```

The *rdf* : *Description* tag contains the description of the resource specified in
the *rdf* : *about* attribute. The properties of the resource are described within
the *rdf* : *Description* element.

8.10 Mobile computing and m-commerce

Mobile computing is potentially the largest growth area of computing use over
the next ten years, with the third generation (3G) of mobile phones currently
being introduced having much greater capacity for executing software applications and using the internet than preceding models. M-commerce is the seg-
ment of e-commerce that makes use of wireless communication, and likewise
has considerable scope for expansion – hopefully in a more useful direction than
merely bombarding mobile phone users with spam text messages in addition
to the existing plague of spam email!

Because of the very recent development of the area, a wide range of (incom-
patible) communication technologies, software platforms/operating systems and
languages for mobile computing and web page construction exist.

8.10.1 Short Message Service (SMS)

One simple mobile technology that can be used in software applications is
the *Short Message Service* (SMS), which allows text messages of up to 160
characters to be sent to and between mobile devices. For example, a home
alarm system could send intruder alerts to the home owner in this way, or
a restaurant booking service could send reminders to someone who booked a

table, the day before their booked meal. J2ME provides SMS facilities as part
of the Java Wireless Messaging API (WMA).

8.10.2 Writing software for mobile phones

Although mobile phones are steadily gaining in processing power and memory
capacity, the present generation of phones are approximately at the level of
1980's home computers, with around 500 KB of RAM. An additional limitation
is the screen size, which may be as small as 128 pixels square. These limitations
mean that special programming techniques are necessary, in order to conserve
memory requirements, both of data and the memory used to store the program
itself. This may require avoiding design patterns such as Mediator, Visitor
or Observer, which use complex inter-reference between objects and extensive
message-passing. Object-oriented structuring may still be used, however.

Java is the most popular programming language for mobile phones, and
the J2ME (Java 2 Micro Edition) provides tools for writing *MIDlets*, the Java
term for J2ME applications. J2ME is a subset of the Java standard edition,
J2SE, in particular there is no floating point numeric type (*double* or *float*)
and calculations on such numbers must be simulated using integers. The Swing
packages are also missing, replaced by mobile device GUI classes. GUI coding
may also take advantage of the facilities offered by the particular mobile phone
range being considered for deployment, although at a possible cost in terms of
later portability.

8.10.3 WAP and WML

One widely-used mobile technology is the Wireless Application Protocol (WAP)
and Wireless Markup Language (WML). WAP is a means by which a wireless
device can communicate with the internet, via WAP gateways. The WML is a
restricted form of HTML designed to display web pages on the small screens of
(2nd generation) mobile phones, which often have space for no more than five
lines of text plus a command button. These micropages are termed 'cards' in
WML, and can be viewed using a browser running on the mobile device. An
example of a WML page is:

```
<wml>
  <card id = "enterName" title = "Enter your name">
  <do type = "accept" label = "Ok">
    <go href = "propscript.wmls#getName()"/>
  </do>
  <p>Enter your name:<br>
  <input name = "name" value = ""/>
  </p>
  </card>

  <card id = "enterEmail" title = "Enter your email">
```

```
<do type = "accept" label = "Login">
 <go href = "propscript.wmls#login()"/>
</do>
<do type = "options" label = "Register">
  <go href = "propscript.wmls#register()"/>
</do>
<p>$emailmessage <br>
<input name = "email" value = ""/>
</p>
</card>
</wml>
```

The first card contains an input field to receive the customer's name, and a
button (created by the *do* tag) labelled "Ok". Entering data into the field
and pressing the button triggers the *go* action of the button, which calls the
getName function. This retrieves the name value that was entered and constructs a message *emailmessage*, and moves the browser on to display the next
card, which prompts for the customer's email, using the message constructed
from their name. At the bottom of this card are two options, one for registering
and another to login.

The *scripts.wml* file contains functions called by the WML pages:

```
extern function getName()
{ var x = WMLBrowser.getVar("name");
  WMLBrowser.setVar("emailmessage",
    "Enter your email, " + x);
  WMLBrowser.go("#enterEmail");
}

extern function register()
{ // move to card with registration dialog }

extern function login()
{ // send login data to server }
```

An alternative approach for user-interface design of m-commerce systems is
to use *Flash Lite*, a restricted subset of the Flash multimedia design language
(http://www.macromedia.com).

8.10.4 Bluetooth

Bluetooth is a technology for short range (30 feet/10 metres) wireless communication between devices, enabling local area networks to be formed between
PDAs, mobile phones, printers, etc. In contrast to infrared communication,
bluetooth is not restricted to line-of-sight links, and can support one-to-many
communication, wheras infrared is only one-to-one.

One application of bluetooth could be for multiplayer games such as chess
to be played by two people on different mobile phones, using bluetooth to
communicate moves between the phones.

Java support for bluetooth operation is defined in the javax.bluetooth and javax.obex packages of the Java Micro Edition.

8.11 Summary

We have described some of the technologies and applications of web service systems, and the two main frameworks, J2EE and .Net for the development of such systems.

8.12 Exercises

1 Represent the dating agency system (exercise 4 of the preceding chapter) in the J2EE architecture.

2 Draw a class diagram and design architecture for the following system which allows someone to remotely monitor their cat(s) via a set of movement sensors and webcams (Figure 8.14). The monitors are polled (sampled) at intervals set by the user, and the cams may also be periodically panned across the area they monitor. Individual sensors or camaras can be switched on or off. There are two interfaces designed as sets of web pages: a set of WML pages for viewing over a mobile phone, and a set of HTML pages for viewing at a PC. The system shows the rooms whose sensors were most recently triggered. Design the WML and XHTML interfaces of this system, identifying what pages are visible to the user and what command options they have.

3 Implement the messaging service of the dating agency system (exercise 4 of the preceding chapter) using JavaMail: the system stores users real email addresses, but does not show these to other users, instead it handles the emailing of messages between users, setting the 'from' address of a message to be the user's nickname on the system.

4 Organise the data of the restaurant management system class diagram in Figure 8.15 into suitable entity beans.

5 (Project) Develop a web-service system for financial information, providing services via the XML SOAP protocol to other web systems/clients. The service answers requests for information about share prices on the UK stock exchange, and about major currency exchange rates.

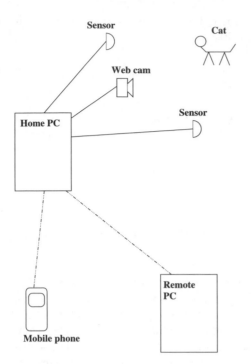

Figure 8.14: Cat monitoring system

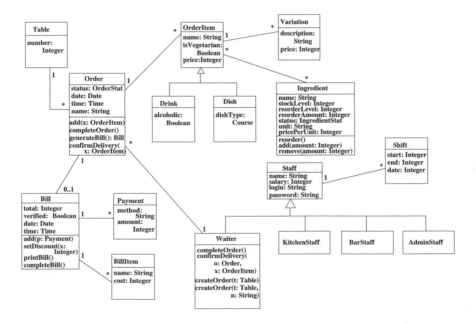

Figure 8.15: Class diagram of restaurant system

Chapter 9

Implementing the Model-Driven Architecture

This chapter describes in detail the concepts and terminology of the MDA, and the role of transformations and refactoring. We show how transformations can be formally represented and justified. We conclude with a survey of current MDA tools.

9.1   MDA terminology

In this section we summarise the key concepts of the MDA.

Computation Independent Model (CIM)   A CIM abstracts completely from implementation details, and uses terminology familiar to practitioners in the domain of the application – it is similar to the concept of a *domain model*, and can be used to assist in establishing requirements and expressing these in detail. It describes the system in terms of the domain in which it must operate.

UML notations such as class diagrams and statecharts can be used to define CIMs. Only declarative constraints should be used to specify functional behaviour.

Model   A model in MDA terms is a representation of a part of the function, structure and/or behaviour of a system [36]. A model must be in a *formal* representation, ie, a notation with a well-defined syntax and semantics. The subset of UML that we have been using satisfies these requirements (at least for class diagram and statechart notations) and all MDA models that we consider in this book will be expressed in UML, but other formal languages could be used instead, in principle.

Model Transformation   Conversion of one model of a system to another model of the same system. The central model transformation of MDA is the PIM to PSM transformation. Figure 9.1 shows two alternative strategies for carrying out this transformation.   Diagram (a) shows the *marking* strategy for model

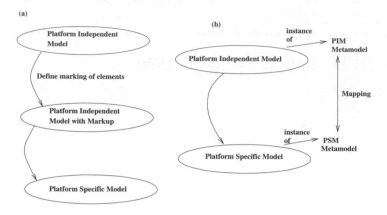

Figure 9.1: PIM to PSM transformation strategies

transformation: a mark may be a stereotype such as ≪ *persistent* ≫, or some other identification of a particular intended implementation of a PIM model element. Several markings may apply to one element, eg, an entity may be marked as both persistent and secure, enforcing password-controlled access to it. Section 9.3 discusses how UML can be extended to support markings for such transformations.

Diagram (b) shows an alternative approach in which the transformation is defined as a mapping of metamodels: we explore this approach in more detail in Section 9.2 below.

Pervasive Services   Services provided by platforms, such as directory services, transactions, security, event handling and notification, which are shared between all applications on that platform.

Platform   A set of technologies and functionalities which are available to any application based on that platform. An example is J2EE.

Platform-Independent Model (PIM)   A PIM captures all the essential inform-ation about and properties of a system, independent of particular implement-ations. The information could include:

- The entities involved, with their attributes and operations;
- The relationships between entities, with multiplicities;
- Life-cycles of objects, expressed as statecharts;
- Logical static properties, expressed as constraints on classes and associ-ations;
- Logical behavioural properties, expressed as pre- and postcondition con-straints on operations.

Static invariants can also implicitly make constraints on the dynamic behaviour of a system, for example a constraint $b = a.size$ linking a role a and attribute *b* of the same class implies that whenever *a* is changed, *b* may have to be changed.

Some assumptions may be made about the eventual implementation platform, eg, that operations such as *addrole* to add an object to a multi-valued role will be available, even if these may be actually implemented in terms of a relational database, as we described in Chapter 7. This is an example of PIM specification in terms of a *virtual machine*.

Platform-Specific Model A version of a PIM tailored to a particular implementation environment. Eg, from a PIM class *E* we may derive a class *ECreateForm* in the PSM which describes an input form on a web page for creating instances of *E*, for an online version of the system. The PSM does not add any new logical properties, but may add computational/algorithmic detail and transform the PIM elements to conform to restrictions of the platform (eg, removing many-many associations to enable representation of a data model in a relational database).

A PSM must include all the details needed to implement a system, or alternatively must only rely on already-implemented specifications of a platform.

The *record of transformation* of the PIM to the PSM is an important product of the process of producing the PSM, describing in particular which PSM elements were derived from what PIM elements, and this record should be retained.

Refactoring A parameterised behaviour-preserving program transformation that updates an application's design and underlying source code [49].

Reverse Engineering The process of extracting a design or specification from an implementation of a system: this is necessary if an organisation wishes to capture business rules which may be embedded in a legacy application.

Round-trip Engineering Reverse-engineering followed by the normal forward engineering PIM to PSM transformation. This is used to port an application from one platform to another.

Virtual Machine A catalogue of operations/services which are independent of any particular platform but can be implemented in several platforms. Defining a PIM in terms of a virtual machine means that the work required to implement the PIM can be reduced, since the virtual machine may already have an implementation on the target platform.

A generalisation of this is to define an application as a hierarchy of layers, each layer depending only on the interface and specification of its supplier layers, not their implementation. This means that, in principle, the PIM to PSM mapping of the application can also be split into separate mappings of each layer, with the interfaces of the layers being preserved by the mappings.

9.2   Model transformations

Transformations on models are fundamental to the MDA approach: either as a means to improve a model to make it more generic and flexible for use as a PIM, or as a means to transform PIMs into PSMs. For reverse-engineering or round-trip engineering, PSM to PIM transformations – essentially ways of abstracting away from model-specific details – are also important.

In this section we describe a number of useful transformations in detail, and give a framework for formally representing and reasoning about transformations.

9.2.1   Models

By a *model*, we mean a collection of UML model elements. A model can be regarded as an instance of the UML metaclass *Subsystem*, linked to objects representing the model elements of that particular model. For example, a simple model containing three classes, two attributes and two associations (Figure 9.2) can be represented as $m1 : Subsystem$ in the (meta) object diagram of Figure 9.3.

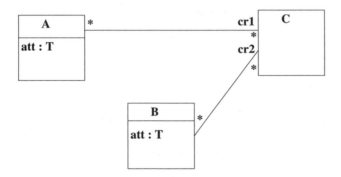

Figure 9.2: Model $m1$

Figure 9.4 shows a portion of the UML 2.0 metamodel. Instances of *Attribute* are actual attributes that are defined in UML class diagrams, likewise for *Class*, *BehaviouralFeature*, etc. A model element is partly defined by the values of its metafeatures: each *Attribute* instance has a *type*, which is a particular *Type*, for example. However, a model element also has a semantics, which defines what its value can be at any time point. For classes, this value is a set, also called the *extent* of the class, consisting of all those instances (objects) of the class that currently exist. Eg, the empty set is a possible extent of the *User* class in the property system PIM, as is a singleton set consisting of a single user.

We will denote the extent of a model element by overlining its name: $\overline{m1.A}$ is the set of objects whose class is $m1.A$ (at a particular time). For an association

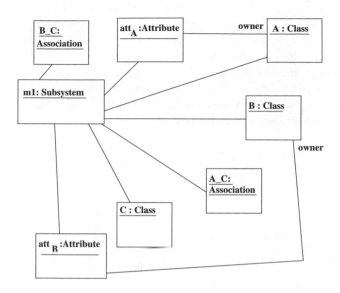

Figure 9.3: Model $m1$ as meta-object

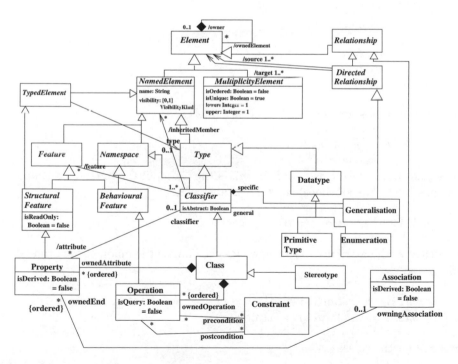

Figure 9.4: UML 2.0 kernal metamodel

end such as $cr1$, $\overline{cr1}$ maps each $x : \overline{A}$ to a set $\overline{cr1}(x)$ of elements of $\overline{C}$ (for a 1-multiplicity end, the extent is a map from objects of the source class to single objects of the target class). The extents $\overline{att}$ of attributes $att : T$ are also maps, mapping from objects of the class of att to elements of T.

Transformations between models can then be expressed as relationships between the corresponding metaobjects. For example, the 'introducing a superclass' transformation is applicable to $m1$, producing a model $m2$ (Figure 9.5). This can be formally expressed by the properties:

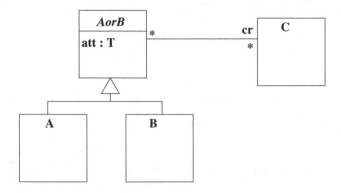

Figure 9.5: Model $m2$

$$m1.A = m2.A$$
$$m1.B = m2.B$$
$$m1.C = m2.C$$

That is, the classes are the same in both models.

$$\overline{m2.AorB} = \overline{m2.A} \cup \overline{m2.B}$$

The extent of the new class $AorB$ in $m2$ is the union of the extents of A and B in this model (at all times) so $AorB$ is abstract:

$$(m2.AorB).isAbstract = true$$

The extent of the attribute of this new class is likewise the union of the original two attributes:

$$x : \overline{m2.A} \;\Rightarrow\; \overline{m2.att}(x) = \overline{m1.att_A}(x)$$
$$x : \overline{m2.B} \;\Rightarrow\; \overline{m2.att}(x) = \overline{m1.att_B}(x)$$

Similarly for the roles:

$$x : \overline{m2.A} \;\Rightarrow\; \overline{m2.cr}(x) = \overline{m1.cr1}(x)$$
$$x : \overline{m2.B} \;\Rightarrow\; \overline{m2.cr}(x) = \overline{m1.cr2}(x)$$

This describes when $(m1, m2)$ are a valid pair of models related by the 'introducing a superclass' transformation for general classes A, B, C with the features shown in Figure 9.2.

In the following section we formalise some other transformations in the same manner.

9.2.2 Transformations

There are three general categories of transformations typically used in MDA development:

1. Quality improvements of models, eg:

   - introducing a superclass;
   - making partial roles into total.

2. Refinements, eg:

   - introducing design patterns;
   - transforming PIM types into PSM types (Integer to int, etc);
   - removing multiple inheritance;
   - removing many-many associations;
   - introducing primary and foreign keys;
   - source/target splitting on statecharts;
   - amalgamating subclasses.

3. Abstractions, eg:

   - replacing PSM types by PIM types.

We will discuss the motivations behind some of these transformations, and illustrate how they can be formally expressed.

Introducing a Superclass   This is used to simplify a class diagram and remove duplicate features from it, by recognising that these features are actually special cases of a feature of a superclass that should be present in the model. This is simple to apply if two classes have a common subset of attributes and/or operations, but the situation for common roles is slightly more subtle.

Consider Figure 9.6, which shows an initial attempt at drawing a class diagram of an ambulance dispatch system. What is noticeable is that there are several associations with the same meaning: *Ambulance_Hospital*, *Ambulance_Incident*, etc, all have the meaning that the ambulance is present at the location concerned. Similarly for the associations from *Patient* to these classes. Thus the diagram can be rationalised by creating a new superclass *Location* and replacing the multiple associations from *Ambulance* and *Patient* to its subclasses by a pair of associations to *Location* (Figure 9.7).

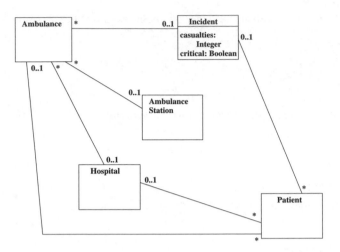

Figure 9.6: Ambulance dispatch class diagram version 0

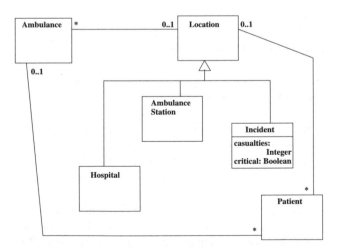

Figure 9.7: Ambulance dispatch class diagram version 1

In general, this transformation should be applied if there are classes A, B and C, and associations A_B and A_C with the same meaning and same multiplicity c at the A end. The result of the transformation is to create a superclass $BorC$ of B and C, and replace the two associations by a single A_BorC association with multiplicity $c1 \cup c2$ at the $BorC$ end, if $c1$ and $c2$ are the corresponding multiplicities of the original associations (Figure 9.8), and those associations were exclusive (an A object could not be associated to both a B and a C – this is the case for the ambulance system, effectively). If the associations were not exclusive, then the multiplicity at the $BorC$ end is $c1 + c2$: the collection of sums $x + y$ where x is in $c1$ and y in $c2$. Table 9.1 shows the rules for combining single interval multiplicities. The new role c is

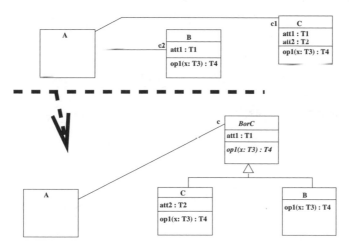

Figure 9.8: Association-based superclass introduction

$c1$	$c2$	$c1 \cup c2$	$c1 + c2$
1..u	n..m	max(l,n)..max(u,m)	(1+n)..(u+m)
1..*	n..m	max(l,n)..*	(1+n)..*
*	n..m	*	n..*
*	*	*	*

Table 9.1: Rules for combining subclass role multiplicities

the union of $c1$ and $c2$:

$$x : \overline{m_2.A} \;\Rightarrow\; \overline{m_2.c}(x) = \overline{m_1.c1}(x) \cup \overline{m_1.c2}(x)$$

Making Partial Roles into Total Figure 9.9 shows an example of this transformation. In the first model we need the condition

$$br = \{\} \;\Rightarrow\; cr \; /= \; \{\}$$

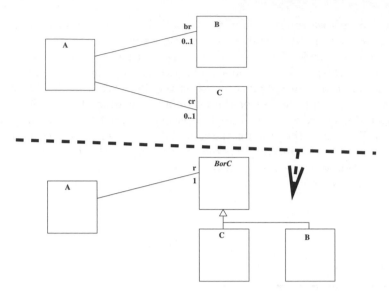

Figure 9.9: Making partial roles total

Then:

$$m_2.A = m_1.A$$
$$m_2.B = m_1.B$$
$$m_2.C = m_1.C$$
$$\overline{m_2.BorC} = \overline{m2.B} \cup \overline{m2.C}$$
$$x : \overline{m_2.A} \implies \overline{m_2.r}(x) = \overline{m_1.br}(x) \cup \overline{m_1.cr}(x)$$

For example, A could be *BankAccount*, B could be *Person* and C could be *Company*. The new superclass could be called *AccountHolder*.

Removal of Many-many Associations This transformation (Figure 9.10) replaces a many-many association with a new class and two many-one associations. In this case, model m_1 has classes A and B, which are unchanged in the new model m_2. m_2 also has a new class C, defined to have the property that

$$c1 : C \ \& \ c2 : C \ \& \ c1.ar = c2.ar \ \& \ c1.br = c2.br \implies c1 = c2$$

The original relation A_B is implemented by the composition of the new relations:

$$x : \overline{A} \ \& \ y : \overline{m1.br}(x) \iff \exists c : \overline{C} \cdot x = \overline{m2.ar}(c) \ \& \ y = \overline{m2.br}(c)$$

Replace Inheritance by Association This transformation (Figure 9.11) is useful to remove situations of multiple inheritance from PIMs. In this case, $m1$ and

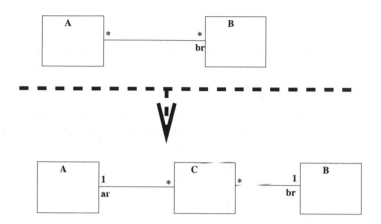

Figure 9.10: Removing a many-many association

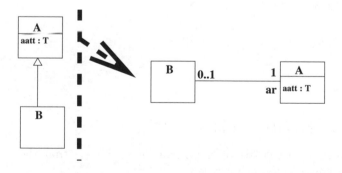

Figure 9.11: Replacing an inheritance by an association

$m2$ have the same classes A and B, but

$$x : \overline{m2.B} \;\Rightarrow\; \overline{m1.aatt}(x) = \overline{m2.aatt}(\overline{m2.ar}(x))$$

and

$$b = \overline{m2.ar}(b)$$

(where the extent $\overline{B}$ of a subclass B is considered as a subset of the extent $\overline{A}$ of its superclass A). In other words, to get the *aatt* value of some $b : B$ in the new model, we need to navigate to $b.ar$ and get its *aatt* value.

Replace Associations by Foreign Keys   This transformation (Figure 9.12) is applicable to any explicit many-one association between persistent classes. It assumes that primary keys already exist for the classes linked by the association. In model $m1$ (the PIM) and model $m2$ (the PSM) the classes are the same, so

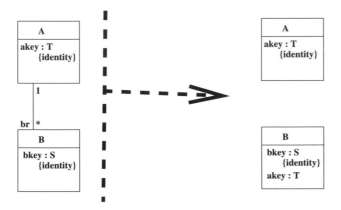

Figure 9.12: Replacing association by foreign key

that

$$\overline{m1.A} = \overline{m2.A}$$
$$\overline{m1.B} = \overline{m2.B}$$

For $a : \overline{A}$, $b : \overline{B}$:

$$b : \overline{m1.br}(a) \;\Leftrightarrow\; \overline{m2.akey_B}(b) = \overline{m2.akey_A}(a)$$

In other words, the association consists of those pairs $a \mapsto b$ such that the foreign key value of b is equal to the primary key value of a.

9.3   UML profiles

UML can be extended with 'profiles', which allow the definition of platform-specific constructs such as 'EntityJavaBean', 'compound key' or 'form'. A profile consists of a set of stereotypes, which are defined in the profile by their name and the (set of) UML metaclasses that they apply to. Figure 9.13 shows the profile we have been using for web systems. A solid-headed arrow from the

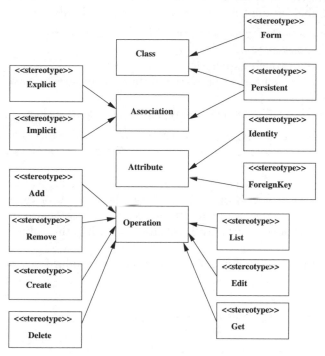

Figure 9.13: Profile for web applications

stereotype to the metaclass indicates that particular instances of the metaclass can be stereotyped (marked) by the stereotype. So, for example, both classes and associations can be marked as 'persistent'.

Profiles can be used to define a PIM to PSM mapping, with the profile stereotypes attached to model elements determining how these elements are transformed.

9.4 Transformations for internet systems

The development process we described in Chapter 7 for online implementation of an information system can also be formally expressed as a transformation of a PIM into a PSM.

This PIM to PSM transformation adopts the 'marking' strategy using a profile, whereby elements of the PIM are given a marking to indicate what elements should be used to implement them. The markings used are the stereotypes:

- *persistent* on classes

- *implicit* and *explicit* on associations
- *create, delete, add, remove, list, check, get, edit* on operations.

The following specific transformations are also used to convert the PIM data model into one suitable for implementation in a relational database:

- Removing inheritance, either by aggregation of classes, or by replacing an inheritance by an association.
- Removing many-many explicit associations.
- Introducing primary keys for persistent classes if they do not already have an identity attribute.
- Introducing foreign keys to implement many-one explicit associations.

A PIM class C which is stereotyped as $\ll$ *persistent* $\gg$ and which has operations stereotyped by $\ll$ *create* $\gg$, $\ll$ *delete* $\gg$, $\ll$ *list* $\gg$, $\ll$ *check* $\gg$, $\ll$ *edit* $\gg$, $\ll$ *get* $\gg$, $\ll$ *add* $\gg$, $\ll$ *remove* $\gg$ will give rise to a number of dependent classes in the PSM, stereotyped as $\ll$ *form* $\gg$ and representing web pages for each of the stereotyped operations of the class. Each of these new classes will have the respective $\ll$ *create* $\gg$, $\ll$ *delete* $\gg$, etc operation describing the action of the form – usually invoked by pressing the submit button of the form.

For each stereotype the corresponding form class has a standard set of attributes:

- *create, edit* – all attributes of C.
- *delete, get* (the value of a role r of C) – the primary key of C.
- *list* – no attributes.
- *add* (to a role r of C) – the primary key of C and the primary key of the class adjacent to r.
- *remove* (from a role r of C) – the primary key of C and the primary key of the class adjacent to r.
- *check* – the primary key of C plus whatever other attributes of C are needed for the check (eg, a password).

The derivation can be made completely precise, eg, if C is the model $m1$ (PIM) class, and *CreateCPage* is the model $m2$ (PSM) class derived from it for its *create* operation, and there is

$$m : CreateCPage.feature \ \& \ m : Operation$$

with $m.stereotype = cs$ with $cs.name =$ "*create*", then $CreateCPage.attribute$ and $C.attribute$ are isomorphic, where $C.attribute \ = \ C.feature \ /\backslash \ Attribute$ – the set of C's features which are attributes.

If att and att' are corresponding attributes under this isomorphism, then they only differ in their names and their classifier, all other properties are the same. In particular

$$att.type = att'.type$$

The constraints of *CreateCPage* are those of C, after renaming of attributes of C to the corresponding attributes of *CreateCPage*. Similarly for the other derived classes.

9.5   Implementing model transformations

Because of the importance of model transformations to the MDA process, techniques for specifying and implementing such transformations need to be considered. We describe three alternative approaches: using XML transformations (XSLT), the inbuilt support (REI) in Rational Rose for UML model transformations, and the Java facilities for metadata manipulation.

9.5.1   Extensible Stylesheet Language Transformations (XSLT)

XSLT is an XML notation which can be used to transform one XML document (the *source* document) into another, the *target* document (Figure 9.14). It is typically used to 'mark up' an XML document into an XHTML document for rendering on a browser, but can also be used for data transformations from XML documents that represent (eg) UML diagrams from a PIM into XML for corresponding PSM diagrams.

Transformation defined by XSL file

Input XML Structure   **Output XML Structure**

Figure 9.14: XSLT process

The standard representation of UML in XML is termed XMI (XML Metadata Interchange) format, which expresses the UML diagrams in terms of their structure according to the UML metamodel (Figure 9.4). For example, an XMI representation of the *Integer* data type could be:

```
<UML:DataType xmi.id = "G.10" name = "Integer"
  visibility = "public" isSpecification = "false"
  isRoot = "false" isLeaf = "false"
  isAbstract = "false"/>
```

Each kind of UML model element (class, association, association end, data type, operation, etc) is represented by an XMI tag, the attributes of this tag correspond to the metamodel attributes of the model element.

An XSLT file defines a transformation as a mapping of tree structures, using the tag and attribute names in the source document to identify what items should be matched against, and then describing the output document in terms of these.

For example, a script which changes the name of every occurrence of an *Integer* data type into 'int', and every real and boolean into their Java types, could be:

```
<xsl:template match = "UML:DataType">
<xsl:if test = "@name = 'Integer'">
<UML:DataType xmi.id = "{@xmi.id}" name = "int"
  visibility = "{@visibility}"
  isSpecification = "{@isSpecification}"
  isRoot = "{@isRoot}" isLeaf = "{@isLeaf}"
  isAbstract = "{@isAbstract}"/>
</xsl:if>
<xsl:if test = "@name = 'Real'">
<UML:DataType xmi.id = "{@xmi.id}" name = "double"
  visibility = "{@visibility}"
  isSpecification = "{@isSpecification}"
  isRoot = "{@isRoot}" isLeaf = "{@isLeaf}"
  isAbstract = "{@isAbstract}"/>
</xsl:if>
<xsl:if test = "@name = 'Boolean'">
<UML:DataType xmi.id = "{@xmi.id}" name = "boolean"
  visibility = "{@visibility}"
  isSpecification = "{@isSpecification}"
  isRoot = "{@isRoot}" isLeaf = "{@isLeaf}"
  isAbstract = "{@isAbstract}"/>
</xsl:if>
</xsl:template>
```

The first two lines specify that the transformation should apply to UML data type model elements, whose name is 'Integer', the body of the first *xsl : if* tag describes the output *UML : DataType* tag in terms of the input matched element: all attribute values of the input are simply copied to the output, except for the name, which is set to 'int'. Similarly for the other *if* tags.

The XSLT approach has the following advantages:

- It is a low cost technology requiring only a text editor to write the XSLT files and a browser such as IE or Mozilla to run them.
- XML has become the standard language of data interchange between tools, so XSLT is widely used and understood.

However it also has several disadvantages:

- It is very verbose, requiring all details of the output (not merely those parts which are changed from the input) to be specified. This means that mappings can become unwieldy and unreadable.
- It is difficult to separate the source and target parts of rules, and the filtering constraints.
- To write the rules, knowledge of the precise textual form of the input and output is needed, rather than the abstract structure of the model languages.
- Debugging of XSLT is very difficult without tools such as Xselerator [54].
- The transformations supported by XSLT are limited to top-down parsing, so that multiple traversals of the input tree structures may be needed in some cases.

- All data is passed by value, resulting in inefficiencies.

9.5.2   Rose Extensibility Interface (REI)

This is an alternative transformation technique, using the Rational Rose CASE tool. Rose provides an extensibility interface, REI, to enable developers to create software which extends and customises the Rose tool for particular purposes [40]. The REI is based on a metamodel of the Rational Rose models, which is very similar to the UML metamodel used in XMI. This enables Rose models to be manipulated and transformed. The actual language used to program such actions is the internal Rose scripting language, BasicScript, which is similar to the Visual Basic language used as the standard Windows scripting language. Rose provides a script editor for writing and debugging BasicScript programs.

A key REI metamodel entity is *Class*, representing class model elements. For this entity there are the BasicScript actions *AddOperation*, *AddParameter*, *AddAttribute*, *DeleteAttribute*, *DeleteOperation*, etc, to modify the features of particular classes in a model.

The following script function performs the same transformation as the XSLT example above:

```
Sub ChangeDataType (inCat As Category)
  Dim aClass As Class
  Dim aAttribute As Attribute

  For i% = 1 To inCat.Classes.Count
    Set aClass = inCat.Classes.GetAt(i%)
    For k% = 1 To aClass.Attributes.Count
      Set aAttribute = aClass.Attributes.GetAt(k%)
      Select Case aAttribute.Type
        Case "Integer"
             aAttribute.Type = "int"
        Case "Real"
             aAttribute.Type = "double"
        Case "Boolean"
             aAttribute.Type = "boolean"
      End Select
    Next k%
  Next i%
End Sub
```

The *inCat.Classes* collection is a list of all the classes in the input model, the outer for loop iterates through each of these, modifying the types of the attributes from PIM to PSM (Java) types.

In comparison to the XSLT approach, the REI method of implementing transformations has the following disadvantages:

- Greater expertise in programming is needed for REI, in particular, knowledge of Visual Basic is necessary.

- It requires use and purchase of Rational Rose.

But REI has the advantages:

- REI scripts are clearer to read and easier to maintain. They only need to refer to the items which are changed in the transformation.
- The programmer is dealing directly with models, not with (very large) chunks of text representing the models.

9.5.3   Java Metadata Interface (JMI)

Another transformation approach is to use the Java Metadata Interface (JMI), which provides Java interfaces to access and manipulate metamodels, including the UML 2.0 metamodel. Using this approach, a UML model to be transformed is stored in XMI format and used to populate a metamodel repository for UML. JMI methods are then used to query and update this repository in order to implement a transformation. Like the REI approach, this works at the level of models and is therefore preferable to a text-based approach such as XSLT. However it does require Java expertise.

JMI is defined in the *javax.jmi.* packages of Java 1.5. Documentation is at: http://java.sun.com/products/jmi/.

9.6   MDA tools

There are as yet relatively few tools which support MDA, due to the recent development of the MDA approach. Some commercial tools are described in the following.

OptimalJ.   This is a product of Compuware [35]. The tool uses standard UML as its modelling notation, and supports the construction of PIMs and J2EE PSMs, and the generation of executable Java code from these PSMs. OptimalJ utilises various design patterns, such as the Facade pattern, to structure the generated code and make it more comprehensible. Models can be imported and exported in XMI format, and checked for violations of UML and OptimalJ rules. Due to the complexity of J2EE, the time saving of automatically generating J2EE applications via OptimalJ, compared to manual code production, is significant. Some limitations of OptimalJ are due to its specific focus on J2EE as a platform: only J2EE PSMs are supported, and restrictions on PIMs reflect the intended implementation (for example, all classes must have primary keys, and Java/SQL keywords such as 'Order' must be avoided).

Codagen Architect.   This tool (http://www.codagen.com/products/architect/) supports UML class, statechart, sequence, collaboration and use case diagrams, and code generation from UML models to Java, C#, C++ and Visual Basic.

J2EE and .Net platforms are supported. Like OptimalJ, it supports select-ive user adaption of generated code, to enable manual maintenance of some sections of the code.

SosyInc Modeller and Transformation Engine. This system (http://www.sosyinc.com) uses a UML-like notation to define class diagrams, from which code in Visual Basic or Java can be generated automatically. It includes some specification of behavioural logic in a 'functional model' in or-der that complete executable code can be produced. Prototype GUIs can be generated, and security controls can be specified at the model level.

9.7   Summary

There has been a long history of research on the use of transformations to carry out design and program refinement. The work of Gries [18] used transforma-tions to map specifications (as postconditions) into programs which established the specifications. Extensive strategies and tool support for design refinement by transformation were developed in the 1980s and 1990s [47], leading to sys-tems such as KIDS. Transformations are the focus of much current work on the MDA, for example, http://qvtp.org/ provide a detailed proposal for transform-ations, queries and views for the prospective OMG MOF 2.0 QVT standard.

9.8   Exercises

1 Formally express the transformation of Figure 9.15 as a relationship between models, where i in the first model is implemented by $br[index]$ in the second. An ordered association such as br has an extent which is a map from objects of the source class to sequences of objects of the target class.

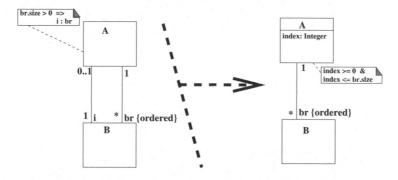

Figure 9.15: Transforming index association into an attribute

2 Explain why the replacement of associations by foreign keys transformation
cannot be applied to many-many associations.

3 (Project) Define a profile and marking transformation strategy to transform
UML PIMs into C++ PSMs and C++ code.

4 If C is a subclass of two classes A and B, how are the extents of these
classes related?

Chapter 10

Case Studies of Web System Development

In this chapter we present a complete development of the online property search system, using the UML2Web synthesis tool. We also illustrate the automated generation of a JSP-based architecture for a web system.

10.1 Property system specification

The use cases of the property search system that we will synthesise code for are shown in Figure 10.1 and the abstract class diagram is shown in Figure 10.2.

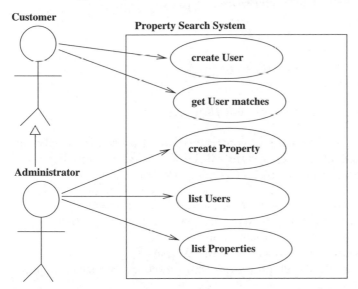

Figure 10.1: PIM use case diagram of property search system

The constraints of this system in LOCA are:

1. $C1$ 'A user's minimum price must be at least 0, and less than or equal to

269

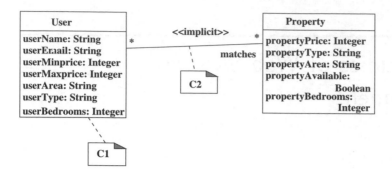

Figure 10.2: PIM class diagram of property search system

their maximum price choice':

$$0 \leq userMinprice \ \&$$
$$userMinprice \leq userMaxprice$$

as a class invariant of *User*.

2. *C*2 'A property matches a user's requirements if its price is in their range, it is available, has at least as many bedrooms as they require, and is of the same type and in the same area as required':

$$userMinprice \leq propertyPrice \ \&$$
$$userMaxprice \geq propertyPrice \ \&$$
$$userArea = propertyArea \ \&$$
$$userType = propertyType \ \&$$
$$userBedrooms \leq propertyBedrooms \ \&$$
$$propertyAvailable = true$$

This defines the implicit association *User_Property*.

In addition to the class diagram and constraints, we also need to specify the operations that a user of the web system will be able to carry out. These are based on the use cases of Figure 10.1. The operations are therefore:

- *createUser* – to define a new user and add it to the system.
- *createProperty* – to define a new property and add it to the system.
- *listUser* – to list all users in the system.
- *listProperty* – to list all properties in the system.
- *getUsermatches* – to list all properties that match a given user's requirements.

Before a web system can be generated, the data model needs to be refined:

- Primary keys need to be introduced for all entities to be persistently represented in the data repository of the system.

- Explicit many-many associations need to be replaced by one-many associations.
- Foreign keys need to be introduced in place of explicit many-one associations.

In this case the *User_Property* association is implicit, so no further refinement other than providing primary keys for the entities is needed. Figure 10.3 shows the refined model.

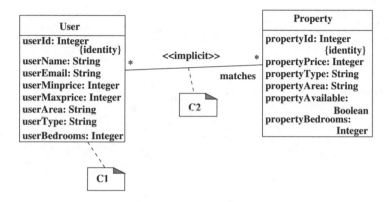

Figure 10.3: Refined class diagram of property search system

10.2 Web system generation

Three kinds of component are generated by the UML2Web tool from the specification described above:

1. Java classes which generate web pages as HTML text, for the interface of the application.
2. Java servlets, which receive requests from these web pages and process them, returning either an error page if some error has occurred in the input data or in processing, or the next page in the interaction sequence of the system.
3. A database interface, which is used by the servlets to update and query the data tables of the application.

Figure 10.4 shows the interaction sequence of the application. Figure 10.5 shows the hierarchy of web page generation classes for the property search application.

Figure 10.6 shows the supplier-clientship dependencies between the property system components.

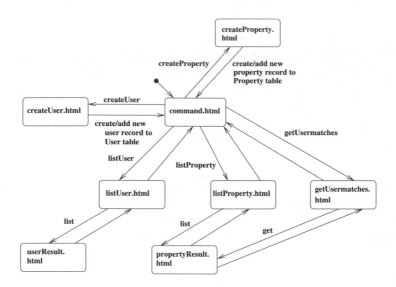

Figure 10.4: Interaction sequence of property search system

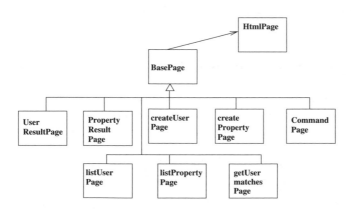

Figure 10.5: Classes for web-page generation

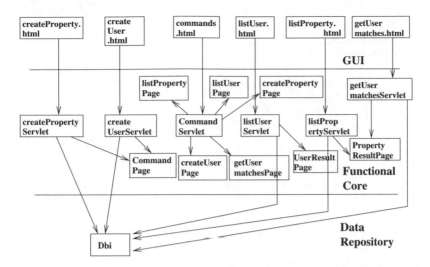

Figure 10.6: Complete architecture of property search system

10.3 Interface components

The base page of the system is defined by the class:

```
public class BasePage
{ protected HtmlPage page = new HtmlPage();
  protected HtmlHead head =
    new HtmlHead("Web System");
 protected HtmlBody body = new HtmlBody();

  public BasePage()
  { page.setHead(head);
    page.setBody(body);
  }

  public String toString()
  { return page.getHtml(); }
}
```

This can be modified as required to construct (for example) a common background image or colour for all the web pages of the system:

```
public class BasePage
{ protected HtmlPage page = new HtmlPage();
  protected HtmlHead head =
    new HtmlHead("Web System");
 protected HtmlBody body = new HtmlBody();

  public BasePage()
  { body.setFooter("Property Search UK <A HREF =
\"http://localhost:8080/commands.html\">Home</A>");
```

```
    body.setAttribute("bgcolor","yellow");
    page.setHead(head);
    page.setBody(body);
  }


  public String toString()
  { return page.getHtml(); }
}
```

This adds a footer with a link back to the command page, and sets the background colour of all the pages to yellow.

The base page class is extended and specialised to produce all the pages used in the system:

- *commands.html*, created by *CommandPage*
- *createUser.html*, created by *createUserPage*
- *createProperty.html*, created by *createPropertyPage*
- *listUser.html*, created by *listUserPage* and its results displayed by *UserResultPage*
- *listProperty.html*, created by *listPropertyPage* and its results displayed by *PropertyResultPage*
- *getUsermatches.html*, created by *getUsermatchesPage* and its results displayed by *PropertyResultPage*.

The command page is created by the following class:

```
public class CommandPage extends BasePage
{ private HtmlForm form = new HtmlForm();
  private HtmlInput createUserbutton = new HtmlInput();
  private HtmlInput createPropertybutton = new HtmlInput();
  private HtmlInput listUserbutton = new HtmlInput();
  private HtmlInput listPropertybutton = new HtmlInput();
  private HtmlInput getUsermatchesbutton = new HtmlInput();

  public CommandPage()
  { super();
    form.setAttribute("method","POST");
        form.setAttribute("action",
                "http://localhost:8080/servlet/CommandServlet");
    createUserbutton.setAttribute("value","createUser");
    createUserbutton.setAttribute("name","createUser");
    createUserbutton.setAttribute("type","submit");
    form.add(createUserbutton);
    createPropertybutton.setAttribute("value","createProperty");
    createPropertybutton.setAttribute("name","createProperty");
    createPropertybutton.setAttribute("type","submit");
    form.add(createPropertybutton);
    listUserbutton.setAttribute("value","listUser");
    listUserbutton.setAttribute("name","listUser");
    listUserbutton.setAttribute("type","submit");
```

```
      form.add(listUserbutton);
      listPropertybutton.setAttribute("value","listProperty");
      listPropertybutton.setAttribute("name","listProperty");
      listPropertybutton.setAttribute("type","submit");
      form.add(listPropertybutton);
      getUsermatchesbutton.setAttribute("value","getUsermatches");
      getUsermatchesbutton.setAttribute("name","getUsermatches");
      getUsermatchesbutton.setAttribute("type","submit");
      form.add(getUsermatchesbutton);
      body.add(form);
   }
}
```

This produces the web page of Figure 10.7.

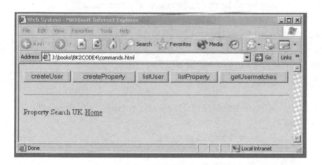

Figure 10.7: commands.html

The page for registering new users is generated by the following class:

```
public class createUserPage extends BasePage
{ protected HtmlForm form = new HtmlForm();
  protected HtmlInput button = new HtmlInput();

  public createUserPage()
  { super();
    HtmlText heading = new HtmlText("create User form","h1");
    body.add(0,heading);
    form.setAttribute("action",
        "http://localhost:8080/servlet/createUserServlet");
    HtmlItem para = new HtmlItem("p");
    form.setAttribute("method","POST");
    button.setAttribute("type","submit");
    button.setAttribute("value","create");
    body.add(form);
```

```
HtmlText userIdLabel = new HtmlText("userId","strong");
form.add(userIdLabel);
HtmlInput userIdField = new HtmlInput();
userIdField.setAttribute("type","text");
userIdField.setAttribute("name","userId");
form.add(userIdField);
form.add(para);
HtmlText userNameLabel = new HtmlText("userName","strong");
form.add(userNameLabel);
HtmlInput userNameField = new HtmlInput();
userNameField.setAttribute("type","text");
userNameField.setAttribute("name","userName");
form.add(userNameField);
form.add(para);
HtmlText userEmailLabel = new HtmlText("userEmail","strong");
form.add(userEmailLabel);
HtmlInput userEmailField = new HtmlInput();
userEmailField.setAttribute("type","text");
userEmailField.setAttribute("name","userEmail");
form.add(userEmailField);
form.add(para);
HtmlText userMinpriceLabel = new HtmlText("userMinprice","strong");
form.add(userMinpriceLabel);
HtmlInput userMinpriceField = new HtmlInput();
userMinpriceField.setAttribute("type","text");
userMinpriceField.setAttribute("name","userMinprice");
form.add(userMinpriceField);
form.add(para);
HtmlText userMaxpriceLabel = new HtmlText("userMaxprice","strong");
form.add(userMaxpriceLabel);
HtmlInput userMaxpriceField = new HtmlInput();
userMaxpriceField.setAttribute("type","text");
userMaxpriceField.setAttribute("name","userMaxprice");
form.add(userMaxpriceField);
form.add(para);
HtmlText userAreaLabel = new HtmlText("userArea","strong");
form.add(userAreaLabel);
HtmlInput userAreaField = new HtmlInput();
userAreaField.setAttribute("type","text");
userAreaField.setAttribute("name","userArea");
form.add(userAreaField);
form.add(para);
HtmlText userTypeLabel = new HtmlText("userType","strong");
form.add(userTypeLabel);
HtmlInput userTypeField = new HtmlInput();
userTypeField.setAttribute("type","text");
userTypeField.setAttribute("name","userType");
form.add(userTypeField);
form.add(para);
HtmlText userBedroomsLabel = new HtmlText("userBedrooms","strong");
```

```
        form.add(userBedroomsLabel);
        HtmlInput userBedroomsField = new HtmlInput();
        userBedroomsField.setAttribute("type","text");
        userBedroomsField.setAttribute("name","userBedrooms");
        form.add(userBedroomsField);
        form.add(para);
        form.add(button);
    }
}
```

This produces the web page of Figure 10.8.

Figure 10.8: createUser.html

The class for generating the *createProperty* web page is very similar to that for users:

```
public class createPropertyPage extends BasePage
{ protected HtmlForm form = new HtmlForm();
  protected HtmlInput button = new HtmlInput();

  public createPropertyPage()
  { super();
    HtmlText heading = new HtmlText("create Property form","h1");
    body.add(0,heading);
    form.setAttribute("action",
      "http://localhost:8080/servlet/createPropertyServlet");
    HtmlItem para = new HtmlItem("p");
```

```
    form.setAttribute("method","POST");
    button.setAttribute("type","submit");
    button.setAttribute("value","create");
    body.add(form);
    HtmlText propertyIdLabel = new HtmlText("propertyId","strong");
    form.add(propertyIdLabel);
    HtmlInput propertyIdField = new HtmlInput();
    propertyIdField.setAttribute("type","text");
    propertyIdField.setAttribute("name","propertyId");
    form.add(propertyIdField);
    form.add(para);
    HtmlText propertyPriceLabel = new HtmlText("propertyPrice","strong");
    form.add(propertyPriceLabel);
    HtmlInput propertyPriceField = new HtmlInput();
    propertyPriceField.setAttribute("type","text");
    propertyPriceField.setAttribute("name","propertyPrice");
    form.add(propertyPriceField);
    form.add(para);
    HtmlText propertyTypeLabel = new HtmlText("propertyType","strong");
    form.add(propertyTypeLabel);
    HtmlInput propertyTypeField = new HtmlInput();
    propertyTypeField.setAttribute("type","text");
    propertyTypeField.setAttribute("name","propertyType");
    form.add(propertyTypeField);
    form.add(para);
    HtmlText propertyAreaLabel = new HtmlText("propertyArea","strong");
    form.add(propertyAreaLabel);
    HtmlInput propertyAreaField = new HtmlInput();
    propertyAreaField.setAttribute("type","text");
    propertyAreaField.setAttribute("name","propertyArea");
    form.add(propertyAreaField);
    form.add(para);
    HtmlText propertyAvailableLabel =
      new HtmlText("propertyAvailable","strong");
    form.add(propertyAvailableLabel);
    HtmlInput propertyAvailableField = new HtmlInput();
    propertyAvailableField.setAttribute("type","text");
    propertyAvailableField.setAttribute("name","propertyAvailable");
    form.add(propertyAvailableField);
    form.add(para);
    HtmlText propertyBedroomsLabel =
      new HtmlText("propertyBedrooms","strong");
    form.add(propertyBedroomsLabel);
    HtmlInput propertyBedroomsField = new HtmlInput();
    propertyBedroomsField.setAttribute("type","text");
    propertyBedroomsField.setAttribute("name","propertyBedrooms");
    form.add(propertyBedroomsField);
    form.add(para);
    form.add(button);
  }
```

```
}
```

The web pages for listing all rows of a database table simply consist of a command button:

```
public class listUserPage extends BasePage
{ protected HtmlForm form = new HtmlForm();
  protected HtmlInput button = new HtmlInput();

  public listUserPage()
  { super();
    HtmlText heading = new HtmlText("list User form","h1");
    body.add(0,heading);
    form.setAttribute("action",
      "http://localhost:8080/servlet/listUserServlet");
    HtmlItem para = new HtmlItem("p");
    form.setAttribute("method","POST");
    button.setAttribute("type","submit");
    button.setAttribute("value","list");
    body.add(form);
    form.add(button);
  }
}
```

GET could be used instead of POST here, to allow browsers to cache the results of the query for later redisplay in the same browsing session.

The results of this command are displayed using the *UserResultPage* class, which generates an HTML table from the rows in a given result set:

```
import java.sql.*;

public class UserResultPage extends BasePage
{ private HtmlTable table = new HtmlTable();
  private HtmlTableRow header = new HtmlTableRow();

  public UserResultPage()
  { table.setAttribute("border","2");
    header.addCell(new HtmlTableData("userId"));
    header.addCell(new HtmlTableData("userName"));
    header.addCell(new HtmlTableData("userEmail"));
    header.addCell(new HtmlTableData("userMinprice"));
    header.addCell(new HtmlTableData("userMaxprice"));
    header.addCell(new HtmlTableData("userArea"));
    header.addCell(new HtmlTableData("userType"));
    header.addCell(new HtmlTableData("userBedrooms"));
    table.addRow(header);
    body.add(table);
  }

  public void addRow(ResultSet resultSet)
  { HtmlTableRow row = new HtmlTableRow();
```

```
    try {
      row.addCell(new HtmlTableData("" +
                    resultSet.getInt("userId")));
      row.addCell(new HtmlTableData("" +
                    resultSet.getString("userName")));
      row.addCell(new HtmlTableData("" +
                    resultSet.getString("userEmail")));
      row.addCell(new HtmlTableData("" +
                    resultSet.getInt("userMinprice")));
      row.addCell(new HtmlTableData("" +
                    resultSet.getInt("userMaxprice")));
      row.addCell(new HtmlTableData("" +
                    resultSet.getString("userArea")));
      row.addCell(new HtmlTableData("" +
                    resultSet.getString("userType")));
      row.addCell(new HtmlTableData("" +
                    resultSet.getInt("userBedrooms")));
    } catch (Exception e) { e.printStackTrace(); }
    table.addRow(row);
  }
}
```

The form for finding all matches of a given user contains a field for entering the user id:

```
public class getUsermatchesPage extends BasePage
{ protected HtmlForm form = new HtmlForm();
  protected HtmlInput button = new HtmlInput();

  public getUsermatchesPage()
  { super();
    HtmlText heading = new HtmlText("get Usermatches form","h1");
    body.add(0,heading);
    form.setAttribute("action",
      "http://localhost:8080/servlet/getUsermatchesServlet");
    HtmlItem para = new HtmlItem("p");
    form.setAttribute("method","POST");
    button.setAttribute("type","submit");
    button.setAttribute("value","get");
    body.add(form);
    HtmlText userIdLabel = new HtmlText("userId","strong");
    form.add(userIdLabel);
    HtmlInput userIdField = new HtmlInput();
    userIdField.setAttribute("type","text");
    userIdField.setAttribute("name","userId");
    form.add(userIdField);
    form.add(para);
    form.add(button);
  }
}
```

Again, GET could be used.

10.4   Servlets

For each input web page there is a servlet which responds to a request from
that page. In the case of the *commands.html* page, the servlet simply returns
the input web page of the requested command:

```java
import java.io.*;
import java.util.*;
import javax.servlet.http.*;
import javax.servlet.*;
public class CommandServlet extends HttpServlet
{ public CommandServlet() {}

  public void init(ServletConfig cfg)
  throws ServletException
  { super.init(cfg); }

  public void doGet(HttpServletRequest req,
            HttpServletResponse res)
  throws ServletException, IOException
  { res.setContentType("text/html");
    PrintWriter pw = res.getWriter();
    String createUserC = req.getParameter("createUser");
    if (createUserC != null)
    { pw.println(new createUserPage()); }
    String createPropertyC = req.getParameter("createProperty");
    if (createPropertyC != null)
    { pw.println(new createPropertyPage()); }
    String listUserC = req.getParameter("listUser");
    if (listUserC != null)
    { pw.println(new listUserPage()); }
    String listPropertyC = req.getParameter("listProperty");
    if (listPropertyC != null)
    { pw.println(new listPropertyPage()); }
    String getUsermatchesC = req.getParameter("getUsermatches");
    if (getUsermatchesC != null)
    { pw.println(new getUsermatchesPage()); }
    pw.close();
  }

  public void doPost(HttpServletRequest req,
            HttpServletResponse res)
  throws ServletException, IOException
  { doGet(req,res); }

}
```

Hard-coded (static) web pages could be used instead of dynamically generated
pages, however for more complex systems dynamic pages are more flexible.
For example, the possible categories of properties could be listed in a database
table, so that *createPropertyPage* and *createUserPage* could look up the current

categories and always generate HTML forms with the correct lists of options
for the property type attribute.

The servlet for the *createUser* operation is:

```
import java.io.*;
import java.util.*;
import javax.servlet.http.*;
import javax.servlet.*;

public class createUserServlet extends HttpServlet
{ private Dbi dbi;

  public createUserServlet() {}

  public void init(ServletConfig cfg)
  throws ServletException
  { super.init(cfg);
    dbi = new Dbi();
  }

  public void doGet(HttpServletRequest req,
              HttpServletResponse res)
  throws ServletException, IOException
  { res.setContentType("text/html");
    PrintWriter pw = res.getWriter();
    ErrorPage errorPage = new ErrorPage();
    String userId = req.getParameter("userId");
    int iuserId = 0;
    try { iuserId = Integer.parseInt(userId); }
    catch (Exception e)
    { errorPage.addMessage(userId + " is not an integer"); }
    String userName = req.getParameter("userName");
    String userEmail = req.getParameter("userEmail");
    String userMinprice = req.getParameter("userMinprice");
    int iuserMinprice = 0;
    try { iuserMinprice = Integer.parseInt(userMinprice); }
    catch (Exception e)
    { errorPage.addMessage(userMinprice + " is not an integer"); }
    String userMaxprice = req.getParameter("userMaxprice");
    int iuserMaxprice = 0;
    try { iuserMaxprice = Integer.parseInt(userMaxprice); }
    catch (Exception e)
    { errorPage.addMessage(userMaxprice + " is not an integer"); }
    String userArea = req.getParameter("userArea");
    String userType = req.getParameter("userType");
    String userBedrooms = req.getParameter("userBedrooms");
    int iuserBedrooms = 0;
    try { iuserBedrooms = Integer.parseInt(userBedrooms); }
    catch (Exception e)
    { errorPage.addMessage(userBedrooms + " is not an integer"); }
    if (0 <= iuserMinprice) { }
```

```
      else
      { errorPage.addMessage("Constraint : 0 <= iuserMinprice failed"); }
      if (iuserMinprice <= iuserMaxprice) { }
      else
      { errorPage.addMessage(
          "Constraint : iuserMinprice <= iuserMaxprice failed"); }
      if (errorPage.hasError())
      { pw.println(errorPage); }
      else
      try
      { dbi.createUser(iuserId, userName, userEmail,
            iuserMinprice, iuserMaxprice, userArea, userType, iuserBedrooms);
        CommandPage cp = new CommandPage();
        pw.println(cp);
      } catch (Exception e)
      { e.printStackTrace();
        errorPage.addMessage("Database error");
        pw.println(errorPage); }
      pw.close();
    }

    public void doPost(HttpServletRequest req,
                HttpServletResponse res)
    throws ServletException, IOException
    { doGet(req,res); }

    public void destroy()
    { dbi.logoff(); }
}
```

This servlet checks type constraints: that the id, price and number of bedroom values entered are integers, and logical invariants of the *User* class:

1. That *userMinprice* ≥ 0
2. That *userMaxprice* $\geq$ *userMinprice*

If any of these constraints fails to be true, then a message is added to the error page, and the error page is returned to the client browser.

The error page is created by the class:

```
public class ErrorPage extends BasePage
{ private int errors = 0;
  HtmlItem para = new HtmlItem("p");

  public void addMessage(String t)
  { body.add(new HtmlText(t,"strong"));
    body.add(para);
    errors++;
  }

  public boolean hasError() { return errors > 0; }
}
```

Data is only added to the database if there have been no errors, in which case the command page is returned to the client.

The servlet for creating properties is similar:

```
import javax.servlet.http.*;
import javax.servlet.*;

public class createPropertyServlet extends HttpServlet
{ private Dbi dbi;

  public createPropertyServlet() {}

  public void init(ServletConfig cfg)
  throws ServletException
  { super.init(cfg);
    dbi = new Dbi();
  }

  public void doGet(HttpServletRequest req,
              HttpServletResponse res)
  throws ServletException, IOException
  { res.setContentType("text/html");
    PrintWriter pw = res.getWriter();
    ErrorPage errorPage = new ErrorPage();
    String propertyId = req.getParameter("propertyId");
    int ipropertyId = 0;
    try { ipropertyId = Integer.parseInt(propertyId); }
    catch (Exception e)
    { errorPage.addMessage(propertyId + " is not an integer"); }
    String propertyPrice = req.getParameter("propertyPrice");
    int ipropertyPrice = 0;
    try { ipropertyPrice = Integer.parseInt(propertyPrice); }
    catch (Exception e)
    { errorPage.addMessage(propertyPrice + " is not an integer"); }
    String propertyType = req.getParameter("propertyType");
    String propertyArea = req.getParameter("propertyArea");
    String propertyAvailable = req.getParameter("propertyAvailable");
    String propertyBedrooms = req.getParameter("propertyBedrooms");
    int ipropertyBedrooms = 0;
    try { ipropertyBedrooms = Integer.parseInt(propertyBedrooms); }
    catch (Exception e)
    { errorPage.addMessage(propertyBedrooms + " is not an integer"); }
    if (errorPage.hasError())
    { pw.println(errorPage); }
    else
    try
    { dbi.createProperty(ipropertyId, ipropertyPrice, propertyType,
          propertyArea, propertyAvailable, ipropertyBedrooms);
      CommandPage cp = new CommandPage();
      pw.println(cp);
    } catch (Exception e)
```

```
      { e.printStackTrace();
        errorPage.addMessage("Database error");
        pw.println(errorPage); }
      pw.close();
    }

    public void doPost(HttpServletRequest req,
                 HttpServletResponse res)
    throws ServletException, IOException
    { doGet(req,res); }

    public void destroy()
    { dbi.logoff(); }
}
```

The servlets for listing all users and properties have no input parameters for the requests they handle, but execute a *SELECT* * query on the relevant database table, and present the result using a *...ResultPage*:

```
import java.io.*;
import java.util.*;
import javax.servlet.http.*;
import javax.servlet.*;
import java.sql.*;

public class listUserServlet extends HttpServlet
{ private Dbi dbi;

    public listUserServlet() {}

    public void init(ServletConfig cfg)
    throws ServletException
    { super.init(cfg);
      dbi = new Dbi();
    }

    public void doGet(HttpServletRequest req,
                 HttpServletResponse res)
    throws ServletException, IOException
    { res.setContentType("text/html");
      PrintWriter pw = res.getWriter();
      try
      { ResultSet resultSet = dbi.listUser();
        UserResultPage userresultpage = new UserResultPage();
        while (resultSet.next())
        { userresultpage.addRow(resultSet); }
        pw.println(userresultpage);
        resultSet.close();
      }
      catch (Exception e)
      { e.printStackTrace(); }
```

```
    pw.close();
  }

  public void doPost(HttpServletRequest req,
              HttpServletResponse res)
  throws ServletException, IOException
  { doGet(req,res); }

  public void destroy()
  { dbi.logoff(); }
}
```

The servlet for obtaining all matching properties that meet a user's requirements is:

```
import java.io.*;
import java.util.*;
import javax.servlet.http.*;
import javax.servlet.*;
import java.sql.*;

public class getUsermatchesServlet extends HttpServlet
{ private Dbi dbi;

  public getUsermatchesServlet() {}

  public void init(ServletConfig cfg)
  throws ServletException
  { super.init(cfg);
    dbi = new Dbi();
  }

  public void doGet(HttpServletRequest req,
              HttpServletResponse res)
  throws ServletException, IOException
  { res.setContentType("text/html");
    PrintWriter pw = res.getWriter();
    ErrorPage errorPage = new ErrorPage();
    String userId = req.getParameter("userId");
    int iuserId = 0;
    try { iuserId = Integer.parseInt(userId); }
    catch (Exception e)
    { errorPage.addMessage(userId + " is not an integer"); }
    if (errorPage.hasError())
    { pw.println(errorPage); }
    else
    try { ResultSet resultSet = dbi.getUsermatches(iuserId);
       PropertyResultPage propertyresultpage = new PropertyResultPage();
       while (resultSet.next())
       { propertyresultpage.addRow(resultSet); }
       pw.println(propertyresultpage);
```

```
      resultSet.close();
  } catch (Exception e)
  { e.printStackTrace();
    errorPage.addMessage("Database error");
    pw.println(errorPage); }
  pw.close();
}

public void doPost(HttpServletRequest req,
            HttpServletResponse res)
throws ServletException, IOException
{ doGet(req,res); }

public void destroy()
{ dbi.logoff(); }
}
```

PropertyResultPage is used to list all the matching properties found.

Figure 10.9 shows the result of selecting the list property command, and Figure 10.10 the result of selecting the get matches command, for a user who wants two-bedroomed flats under £100,000 in the central area.

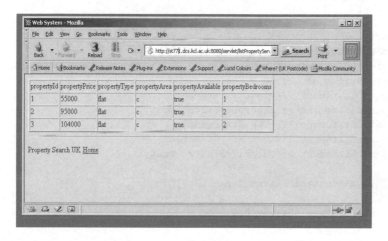

Figure 10.9: Result of *listProperty*

10.5   Database

The data repository of the system consists of a database, and a database interface class, in which the queries required by the property search application are defined as SQL prepared statements:

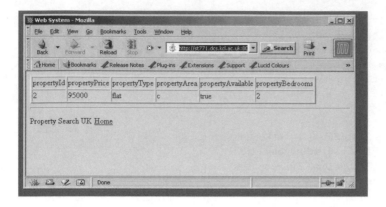

Figure 10.10: Result of *getUsermatches*

```java
import java.sql.*;

public class Dbi
{ private Connection connection;
  private static String defaultDriver = "";
  private static String defaultDb = "";
  private PreparedStatement createUserStatement;
  private PreparedStatement createPropertyStatement;
  private PreparedStatement listUserStatement;
  private PreparedStatement listPropertyStatement;
  private PreparedStatement getUsermatchesStatement;

  public Dbi() { this(defaultDriver,defaultDb); }

  public Dbi(String driver, String db)
  { try
    { Class.forName(driver);
      connection = DriverManager.getConnection(db);
      createUserStatement =
        connection.prepareStatement("INSERT INTO User " +
          "(userId,userName,userEmail,userMinprice," +
          "userMaxprice,userArea,userType,userBedrooms) VALUES " +
          "(?,?,?,?,?,?,?,?)");
      createPropertyStatement =
        connection.prepareStatement("INSERT INTO Property " +
          "(propertyId,propertyPrice,propertyType,propertyArea," +
          "propertyAvailable,propertyBedrooms) VALUES (?,?,?,?,?,?)");
      listUserStatement =
        connection.prepareStatement("SELECT * FROM User");
```

```
      listPropertyStatement =
        connection.prepareStatement("SELECT * FROM Property");
      getUsermatchesStatement =
        connection.prepareStatement("SELECT propertyId,propertyPrice," +
          "propertyType,propertyArea,propertyAvailable," +
          "propertyBedrooms FROM User,Property " +
          "WHERE (User.userMinprice <= Property.propertyPrice AND " +
          "User.userMaxprice >= Property.propertyPrice AND " +
          "User.userArea = Property.propertyArea AND " +
          "User.userType = Property.propertyType AND " +
          "User.userBedrooms <= Property.propertyBedrooms AND " +
          "Property.propertyAvailable = 'true') AND User.userId = ?");
  } catch (Exception e) { }
}

public synchronized void createUser(int userId, String userName,
  String userEmail, int userMinprice, int userMaxprice,
  String userArea, String userType, int userBedrooms)
{ try
  { createUserStatement.setInt(1, userId);
    createUserStatement.setString(2, userName);
    createUserStatement.setString(3, userEmail);
    createUserStatement.setInt(4, userMinprice);
    createUserStatement.setInt(5, userMaxprice);
    createUserStatement.setString(6, userArea);
    createUserStatement.setString(7, userType);
    createUserStatement.setInt(8, userBedrooms);
    createUserStatement.executeUpdate();
    connection.commit();
  } catch (Exception e) { e.printStackTrace(); }
}

public synchronized void createProperty(int propertyId,
  int propertyPrice,
  String propertyType, String propertyArea,
  String propertyAvailable, int propertyBedrooms)
{ try
  { createPropertyStatement.setInt(1, propertyId);
    createPropertyStatement.setInt(2, propertyPrice);
    createPropertyStatement.setString(3, propertyType);
    createPropertyStatement.setString(4, propertyArea);
    createPropertyStatement.setString(5, propertyAvailable);
    createPropertyStatement.setInt(6, propertyBedrooms);
    createPropertyStatement.executeUpdate();
    connection.commit();
  } catch (Exception e) { e.printStackTrace(); }
}

public synchronized ResultSet listUser()
{ try
```

```
   { return listUserStatement.executeQuery();
   } catch (Exception e) { e.printStackTrace(); }
 return null; }

public synchronized ResultSet listProperty()
{ try
  { return listPropertyStatement.executeQuery();
  } catch (Exception e) { e.printStackTrace(); }
 return null; }

public synchronized ResultSet getUsermatches(int userId)
{ try
  { getUsermatchesStatement.setInt(1, userId);
    return getUsermatchesStatement.executeQuery();
  } catch (Exception e) { e.printStackTrace(); }
 return null; }

public synchronized void logoff()
{ try { connection.close(); }
  catch (Exception e) { e.printStackTrace(); }
}
}
```

SELECT * may not return the fields of the table in the order they are defined
in the table. It is more portable to name all the fields of the table directly,
and UML2Web has an option for generating this version of prepared SQL
statements.

To specify a particular database, we set the driver and database name
variables as required. For a postgres database, for example, we could have:

```
import java.sql.*;

public class Dbi
{ private Connection connection;
  private static String defaultDriver = "org.postgresql.Driver";
  private static String defaultDb = "jdbc:postgresql:propdb";
  ...
```

To create the property system tables, the *psql* interactive database program
is used:

```
kcl@pc109 ~/pgdata $ psql propdb
Welcome to psql, the PostgreSQL interactive terminal.

Type:  \copyright for distribution terms
       \h for help with SQL commands
       \? for help on internal slash commands
       \g or terminate with semicolon to execute query
       \q to quit

propdb=# CREATE TABLE Property
```

```
propdb-# (propertyId INT2,
propdb(#  propertyPrice INT,
propdb(#  propertyType CHAR(30),
propdb(#  propertyArea CHAR(30),
propdb(#  propertyAvailable CHAR(10),
propdb(#  propertyBedrooms INT);
```

This statement creates an empty property table with the specified columns.

10.6 JSP architecture example: Cat database

This example illustrates the generation of a web architecture based on JSPs instead of servlets, and provides another example of how class invariants are encoded as constraint checking code in the generated web system.

The specification class diagram is shown in Figure 10.11. The system records information on cats, eg, as insured by a pet insurance company, and maintains a business rule that if a cat is under five years old, its monthly insurance fee is £5, otherwise its fee is £8.

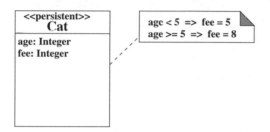

Figure 10.11: Specification class diagram of cat records system

The use cases are to create a new cat and to list all cats. The design class diagram (Figure 10.12) adds an integer *catId : Integer* identity attribute to the *Cat* entity.

Figure 10.13 shows the statechart of the system, with error pages omitted.

The architecture of the generated web system is shown in Figure 10.14. The HTML files *createCat.html* and *listCat.html* give input forms for these operations, and invoke corresponding JSPs *createCat.jsp* and *listCat.jsp*. The file *commands.html* is included in each JSP to provide navigation to the command options:

```
<p><a href="createCat.html">createCat</a></p>
<p><a href="listCat.html">listCat</a></p>
```

createCat.jsp copies the form data to the *CatBean*, a statefull session bean, checks if the data was correct (of the correct type and satisfying the invariants) using the *iscreateCaterror* method, and displays any errors. If there are no errors it updates the database via the bean:

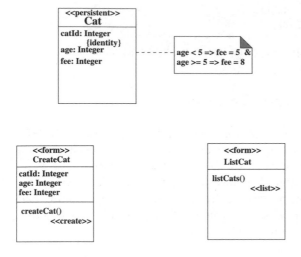

Figure 10.12: Design class diagram of cat records system

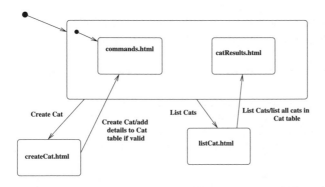

Figure 10.13: Interaction statechart of cat records system

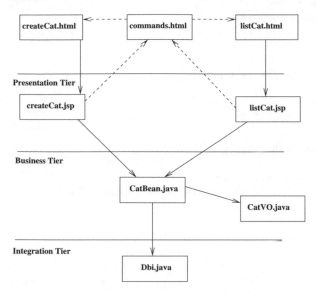

Figure 10.14: Architecture of cat records system

```
<jsp:useBean id="cat" scope="session"
 class="beans.CatBean"/>
<jsp:setProperty name="cat"  property="catId"  param="catId"/>
<jsp:setProperty name="cat"  property="age"  param="age"/>
<jsp:setProperty name="cat"  property="fee"  param="fee"/>

<html>
<head><title>createCat</title></head>
<body>
<h1>createCat</h1>
<% if (cat.iscreateCaterror())
{ %> <h2>Error in data: <%= cat.errors() %></h2>
<h2>Press Back to re-enter</h2> <% }
else { cat.createCat(); %>
<h2>createCat performed</h2>
<% } %>

<hr>

<%@ include file="commands.html" %>
</body>
</html>
```

listCat.jsp obtains the current list of cat objects from the bean and formats them into a table:

```
<%@ page import = "java.util.*" %>
```

```
<%@ page import = "beans.*" %>
<jsp:useBean id="cat" scope="session"
 class="beans.CatBean"/>

<html>
<head><title>listCat results</title></head>
<body>
<h1>listCat results</h1>
<% Iterator cats = cat.listCat(); %>
<table border="1">
<tr><th>catId</th> <th>age</th> <th>fee</th></tr>
<% while (cats.hasNext())
{ CatVO catVO = (CatVO) cats.next(); %>
<tr><td><%= catVO.getcatId() %></td> <td><%= catVO.getage() %></td>
<td><%= catVO.getfee() %></td></tr>
<% } %>
</table>

<hr>

<%@ include file="commands.html" %>
</body>
</html>
```

The *CatBean* performs type and invariant checking of attributes, and interfaces to the *Dbi* to update and query the database table for *Cat*:

```
package beans;

import java.util.*;
import java.sql.*;

public class CatBean
{ Dbi dbi = new Dbi();
 private String catId = "";
 private int icatId = 0;
 private String age = "";
 private int iage = 0;
 private String fee = "";
 private int ifee = 0;
  private Vector errors = new Vector();

  public CatBean() {}

  public void setcatId(String catIdx)
  { catId = catIdx; }

  public void setage(String agex)
  { age = agex; }

  public void setfee(String feex)
```

```
{ fee = feex; }

public void resetData()
{ catId = "";
age = "";
fee = "";
}

public boolean iscreateCaterror()
{ errors.clear();
  try { icatId = Integer.parseInt(catId); }
  catch (Exception e)
  { errors.add(catId + " is not an integer"); }
  try { iage = Integer.parseInt(age); }
  catch (Exception e)
  { errors.add(age + " is not an integer"); }
  try { ifee = Integer.parseInt(fee); }
  catch (Exception e)
  { errors.add(fee + " is not an integer"); }
  if (!(iage < 5) || (ifee == 5)) { }
  else { errors.add("Constraint: !(iage < 5) || (ifee == 5) failed"); }
  if (!(iage >= 5) || (ifee == 8)) { }
  else { errors.add("Constraint: !(iage >= 5) || (ifee == 8) failed"); }
return errors.size() > 0; }

public boolean islistCaterror()
{ errors.clear();
return errors.size() > 0; }

public String errors() { return errors.toString(); }

public void createCat()
{ dbi.createCat(icatId, iage, ifee);
  resetData(); }

public Iterator listCat()
{ ResultSet rs = dbi.listCat();
 List rs_list = new ArrayList();
 try
 { while (rs.next())
   { rs_list.add(new CatVO(rs.getInt("catId"),rs.getInt("age"),
                     rs.getInt("fee")));
   }
 } catch (Exception e) { }
 resetData();
 return rs_list.iterator();
 }
}
```

In this case the bean only checks that the invariants are true before permitting an update, however a more proactive approach which enforces a change in *fee* if a change in *age* occurs could also be adopted. The business tier is the correct place for such business rule related code, and components such as J2EE entity beans may be necessary to ensure that such invariant-maintenance code is carried out in a transactional manner.

CatVO is a 'Value Object' for the Cat entity [12], and is simply used to transfer data between the presentation and business tier (to avoid exposing classes such as *ResultSet* to the presentation tier):

```
package beans;

public class CatVO
{ private int catId;
  private int age;
  private int fee;

  public CatVO(int catIdx,int agex,
               int feex)
  { catId = catIdx;
    age = agex;
    fee = feex;
  }

  public int getcatId()
  { return catId; }

  public int getage()
  { return age; }

  public int getfee()
  { return fee; }
}
```

10.7   Summary

We have presented two simple examples of development of web systems from abstract UML models, using the UML2Web tool. Further variations on this process are possible, such as generation of J2EE components and interfaces.

Chapter 11

Catalogue of Model Transformations

In this chapter we summarise all the transformations that have been used in previous chapters, together with other well-known model transformations. A standard format is used:

Name
Description Summary of the transformation effect
Motivation Situations when the transformation could or should be used
Diagram Illustration of typical application of the transformation
Conditions Properties that must be satisfied for the transformation to be correct.

As with design patterns (which can be considered a special kind of model transformation), there are often many variants on model transformations that are possible, and some of these will also be described.

The five main categories of model transformation are:

1. Quality Improvement Transformations
2. Elaborations
3. Refinements
4. Abstractions
5. Design Patterns

11.1 Quality improvement transformations

The transformations in this category aim to improve the structure of a model, making it conform more closely to normal uses of UML notation, or improving its precision or its flexibility for extension and adaption.

Two general categories of quality improvement transformation are the removal of redundancy and the factoring out/decomposition of elements.

11.1.1 Removal of redundancies

The 'introduce superclass' transformation is one example of the removal of redundancies from a model. Normally redundancies should be eliminated – they complicate a model unnecessarily and, if implemented, lead to extra work and possibilities for program flaws. Other examples of such transformations are the removal of redundant inheritances and associations.

Name *Introduce Superclass*

Description Introduces a superclass of several existing classes, to enable common features of these classes to be factored out and placed in a single location.

Motivation In general, this transformation should be applied if there are several classes A, B, ... which have common features, and there is no existing common superclass of these classes.

Diagram Figure 11.1 shows a generic example, where the existing classes have both common attributes, operations and roles.

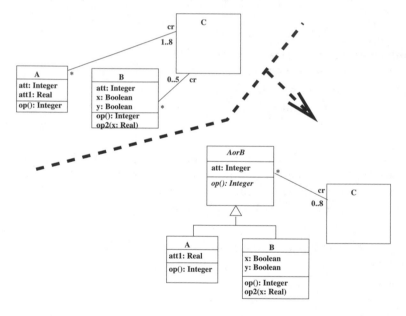

Figure 11.1: General superclass introduction

Conditions The features that are placed in the superclass must have the same intended meaning in the different subclasses, rather than an accidental coincidence of names.

The properties of the features in the superclass are the disjunction of their properties in the individual subclasses. For common roles, this means that their multiplicity on the association from the superclass is the 'strongest common generalisation' of their multiplicities on the subclass associations. Eg, if the subclass multiplicities were $m1..n1$ and

$m2..n2$, the superclass multiplicity would be $min(m1, m2)..max(n1, n2)$. For common operations, the conjunction of the individual preconditions can be used as the superclass operation precondition, and the disjunction of the individual postconditions as the superclass operation postcondition.

Common constraints of the subclasses can also be placed on the superclass.

Variations include situations where a common superclass already exists, but some common features of its subclasses are missing from it. In this case the common features are simply moved up to the superclass.

Name *Remove Redundant Association*

Description An explicit association which can be computed as a derived association from other model elements is made implicit and derived, or eliminated completely.

Motivation Such associations duplicate information needlessly. In an implementation the overhead of maintaining consistency between the association and the information it duplicates could be considerable, and prone to errors.

Diagram Figure 11.2 shows a situation where the redundant association is the relational composition of two others, in Figure 11.3 it is the inverse of another association.

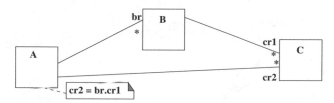

Figure 11.2: Redundant composition association

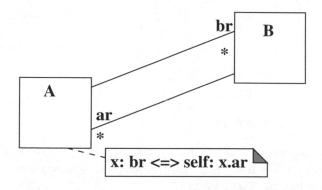

Figure 11.3: Redundant inverse association

Conditions The removed explicit association must be expressible as a derived
   association, ie, there must be a simple rule for computing it in terms of
   other model elements.

In certain cases, eg, the Observer pattern, maintaining explicit inverse associations is a valid decision, however even in these cases it is preferable to
avoid such bidirectional dependence and communication if possible, eg, by
the *update* method providing all needed information to the observer objects
directly, without the need for the observers to callback to the observable.

Name *Eliminate Redundant Inheritance*
Description If a class inherits another by two or more different paths of inheritance, remove all but one path, if possible.
Motivation A redundant inheritance conveys no extra information, but simply
   serves to complicate the model.
Diagram Figure 11.4 shows a typical situation where class A directly inherits
   from class C, and also indirectly via a more specific class B. The first
   inheritance is redundant and can be removed. (In some languages, such
   as Java, such inheritances would actually be invalid.)

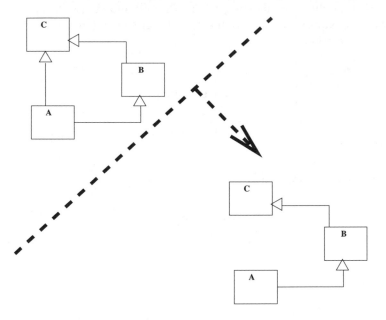

Figure 11.4: Redundant inheritance removal

Conditions The removed inheritance, eg, of E inheriting from F, must be
   genuinely redundant, ie, there must exist another chain of inheritances
   from E to F via other intermediary classes.

Name *Remove Redundant Classes*

Description Classes may be redundant because they are essentially duplicates of other classes in the model but with a different name (synonyms), or because they are not needed in the system being defined.

Motivation Duplication of classes will lead to over-complex models which are difficult to modify and analyse.

Diagram Figure 11.5 shows a typical case where class *A* and class *B* are almost identical and can be replaced by a single class.

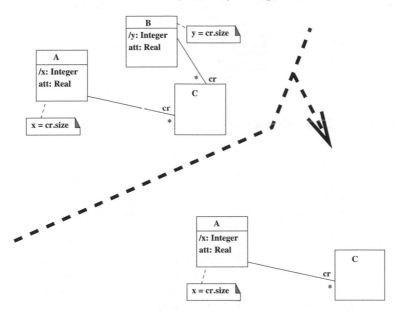

Figure 11.5: Redundant class removal

Name *Merge Partial Classes*

Description Classes may define only part of a coherent concept, other parts may be expressed in different classes and their commonalities have not been recognised. This transformation merges such classes into a single class.

Diagram Figure 11.6 shows a typical case where class *User* and class *Person* represent parts of the same concept and can probably be merged into a single class. The existence of 1-1 or 1-0..1 associations between classes is often an indicator of unnecessary separation of a single concept into two classes (in the second case it may indicate a missing specialisation-generalisation relationship, with the superclass being at the 1 end of the association).

An example in the Scrabble system could be *Row* (for horizontal words) and *Column* (for vertical words), which can be merged into the *Word* class.

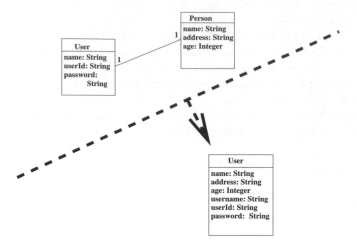

Figure 11.6: Merging partial classes

11.1.2   Factorings

Another group of transformations improve a model by factoring out certain groups of features from a class into new classes or interfaces, or factoring common features of a set of states into a new superstate.

Name *Introduce Interface(s) for Supplier Class(es)*

Description If class A is a client of class B, but only uses some of B's features, introduce an interface B_I of B which has the subset of operations of B that are used by A. Make A a client of B_I instead of B.

Motivation This reduces the dependencies in the model and enables separate development of A and B, and permits them to be placed in different layers or tiers of the system.

Diagram Figure 11.7 shows this transformation.

Conditions A must only depend on the specifications of operations of B, not on their implementation.

An example where it is important to factor out different interfaces of a class for different clients is a password database (Figure 11.8): general users can only use the *check* and *setPassword* operations, whilst the system administrator can delete and create user records.

Name *Disaggregation*

Description A class is factored into component classes.

Motivation A class may become large and unmanageable, with several loosely connected functionalities. It should be split into several classes, such as a master/controller class and helper classes, which have more coherent functionalities and data.

Diagram Figure 11.9 shows a generic example.

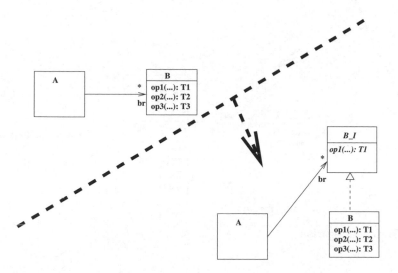

Figure 11.7: Introducing an interface

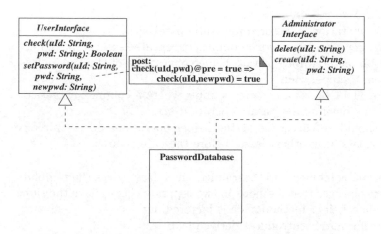

Figure 11.8: Example of interface factoring

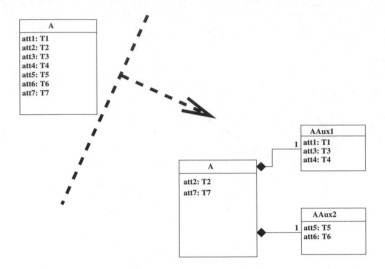

Figure 11.9: Disaggregation

Conditions The helper/component objects always exist when the master object delegates operations to them.

We used an example of this transformation to separate helper classes *EditUserPage*, *LoginPage*, etc, from servlets in the property system. Another case where it arises is in breaking up large web forms into several smaller forms (Figure 11.10 shows an example for a student accommodation agency).

Name *Factor out Sub-operations*
Description An operation is factored into sub-operations.
Motivation An operation may involve complex or repeated sub-computations. These can be factored into private helper operations of the same class, invoked from the operation.
Diagram Figure 11.11 shows a generic example where a complex expression *exp* is factored out into a separate operation *m1*.
Conditions It should be checked that the helper operations do not already exist in the class or in other classes before they are created.

This transformation, combined with 'introduce superclass', gives the template method pattern in the case that methods in two separate classes have the same remainder after their helper method code is factored out.

A similar transformation introduces derived features:

Name *Introduce Derived Features*
Description An expression *e* built from local features of a class, which reoccurs several times in a specification, is replaced by a new derived feature *f* of the class, plus the constraint $f = e$.

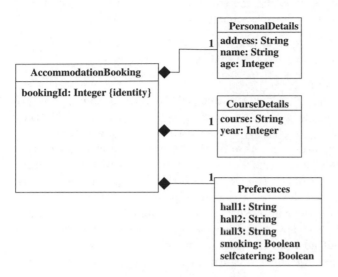

Figure 11.10: Disaggregation for web forms

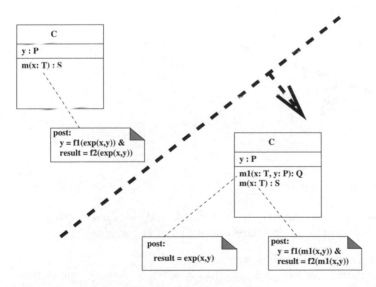

Figure 11.11: Factoring an operation

Motivation Complex repeated expressions lead to inefficient implementations. A derived feature representing the expression need only be recomputed when one of its defining features changes value.

An example in the Scrabble system is the introduction of *rackSize* in place of *rackLetters.size*.

Name *Introduce Superstate*

Description If states s_1, ..., s_n of a statechart all have a common set of outgoing transitions, ie, for a non-empty set α_1, ..., α_m of events they have transitions t_{s_1,α_1}, ..., t_{s_n,α_1}, etc, such that, for a given j, the t_{s_i,α_j} all have the same guards, actions and target states, then introduce a new superstate s of the s_i, and replace the t_{s_i,α_j} by new transitions t_{s,α_j} from s to the common target of the t_{s_i,α_j}, and with the same guard and actions. Common invariants of the substates can be placed on the superstate.

Motivation This reduces the complexity of the diagram (the number of transitions is reduced by $(n-1)*m$) and may identify a conceptually significant state that was omitted from the original model.

Diagram Figure 11.12 shows this transformation.

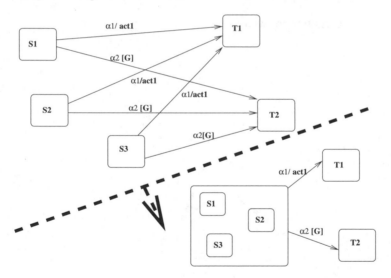

Figure 11.12: Introduce superstate

Conditions The new state can only be introduced if it does not overlap with other states (except those it entirely contains or is contained by).

Name *Introduce Entry or Exit Actions of a State*

Description If all transitions t_1, ..., t_n into a state s have the same final sequence *act* of actions, factor these out and define the entry action of s to be *act* instead.

Likewise, if all transitions with source s have a common initial action act', this can become the exit action of s.

Motivation This reduces the complexity and redundancy of the diagram. It may correspond to a more efficient implementation.

Diagram Figure 11.13 shows an example of this transformation.

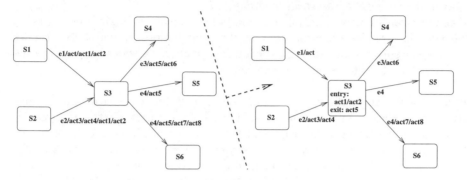

Figure 11.13: Introducing entry and exit actions

11.1.3 Other quality enhancement transformations

Name *Raise Supplier Abstraction Level*

Description If class A is a client of class B, a subclass of C, make A a client of C instead if A only uses features and properties of C.

Motivation If A depends on an over-specific class, this reduces the independence of parts of the system and makes it less easy to modify.

Diagram Figure 11.14 shows this transformation.

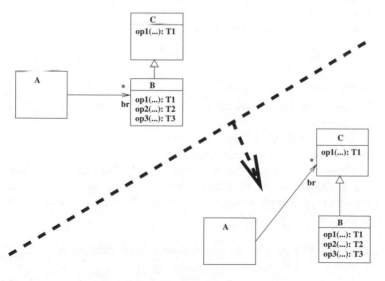

Figure 11.14: Raise supplier abstraction

Conditions The client must genuinely be independent of the specific features of its current supplier.

Name *Express OCL Constraints Graphically*
Description Replaces textual constraints by equivalent diagram elements.
Motivation Makes the properties of the model more immediately visually apparent, more readable and comprehensible by a wider range of people and analysis tools, and more concise.

Examples are multiplicity constraints on association ends, cardinality constraints on classes, subset constraints between associations, etc. If a particular kind of constraint is needed frequently in a domain or system, then a new UML stereotype abbreviating the constraint can be introduced by means of a profile, and used in the diagram instead of the constraint formula. The 'identity' stereotype of attributes is an example of this approach. UML allows new graphical icons or display styles to be used to indicate stereotyping, in addition (eg, the identity attributes could be written in bold font, instead of labelling them with '{*identity*}').

Name *Make Partial Roles Total*
Description A 0..1 multiplicity role of a class A may be turned into a 1 multiplicity role by either moving the role to a superclass of its current target, or by moving the other end to a subclass of A on which the association is total.
Motivation Total associations are generally easier to implement and manage than partial associations.
Diagram Figure 11.15 shows the 'generalise target' version of this transformation. Figure 11.16 the 'specialise source' version.
Conditions In the first version we need the condition

$$ br = \{\} \ \Rightarrow \ cr \ / = \ \{\} $$

Name *Introduce Module*
Description Groups together related classes into a single unit (eg, a UML package or subsystem).
Motivation Improves modularity of model.
Diagram Figure 11.17 shows this transformation.
Conditions The classes must represent a coherent unit. Normally if a class is included in a module so are its subclasses, aggregate part classes, and those classes which are suppliers to it and not suppliers to any other class (ie, subordinate/auxiliary classes).

This transformation can also be used to group data classes into EJBs.

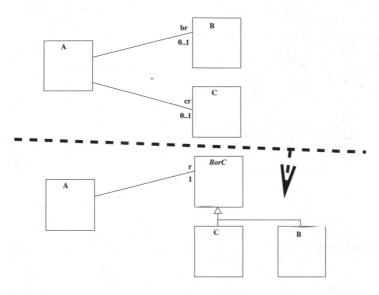

Figure 11.15: Making partial roles total (a)

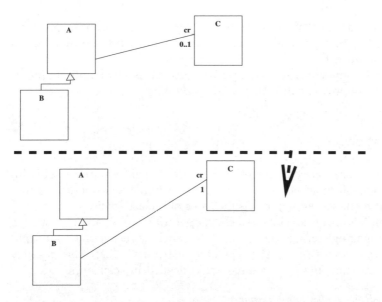

Figure 11.16: Making partial roles total (b)

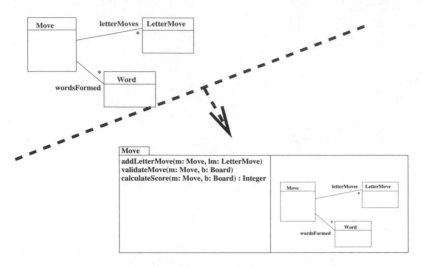

Figure 11.17: Introducing modules

Name *Simplify Postconditions*

Description A number of logical transformations can be made on postconditions of an operation to simplify its specification.

Two postconditions with the forms $A \Rightarrow B$, $A \Rightarrow C$ can be combined into a single postcondition $A \Rightarrow B \ \& \ C$.

Two postconditions with the forms $A \Rightarrow C$, $B \Rightarrow C$ can be combined into $A \ or \ B \Rightarrow C$.

If the left hand side P of a postcondition $P \Rightarrow Q$ is a test on the prestate, and is implied by a precondition of the operation, then the postcondition can be simplified to Q.

Motivation It is important to make postconditions as clear and simple as possible, to improve analysability and readability.

11.2   Elaborations

These transformations enrich a model with additional information. This includes obvious transformations such as adding attributes and operations to a class, adding new classes, adding new subclasses of a class (valid if the class is not a *leaf* class), adding constraints to a class, operation, state, association, etc. It also includes making constraints more precise, such as restricting a multiplicity range of a role, or restricting the type of an attribute. These changes may introduce inconsistency into a model, so care is needed in their application.

Name *Reduce Role Multiplicity Range*

Description A * or $a..b$ multiplicity role of a class A to class B may be reduced to a $0..p$ or $a..min(b, p)$ role, if we know from domain or other knowledge that p is the maximum possible number of B objects that the association can link to one *A* object. In particular, if *B* has cardinality *p*.

Motivation Reducing multiplicities reduces the data storage requirements of the system and may enable the use of simpler data structures (eg, arrays instead of lists). It also improves the possibility of verification via tools such as model checkers [25].

Diagram Figure 11.18 shows this transformation.

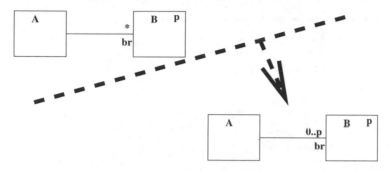

Figure 11.18: Reducing multiplicities

11.3 Refinements

These transformations are used to transform a PIM to a PSM, or to make the PIM more easy to transform to a PSM.

Name *Removal of Many-many Associations*
Description This transformation replaces a many-many association with a new class and two many-one associations.
Motivation Explicit many-many associations cannot be implemented using foreign keys in a relational database – an intermediary table would need to be used instead. This transformation is the object-oriented equivalent of introducing such a table.
Diagram This is shown in Figure 11.19.
Conditions The new class must link exactly those objects that were connected by the original association, and must not duplicate such links:

$$c1 : C \ \& \ c2 : C \ \& \ c1.ar = c2.ar \ \& \ c1.br = c2.br \ \Rightarrow \ c1 = c2$$

Name *Removal of Association Classes*
Description This transformation replaces an association class with a new class and two associations.
Motivation Association classes cannot be represented directly in many object-oriented programming languages.
Diagram This is shown in Figure 11.20.

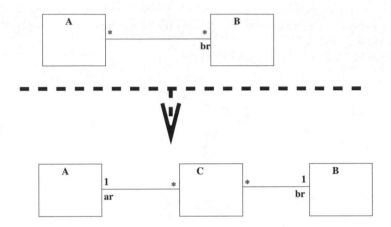

Figure 11.19: Removing a many-many association

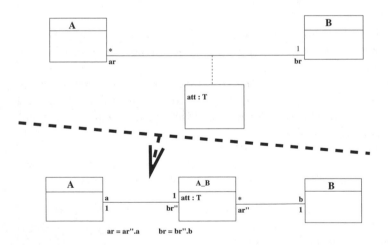

Figure 11.20: Removing an association class

Conditions The new class must link exactly those objects that were connected by the original association, and must not duplicate such links:

$$c1 : A\_B \ \& \ c2 : A\_B \ \& \ c1.a = c2.a \ \& \ c1.b = c2.b \ \Rightarrow \ c1 = c2$$

Name *Weakening preconditions or strengthening postconditions*

Description An operation precondition can be weakened (so that it is able to be applied in more situations without error) and/or its postcondition strengthened (so that its effect is determined more precisely). Both potentially move the method closer to implementation.

Diagram Figure 11.21 shows a general situation.

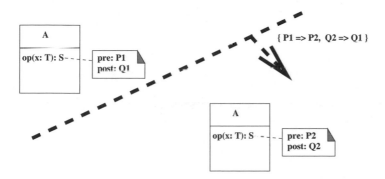

Figure 11.21: Weakening preconditions/strengthening postconditions

It should be borne in mind that the precondition of the operation in any interface used by a client will be the only precondition that such a client can assume. Working to a more general (weaker) precondition in a subclass is an issue of *defensive programming*: improving the robustness of the actual implementation of the operation so that even if the client does call it in an apparently invalid state (according to the interface), the operation will still have defined behaviour.

Name *Replace Inheritance by Association*

Description This transformation replaces inheritance of one class on another by an association from the subclass to the superclass.

Motivation This is useful to remove situations of multiple inheritance from PIMs, eg, for transformation to a Java-specific PSM, or for construction of a relational database schema.

Diagram This is shown in Figure 11.22.

Name *Replace Association by Attribute*

Description In UML 2.0, attributes of a class are equivalent to certain forms of association from the class. Embedding an association into a class as an attribute can be used as a step towards implementing it as an attribute of the class.

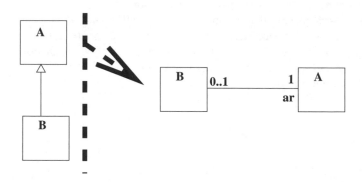

Figure 11.22: Replacing an inheritance by an association

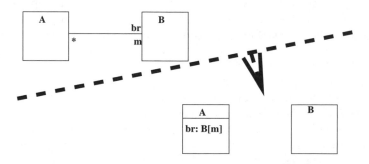

Figure 11.23: Equivalence of attributes and associations

Diagram Figure 11.23 shows the equivalence of associations and attributes. Multiplicities, visibilities, the {*ordered*} and {*unique*} constraints, and the indication / that the feature is derived, can all be mapped from the association notation into identical attribute notation.

Conditions Qualified associations cannot be represented as attributes, as there is no corresponding attribute notation, ie, for specifying map data structures. In addition the multiplicity at the owning entity end of an association cannot be generally expressed in the attribute version. For an ordinary attribute this multiplicity is ∗ and for an identity attribute it is 0..1.

Name *Introduce Primary Key*

Description This transformation applies to any persistent class. If the class does not already have a primary key, it introduces a new identity attribute, of integer type, for this class, together with extensions of the constructor of the class, and a new *get* method, to allow initialisation and read access of this attribute.

Motivation This is an essential step for implementation of a data model in a relational database.

Diagram This is shown in Figure 11.24.

Figure 11.24: Introduce primary key

Name *Replace Associations by Foreign Keys*

Description This transformation applies to any explicit many-one association between persistent classes. It assumes that primary keys already exist for the classes linked by the association. It replaces the association by embedding values of the key of the entity at the 'one' end of the association into the entity at the 'many' end.

Motivation This is an essential step for implementation of a data model in a relational database.

Diagram This is shown in Figure 11.25.

Conditions *b.akey* is equal to *a.akey* exactly when $a \mapsto b$ is in the original association. This correspondence must be maintained by implementing *addbr* and *removebr* operations in terms of the foreign key values.

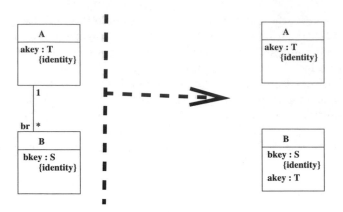

Figure 11.25: Replacing association by foreign key

Name *Amalgamate Subclasses into Superclass*
Description This transformation is the opposite of good object-oriented design,
it amalgamates all subclass features into one class, and includes a flag to
indicate which class the current object really belongs to.
Motivation This is one strategy for representing a class hierarchy in a relational database.
Diagram This is shown in Figure 11.26.

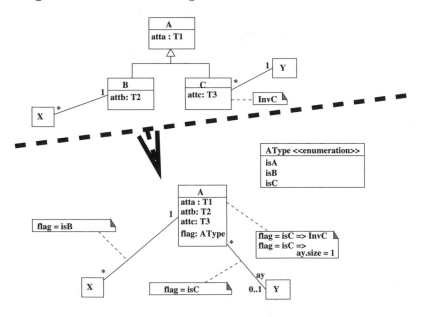

Figure 11.26: Amalgamation of subclasses transformation

Name *Make Association into Index*

Description This replaces an association i that identifies a member of another role set to the same class, by an integer index.

Motivation The resulting data structures are simpler and more efficient to implement.

Diagram Figure 11.27 shows this transformation where i in the first model is implemented by $br[index]$ in the second.

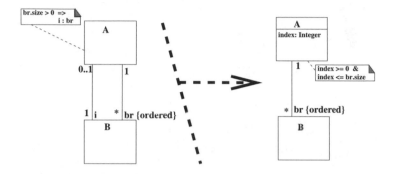

Figure 11.27: Transforming index association into an attribute

Name *Target Splitting*

Description This transformation refines the behaviour of a statechart by introducing substates of a state s and splitting a transition to s into cases for some or all of these substates.

Motivation A simple behaviour may need to be refined into subcases.

Diagram A simple case with two states is shown in Figure 11.28.

Conditions The guard G is split into disjoint guards for each of the new transitions. Here this means $G \equiv G1 \vee G2$ and $G1 \Rightarrow \neg G2$.

Name *Source Splitting*

Description This transformation refines the behaviour of a statechart by introducing substates of a state s and splitting a transition from s into cases for each of these substates.

Motivation A simple behaviour may need to be refined into subcases.

Diagram A simple case with two states is shown in Figure 11.29.

Name *Express Statechart in Pre/Post Constraints*

Description This transformation turns the statechart of a class C into a new enumerated type: $States_C$, with an element for each basic state configuration of the statechart, and an attribute $stateC : States_C$ of C, together with operation pre- and postconditions expressing the behaviour of all the statechart transitions.

If event $\alpha()$ has transitions $t\alpha_1, ..., t\alpha_{n\alpha}$ from state configurations $s\alpha_1, ..., s\alpha_{n\alpha}$ to state configurations $p\alpha_1, ..., p\alpha_{n\alpha}$ with guards $G\alpha_1, ..., G\alpha_{n\alpha}$,

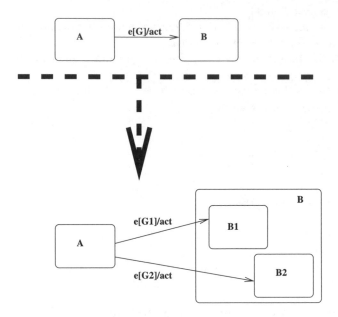

Figure 11.28: Target splitting

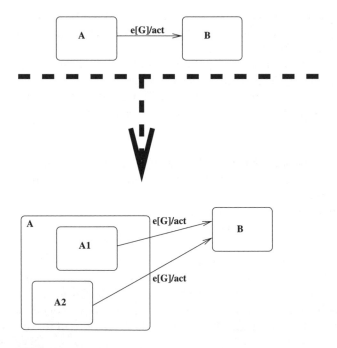

Figure 11.29: Source splitting

then the precondition of α is augmented with the condition

$$(stateC = s\alpha_1 \ \& \ G\alpha_1) \ or \ ... \ or \ (stateC = s\alpha_{n\alpha} \ \& \ G\alpha_{n\alpha})$$

and the postcondition is augmented by conjuncts

$$(stateC@pre = s\alpha_i \ \& \ G\alpha_i@pre) \ \Rightarrow \ stateC = p\alpha_i$$

for $i = 1, ..., n\alpha$.

Motivation The encoding of the statechart as explicit data and updates to this can facilitate the generation of executable code to ensure that objects of the class obey the dynamic behaviour it describes.

Name *Flattening a Statechart*

Description This transformation removes composite states and expresses their semantics in terms of their substates instead: a transition from a composite state boundary becomes duplicated as a transition from each of the enclosed states (if they do not already have a transition for that event). A transition to the composite state boundary becomes a transition to its default initial state.

Motivation The transformation reduces the complexity of the constructs used to express dynamic behaviour, making this behaviour easier to verify, although the size of the model will be increased.

Diagram Figure 11.30 shows a typical case of elimination of a composite state, Figure 11.31 shows the elimination of a concurrent composite state. Note that transitions for the same event in two components of the same concurrent composite state must synchronise (this is a semantic variation point in UML – semantics in which transitions for the same event can also occur independently are also possible).

11.4 Design patterns

Many design patterns can be viewed as model transformations, either as refinements, or as model enhancements. For example, the builder pattern can be introduced as a segregation of construction code from other parts of a class, according to the 'disaggregation' transformation. The template method pattern can be introduced by the 'factor operations' and 'introduce superclass' patterns, as described above.

Name *Introduce State Pattern*

Description An operation may consist of many cases, one for each element of an enumerated type. This explicit conditional choice can be made implicit by using polymorphism and separating the behaviour for each case into a separate subclass.

Diagram Figure 11.32 shows a general situation.

Condition Membership of the subclass for a state (eg, *A1* for *state1*) in the refined model should coincide with the state attribute having that state as its value ($att = state1$) in the original model.

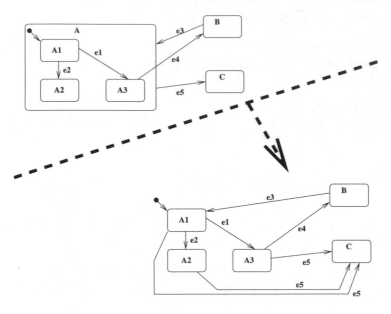

Figure 11.30: Eliminating a composite state

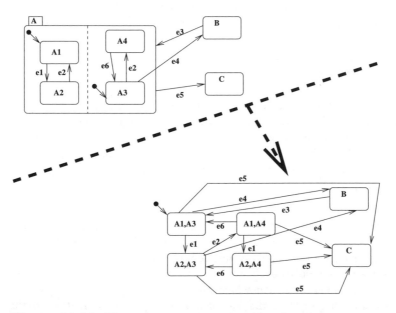

Figure 11.31: Flattening a concurrent composite state

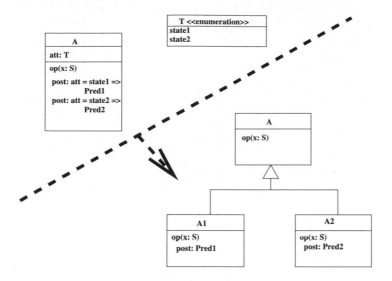

Figure 11.32: Introducing the state pattern

Bibliography

[1] C Alexander. *The Timeless Way of Building*. Oxford University Press, 1979.

[2] C Alexander, S Ishikawa, M Silverstein, M Jacobson, I Fiskdahl-King, and S Angel. *A Pattern Language*. Oxford University Press, 1977.

[3] B Anderson. The architecture handbook. In *OOPSLA Workshops*, 1991–1992.

[4] K Beck. *Extreme Programming Explained*. Addison-Wesley, 1999.

[5] B Boehm. A spiral model of software development and enhancement. *IEEE Computer*, May 1988.

[6] G Booch. *Object-oriented Analysis and Design with Applications*. Prentice Hall, 1994.

[7] G Booch, J Rumbaugh, and I Jacobson. *The Unified Modeling Language User Guide*. Addison-Wesley, 1998.

[8] B-Core UK Ltd, The BToolkit, 2002.

[9] J Cato. *User-Centered Web Design*. Addison-Wesley, 2001.

[10] S Cook and J Daniels. *Designing Object Systems: Object-Oriented Modelling with Syntropy*. Prentice Hall, Sept 1994.

[11] J Coplien. *Advanced C++ Programming Styles and Idioms*. Addison Wesley, 1991.

[12] J Crupi, D Alur, and D Malks. *Core J2EE Patterns*. Prentice Hall, 2001.

[13] CS-RR Software User Requirements Document, 1994.

[14] T DeMarco. *Structured Analysis and System Specification*. Prentice Hall, 1979.

[15] A Dix, J Finlay, G Abowd, and R Beale. *Human-Computer Interaction*. Prentice Hall, 1998.

[16] E Gamma, R Helm, R Johnson, and J Vlissides. *Design Patterns: Elements of Reusable Object-Oriented Software*. Addison Wesley, 1995.

[17] M Grand. *Patterns in Java, Vol. 1*. Wiley, 1998.

[18] D Gries. *The Science of Programming*. Springer-Verlag, 1981.

[19] http://www-136.ibm.com/developerworks/webservices/.

[20] Independent Living Institute, http://www.independentliving.org/.

[21] Java 2 Platform, Enterprise Edition, http://www.java.sun.com/j2ee/, 2004.

[22] I Jacobson. *Object-Oriented Software Engineering: A Use Case Driven Approach*. Addison-Wesley, 1992.

[23] Javaserver pages technology. http://www.java.sun.com/products/jsp/, Sun Microsystems, 2004.

[24] K Lano. *The B Language and Method: A Guide to Practical Formal Development*. Springer Verlag, 1996.

[25] K Lano, D Clark, and K Androutsopoulos. UML to B: Formal verification of object-oriented models. In *IFM 2004*, LNCS. Springer-Verlag, 2004.

[26] K Lano and H Haughton. *Object-Oriented Specification Case Studies*. Prentice Hall, 1993.

[27] T Mandel. *The Elements of User Interface Design*. Wiley, 1997.

[28] OMG model-driven architecture. OMG, http://www.omg.org/mda/, 2004.

[29] S Mellor. Agile MDA, http://www.omg.org/agile/, 2004.

[30] B Meyer. Applying design by contract. *IEEE Computer*, pages 40–51, Oct 1992.

[31] B Meyer. *Object-Oriented Software Construction*. Addison-Wesley, 1992.

[32] B Momjian. *PostgreSQL: Introduction and Concepts*. Pearson Education, 2001.

[33] http://msdn.microsoft.com/webservices/.

[34] The object constraint language version 2.0. http://www.omg.org/.

[35] Compuware OptimalJ Home Page, www.compuware.com/products/optimalj/.

[36] Architecture board ormsc. Model Driven Architecture (MDA), OMG document ormsc/2001-07-01, 2001.

[37] OWL Web Ontology Language, http://www.w3.org/TR/owl-ref/.

[38] PayPal, http://www.paypal.com.

[39] R Pressman. *Software Engineering: A Practitioner's Approach*. McGraw Hill, 2000.

[40] Rational Rose Extensibility Interface (REI), http://www-306.ibm.com/software/rational/.

[41] W Royce. Managing the development of large software systems. In *Proceedings of IEEE WESCON*. IEEE Press, 1970.

[42] J Rumbaugh, M Blaha, W Lorensen, F Eddy, and W Premerlani. *Object-Oriented Modeling and Design*. Prentice Hall, 1994.

[43] The Rational Unified Process, http://www.rational.com/products/rup/, 2002.

[44] Java servlet technology. http://www.java.sun.com/servlets/, Sun Microsystems, 2004.

[45] The user interface hall of shame. http://www.iarchitect.com/shame.htm.

[46] B Sheppard. World-championship-caliber scrabble. *Artificial Intelligence*, (134): 241–275, 2002.

[47] D Smith and C Green. Toward practical applications of software synthesis. In *FMSP '96, Formal Methods in Software Practice*, pages 31–39, 1996.

[48] http://java.sun.com/webservices/.

[49] L Tokuda and D Batory. Evolving object-oriented design with refactorings. Technical report, University of Texas.

[50] J Tukey. The teaching of concrete mathematics. *American Mathematical Monthly*, (65): 1–9, January.

[51] OMG unified modelling language specification 2.0. OMG, http://www.omg.org/technology/documents/formal/uml.htm, 2004.

[52] Web services architecture overview – the next stage of evolution for e-business, September 2000. www106.ibm.com/developerswork/web/library.

[53] Extensible markup language (xml). http://www.w3.org/XML/.

[54] Xsclerator, http://www.marrowsoft.com.

[55] XUI, http://xui.sourceforge.net/.

Scrabble History and Rules

A.1 The history of Scrabble

The original form of Scrabble was invented by American architect Alfred Mosher Butts, in the 1930s. He wanted to create a game which combined the elements of skill – in finding good moves – and chance – the random selection of letters from the bag. He based the letter frequencies on analysis of how often the different letters appeared in the *New York Times* cover, although he reduced the number of 'S' letters to make the game harder. His ideas were rejected by games manufacturers however, and it was not until James Brunot started to independently manufacture the game in 1948 that it began to be commercially marketed. By 1953 it had become so popular, through word of mouth and its adoption by Macy's department store, that Brunot had to license manufacture to a major American games manufacturer. The game rapidly spread in popularity throughout the English-speaking world, and more recently to other countries as well, with versions existing in most of the major languages of the world. The first Scrabble world championship took place in London in 1991.

A.2 Official Scrabble rules

These are summarised from the Scrabble guidebook. The physical contents of the game consist of:

Game board The game is played on a board of 15 squares by 15 squares (Figure 2.22). Certain squares are designated as premium squares, and are marked as such and coloured differently on the board: ordinary squares are plain green, double letter squares are light blue, triple letter squares are dark blue, double word squares are light red, triple word squares are dark red.

Letter tiles There are 100 letter tiles, each marked with a letter of the alphabet (or blank) and the score of the tile. For English Scrabble, there are the following tiles (Table A.1).

Bag This initially holds all the tiles.

Racks Four racks, each able to hold seven tiles. Each player will have their
own rack during the game, from which they select tiles to make a move.

Players Either 2, 3 or 4 players are allowed. One is nominated as the score-
keeper, and keeps track of the player's scores as the game progresses.

Letter	Score	Number of tiles
blank	0	2
A	1	9
B	3	2
C	3	2
D	2	4
E	1	12
F	4	2
G	2	3
H	4	2
I	1	9
J	8	1
K	5	1
L	1	4
M	3	2
N	1	6
O	1	8
P	3	2
Q	10	1
R	1	6
S	1	4
T	1	6
U	1	4
V	4	2
W	4	2
X	8	1
Y	4	2
Z	10	1

Table A.1: Scrabble tiles (English version)

A game may conveniently be divided into three stages:

1. Starting the game: The players each choose one tile from the bag. The
   player with the alphabetically earliest tile (with the blank preceding 'a')
   becomes the player with the first turn. The other players are given turn
   numbers in the order in which they sit, going clockwise, from the first turn
   player. The letters are returned to the bag, which is then shaken/shuffled.
2. Main game: Each player, starting with the first turn player, draws letters
   from the bag until their rack is full. The first turn player plays first, by

placing tiles from their rack in a straight line vertically or horizontally on the board in order to form a new word or words. In the very first move at least one tile must be placed on the centre square. On subsequent moves at least one tile must be placed beside or immediately above or below a square that is already occupied by a tile. The move is checked for validity, and if valid, is accepted and its score calculated and recorded by the scorekeeper and added to that player's total score. Once the player has finished their move, the next player fills their rack and moves.

3. Ending the game: When one player has used all the tiles on their rack and the bag is empty, the game must end. It must also end if all the players have passed twice in succession. The game can also end by agreement of all the players. The scores of the letters remaining on each player's rack are added up and subtracted from their total score. The total score of all remaining letters is added to the total score of the player with the empty rack.

Figure A.1 shows an example move midway through a game.

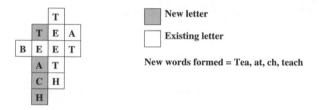

Figure A.1: Typical Scrabble move

The validity conditions for a move are:

- All letters played in a move must be co-linear, either vertically or horizontally, and must be placed on previously vacant squares of the board.
- The letters played do not need to be all next to each other, however if two letters $t1$ and $t2$ are played in a move, then every square between them must also be occupied by a letter by the end of the move.
- All words formed by the move must be in the standard Scrabble word list. The words formed by the move are all maximal vertical or horizontal sequences of letters on the board, read from left to right and from top to bottom, which include at least one letter added during the move.

The scoring calculation is as follows:

1. The score of a move is the sum of the scores of the words formed by the move, plus 50, if the move used all seven letters from the rack.
2. The score of an individual word is the sum of the letter scores of the letters in the move, this sum is multiplied by two for each double word score square covered in the move, and multiplied by three for each triple word score square covered in the move.

3. An individual letter score is either: the score of the letter, if the letter is placed on an ordinary square, double word or triple word square, or was not placed during the move, or, if the letter was placed on a double letter square, it is twice the basic letter score, or if the letter was placed on a triple letter score its score is three times the basic letter score.

Some important ancillary rules are:

1. A player can pass their turn, by not making a move, or they can replace one or more letters from their rack. In either case the turn then passes to the next player.
2. Once a letter is drawn from the bag it cannot be replaced except as part of a specific 'letter swap' move.
3. The blank tile can be used as any letter as needed, however it cannot be reused: once a letter is assigned to it in a move and it is placed on the board as part of a valid move, then it cannot be assigned a different letter in the same game. Its score is always zero.

SCRABBLE is a registered trade mark of J. W. Spear & Sons PLC.

Web Application Development Support Package

This appendix describes the Java classes *HtmlPage*, *HtmlForm*, etc, which can be used (particularly in Servlet-based systems) to generate web pages as part of an internet application.

Figure B.1 shows the classes involved and their relationships.

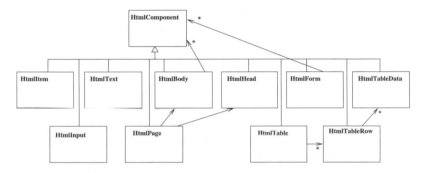

Figure B.1: Classes for HTML generation

HtmlBody This describes the body of an HTML page, as a sequence of HTML components. A component is added to the end of the body by the *add(component : HtmlComponent)* method.

HtmlComponent This is the superclass of all the classes describing HTML elements. It defines a collection of attribute-value pairs which can be altered by the *setAttribute(att : String, val : String)* method. Such pairs appear as HTML attribute settings *att = val* in the tag of the HTML component.

The method *getHtml() : String* returns the ASCII text of the HTML component, which can then be sent to a web browser for display.

HtmlForm This class describes HTML forms, as a list of HTML components within < *form* > and < */form* > tags. The *method* and *action* of the form can be set as attributes using *setAttribute*.

HtmlHead   This class describes the *head* tag of an HTML page. The title of the document is supplied as a string parameter in the constructor, eg:

```
HtmlHead head = new HtmlHead("Add entry");
```

HtmlInput   Describes an *input* element such as a text entry field or button for use within a form. The *type* (such as *text*, *password* or *submit*) is defined using *setAttribute*, as are the other attributes of the element.

HtmlItem   This describes single-line HTML elements such as the paragraph marker $< p >$ or horizontal rule $< hr >$. The tag is specified in the constructor, eg:

```
HtmlItem para = new HtmlItem("p");
```

for a paragraph.

HtmlPage   This class describes complete web pages, with a header in *HtmlHead* and a body in *HtmlBody*.   The methods *setHead(head : HtmlHead)* and *setBody(body : HtmlBody)* set these elements of the page.

HtmlTable   This represents HTML tables. It consists of a list of *HtmlTableRow* instances, a new row is added at the end of the table by the method *addRow(row : HtmlTableRow)*.

HtmlTableData   This represents a cell in an HTML table, most commonly, a single piece of text. In the latter case the text is supplied as a parameter of the constructor: *HtmlTableData(text : String)*.

HtmlTableRow   This represents a row of an HTML table. It consists of a list of cells which are *HtmlTableData* instances. A new cell is added to the end of the row by the method *addCell(cell : HtmlTableData)*.

HtmlText   This describes text components. The text string and the tag are supplied in the constructor *HtmlText(text : String, tag : String)*. For example:

```
HtmlText nameLabel = new HtmlText("Name:","strong");
```

generates the text "Name:" in boldface font. Other qualifiers, such as font size and colour, can be defined using *setAttribute*.

Appendix C

Using Standard OCL

The constraint language LOCA that we have used here is an alternative concrete syntax for a subset of the OCL 2.0 specification notation.

In LOCA we only use the OCL types *OclAny* (the supertype of booleans, numerics and strings), *Boolean*, *Integer*, *Real* and *String*, and the parameterised types *Collection* $< T >$, *Set* $< T >$ and *Sequence* $< T >$ (Figure C.1). *Integer* is a true subtype of *Real* since all operations of reals are applicable to integers and have the same results on integers.

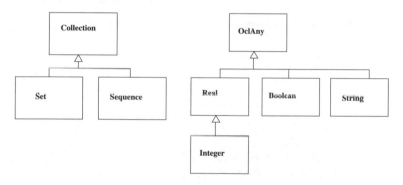

Figure C.1: LOCA type hierarchy

Table C.1 shows the mapping of LOCA syntax to normal OCL syntax. e' denotes the translation of e.

The translated form of numeric operators $/$, $+$, $*$, $-$, $<$, $>=$, $>$, $<=$ on numeric expressions is identical in OCL and LOCA. Comparisons $coll < x$ where *coll* is a collection of numerics, map to

$$coll \rightarrow forAll(y \mid P)$$

where P is the translation of $y < x$. Likewise for other comparison operators between collections and collections, or collections and individual elements.

Navigation expressions differ slightly:

331

LOCA	OCL	Note
OclAny		
$x = y$	$x' = y'$	
$x \; / = \; y$	$x' <> y'$	
Real		
$x + y$	$x' + y'$	Likewise for $-$, $/$, $*$
$x < y$	$x' < y'$	Likewise for $>$, $<=$, $>=$
$x.abs$	$x'.abs()$	Likewise for *floor*, *round*, *sqrt*, *sqr*
$\{n_1, \ldots, n_m\}.max$	$n'_1.max(n'_2.max(\ldots n'_m \ldots))$	Numeric expressions $n_1, \ldots, n_m$
$\{n_1, \ldots, n_m\}.min$	$n'_1.min(n'_2.min(\ldots n'_m \ldots))$	Numeric expressions $n_1, \ldots, n_m$
$\{n_1, \ldots, n_m\}.sum$	$n'_1 + \ldots + n'_m$	No duplicates in $n_1, \ldots, n_m$
Integer		Above operations as for *Real*
$x \; div \; y$	$x'.div(y')$	Likewise for *mod*
String		
$str.size$	$str'.size()$	
$str1 + str2$	$str1'.concat(str2')$	
Boolean		
$b1$ & $b2$	$b1'$ *and* $b2'$	
$b1$ *or* $b2$	$b1'$ *or* $b2'$	
$b1 \Rightarrow b2$	$b1'$ *implies* $b2'$	
Collection		
$c.size$	$c' \rightarrow size()$	
$x : c$	$c' \rightarrow includes(x')$	
$x \; /: \; c$	$c' \rightarrow excludes(x')$	
$c1 <: c2$	$c2' \rightarrow includesAll(c1')$	
$coll \mid (P)$	$coll' \rightarrow select(P')$	
$c.sum$	$c' \rightarrow sum()$	
Set		
$s = \{\}$	$s' \rightarrow isEmpty()$	
$\{x_1, \ldots, x_m\}$	$Set\{x'_1, \ldots, x'_m\}$	
$set \; \backslash/ \; set2$	$set' \rightarrow union(set2')$	
$set \; /\backslash \; set2$	$set' \rightarrow intersection(set2')$	
$set \; \backslash/ \; \{elem\}$	$set' \rightarrow including(elem')$	
$set - \{elem\}$	$set' \rightarrow excluding(elem')$	
$set1 - set2$	$set1' - set2'$	
Sequence		
$Sequence\{x_1, \ldots, x_m\}$	$Sequence\{x'_1, \ldots, x'_m\}$	
$seq[i]$	$seq' \rightarrow at(i')$	
$seq.asSet$	$seq' \rightarrow asSet()$	
$seq1 \frown seq2$	$seq1' \rightarrow union(seq2')$	
Other		
C	C.allInstances()	
self	self	

Table C.1: Correspondence of OCL and LOCA

- *set.role* where *set* is a LOCA set of objects with role *role*, translates to *set'.role* → *asSet*() in OCL.
- *seq.role* where *seq* is a sequence, translates to *seq'.role*→*asSequence*() if *role* is of 1 multiplicity or is ordered, and as *seq'.role*→*asSet*() otherwise.
- *set.att* translates to *set'.att*→*asSet*().
- *seq.att* translates to *seq'.att*→*asSequence*().

This means that a sequence-valued collection in LOCA always corresponds to an OCL Sequence, and set-valued collections to OCL Sets. There are no Bag values explicitly in LOCA (bags can be encoded as sequences, of course).

Likewise for query operations used in a navigation expression (operations with a single-valued result behave as for attributes, operations with a many-valued result behave as for roles of the same multiplicity).

Other numeric, boolean, set or sequence operators can easily be added to the constraint language from OCL if required. The UML2Web tool only accepts the syntax of LOCA described in Chapter 3, however.

For LOCA constraints C on a set ast_1, ..., ast_n of associations, linking classes E_1, ..., E_m, we translate C to OCL by defining variables ex_1, ..., ex_m for each of the classes, and forming an assumption context P as follows:

1. If association ast_k links E_i to E_j with role $role_k$ at the E_j end, add the quantifier

$$ex_i.role_k \rightarrow forAll(ex_j \mid ...)$$

to P, if $role_k$ is not of 1 multiplicity, and add assumption

$$ex_i.role_k = ex_j \text{ implies } ...$$

if $role_k$ is of 1 multiplicity.
2. If for entity E_p there is no bound occurrence of ex_p in the translation of C, then add the quantification

$$E_p.allInstances() \rightarrow forAll(ex_p \mid ...)$$

to P.

The translation is then

$$P(C')$$

where features f of class E in C are translated as $ex.f$ in C'.

For example,

$$e1att = v1 \Rightarrow e2att = v2$$

on an association between $E1$ and $E2$ translates as

$$E1.allInstances() \rightarrow forAll(e1x \mid \\ e1x.role2 \rightarrow forAll(e2x \mid \\ e1x.e1att = v1 \text{ implies } e2x.e2att = v2))$$

if $role2$ is many-valued and at the $E2$ end of the association between $E1$ and $E2$.

C.1   Why use LOCA?

LOCA is designed as a simplified subset of OCL, without OCL's complicated type structure and mathematical operations such as quantifiers. The only new mechanism, of constraints attached to associations and multiple classes/associations, is close in intent to the predicates that may be placed in WHERE clauses in SQL statements. LOCA may be more suitable than full OCL as a notation for undergraduate teaching, or for applications where the full power of general OCL is not needed.

Notationally, we have used $\Rightarrow$ instead of *implies* and & instead of *and*, to increase the visual distinction between operators such as these and the (predominantly identifier) symbols they connect. Likewise for the operators on set and sequence data, etc.

Large OCL specifications can become as unreadable as large programs in a functional programming language, which leads to the risk that they will rarely be checked for errors. The LOCA notation has been designed for translation to the B formal analysis and animation tool [8], enabling constraint errors to be detected and corrected at an early stage.

Appendix D

Exercise Solutions

All the solutions from the exercises in the book are given here. More exercise material is available from the accompaning website.

D.1 Solutions: Chapter 2

1 The use case diagram is given in Figure D.1 and the class diagram in Figure D.2.

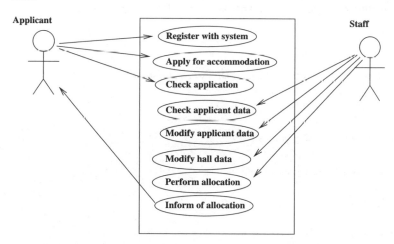

Figure D.1: Accomodation system use cases

2 No: each A that is created requires that five different A objects already exist – so it is impossible to create the first A.

3 Different users can have no aliases in common, because of the 0..1 multiplicity at the user end of the association, so there can be at most 20 different

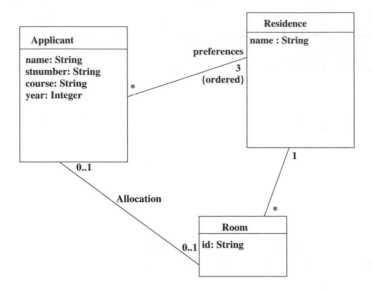

Figure D.2: Accommodation system class diagram

users (the 100 aliases are divided into 20 disjoint sets of size 5).

4 Figure D.3 shows the class diagram. A constraint

$mstyle = style$ &
$mglassType = glassType$

could be attached to the *Conservatory_Module* association.

5 Figure D.4 shows the class diagram.

6 Figure D.5 shows the object diagram.

7 Figure D.6 shows the object diagram.

8 Figure D.7 shows the use case diagram.

9 Figure D.8 shows the class diagram.

10 Figure D.9 shows the class diagram.

11 Both ends have 0..1 multiplicity: at most one spouse is permitted to men or women in UK or USA law. In some countries the multiplicity could be higher at the *Female* end (a man may have several wives) but remain 0..1 at the *Male* end.

When the association is represented as a self-association on *Person* the additional constraint *self* / : *spouses* should be added.

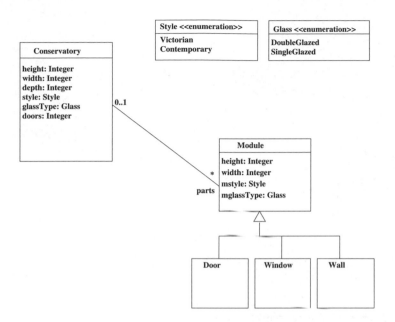

Figure D.3: Conservatory system class diagram

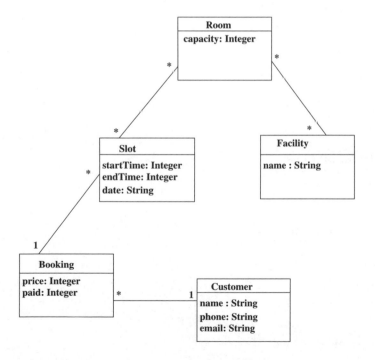

Figure D.4: Conference system class diagram

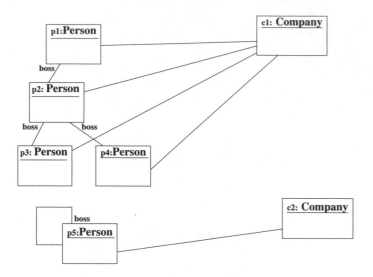

Figure D.5: *Person-Company* object model

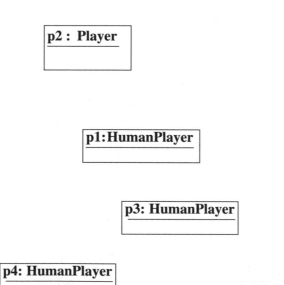

Figure D.6: *Player* object model

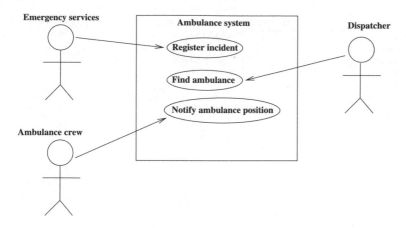

Figure D.7: Ambulance dispatch use case diagram

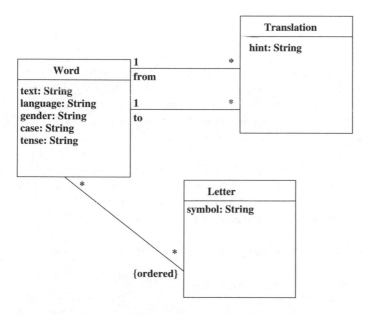

Figure D.8: Translation system class diagram

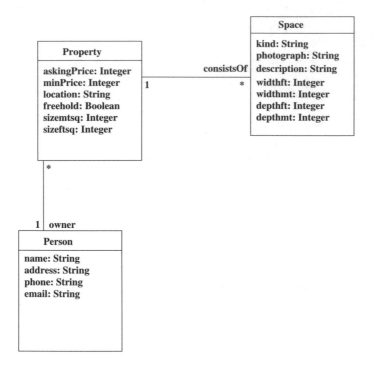

Figure D.9: Estate agent system class diagram

D.2   Solutions: Chapter 3

1   A possible arrangement could be as in Figure D.10. There are two *A* objects and 12 *B* objects, two *B* objects are unattached to any *A*. In general, $B.size \geq 5 * A.size$: there must be five *B* objects for each *A*, and these cannot be shared between two different *A*s (the maximum multiplicity at the *A* end is 1), but extra *B*s could exist.

2   If *x* is an identity attribute of a class *C*, and *D* is a subclass of *C*, then any two objects $obj1$, $obj2$ of *D* with the same value $obj1.x = obj2.x$ for *x* are also instances of *C*, so, since *x* is an identity attribute of *C*, $obj1 = obj2$.

   Therefore, *x* is also an identity attribute of *D*.

3   The revised model is shown in Figure D.11. The constraint

$$age > children.age$$

abbreviates

$$x : children \;\Rightarrow\; age > x.age$$

4   The modified diagram is shown in Figure D.12.

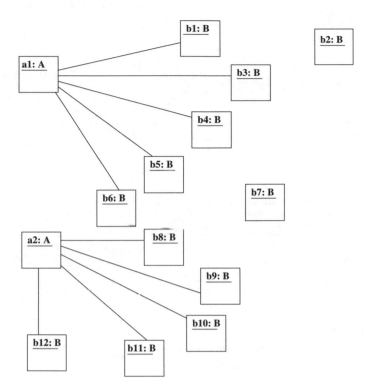

Figure D.10: Example of zero-one to five association

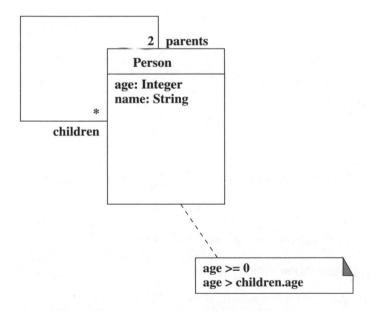

Figure D.11: Modified *Person* model

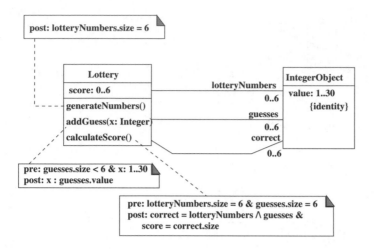

Figure D.12: Modified *Lottery* model

5 These are:

1. $Sequence\{1, 4, 7, 2, 3, 5\}$
2. *false* (7 is not an element of the second sequence)
3. $\{2\}$
4. *true*
5. $\{1, 4\}$

6 This is:

$$i : Integer \;\Rightarrow\; i * i \;>=\; i$$

7 This could be:

$$(A \mid (x > r.y)) \;/=\; \{\}$$

8 This is:

```
sq1.size = sq2.size  &
(i >= 1 & i <= sq1.size  =>  sq1[i] = sq2[sq1.size - i + 1])
```

9 This could be:

$$i : 1..sq.size - 1 \;\Rightarrow\; sq[i].value \;>=\; sq[i+1].value$$

10 For *delete* the postcondition could be:

$$p : String \;\Rightarrow\; check(uId, p) = false$$

Ie, no password p is valid.

For *create* we could have:

$$check(uId, pwd) \; \& \; (p : String \; \& \; check(uId, p)) \; \Rightarrow \; p = pwd$$

The second formula expresses that *pwd* is the only valid password for the new user.

11 This is false because there could be common values in $x.f$ and $y.f$ without there being any common elements in x and y at all. So $(x \cap y).f$ could be empty and $x.f \cap y.f$ non-empty.

However, if f is an identity attribute and $val : x.f \cap y.f$, then $val = xx.f$ and $val = yy.f$ for some $xx : x$ and $yy : y$, and $xx = yy$ because of the identity property of f, so $val : (x \cap y).f$.

The same reasoning gives that

$$(x - y).f = x.f - y.f$$

for identity attributes f.

12 The cardinality of a subclass is at most that of its superclass, since every instance of the subclass is also an instance of the superclass. For an abstract class, its cardinality is the sum of the cardinalities of its subclasses, if these are disjoint.

For *Square*, its cardinality is 225, for *TripleWordSquare* the cardinality is 8, for *TripleLetterSquare* the cardinality is 12, for *DoubleWordSquare* the cardinality is 17, for *DoubleLetterSquare* it is 24, and for *OrdinarySquare* it is 164.

D.3 Solutions: Chapter 4

1 There would be no transition from *Divorced* to *Married*, and therefore the *Divorced* state should not be a substate of *Marriageable*. Figure D.13 shows the revised model.

2 This is shown in Figure D.14.

3 This is shown in Figure D.15.

4 This is shown in Figure D.16.

5 The statechart is shown in Figure D.17.

6 The operation *setlevel* violates the second part of the definition of class consistency: if *setlevel*(l) is invoked with $l >= 10$ and *pump = true* initially, then the state at termination of the operation has

$$level \geq 10 \; \& \; pump = true$$

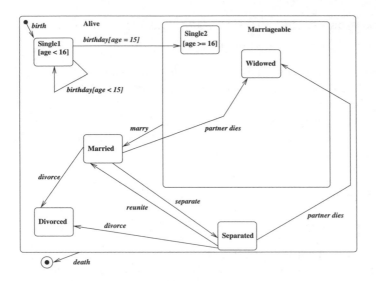

Figure D.13: Revised marriage statechart

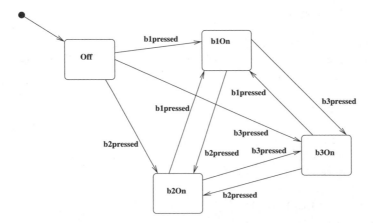

Figure D.14: Radio button statechart

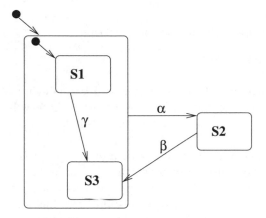

Figure D.15: Revised exercise three statechart

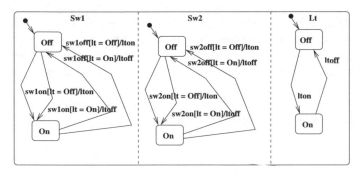

Figure D.16: Light statechart

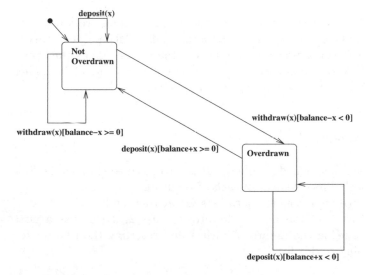

Figure D.17: Bank account statechart

contradicting the second class invariant.

The postcondition of *setlevel* should also include the constraint:

```
post: l >= 10   =>   pump = false
```

7 Since each scoring move must involve at least one letter, and letters cannot be reused, there can be at most 100 scoring moves. In practice there will normally be considerably fewer, but this is an absolute upper bound.

8 The association from B to C seems to be redundant, and a copy of the association from A to C, however the multiplicity constraints are more lax at the B end, which is not possible (an association's multiplicity constraints on subclasses must be at least as strong as on the superclass – since every instance of the subclass is also an instance of the superclass). In addition, attribute *att* of C is redefined in D, which is invalid in some object-oriented languages.

9 A class scope attribute *att* has the property that $obj1.att = obj2.att$ for any two objects $obj1$ and $obj2$ of the class – because there is only a single *att* 'variable' (slot in memory), and all instances share this. But if *att* is also an identity for the class, this means that $obj1 = obj2$, ie, the class can have at most one instance, ie, it is a *Singleton* class.

This is a rather obscure way of expressing the cardinality bound, and it is preferable to express cardinality bounds directly by cardinality annotations or by

$$C.size \leq maxC$$

rather than defining an identity attribute of C with range $1..maxC$.

10 The multiplicities at the ends of a descendent association are lower subranges of the multiplicities of the corresponding ends of its parent: this is because all links in the subassociation are also in the parent. Thus the upper multiplicity bound for the subassociation at a particular end cannot be higher than for its parent, but the lower bound could be lower.

D.4   Solutions: Chapter 5

1 *PairIterator* could be defined as follows: It is initialised to start at the first pair – consisting of the first element of each of the lists.

AtEnd is true if the iterators for both lists are at their ends.

Next steps on by (i) advancing the iterator for list 2, if this has a next element, or (ii) advancing the iterator for list 1 and resetting the iterator for list 2 to the beginning of this list.

In Java this is:

```
import java.util.List;
```

```
import java.util.ArrayList;
import java.util.Iterator;
import java.util.ListIterator;

public class PairIterator implements Iterator
{ private Iterator it1;
  private Iterator it2;
  private Object x1;
  private Object x2;
  private boolean unpositioned = true;
  private List list2;

  public PairIterator(List l1, List l2)
  { it1 = l1.iterator();
    it2 = l2.iterator();
    unpositioned = true;
    list2 = l2;
  }

  public boolean hasNext()
  { return it1.hasNext() || it2.hasNext(); }

  public Object next()
  { List res = new ArrayList();
    if (unpositioned)  // Get first pair:
    { x1 = it1.next();
      x2 = it2.next();
      unpositioned = false;
      res.add(x1);
      res.add(x2);
      return res;
    }
    if (it2.hasNext())
    { x2 = it2.next();
      res.add(x1);
      res.add(x2);
      return res;
    }
    if (it1.hasNext())
    { x1 = it1.next();
      it2 = list2.iterator();
      x2 = it2.next();
      res.add(x1);
      res.add(x2);
      return res;
    }
    res.add(x1);
    res.add(x2);
    return res;
  }
```

```
   public void remove() { }

   public static void main(String[] args)
   { List l = new ArrayList();
     List m = new ArrayList();
     l.add("1"); l.add("2"); l.add("3");
     m.add("a"); m.add("b");
     PairIterator p = new PairIterator(l,m);
     List x = new ArrayList();
     while (p.hasNext())
     { x = (List) p.next();
       System.out.println(x);
     }
   }
 }
```

2 SublistIterator could be defined as follows. The idea is that the sublists of a list *l* are:

1. All sublists of the list formed by removing the first element of *l*, plus
2. all sublists of the list formed by removing the second element of *l*, plus
    ...
3. all sublists of the list formed by removing the last element of *l*.

An index is kept to indicate which of these cases (which element is removed) is being considered at any point.

The initial sublist is the list itself. *atEnd* is true if the index is at the end of the list, and all sublists of the remainder of the list have been produced.

next increments the index if the current sublist iterator is at its end, otherwise the sublist iterator is advanced.

In Java this could be:

```
import java.util.*;

public class SublistIterator
{ private List l; // list whose sublists are being
                  // iterated over
  private int index = 0; // position in l
  private List current = new ArrayList();
  private Object head;         // head of the list
  private List sublist = null;  // tail of the list
  private SublistIterator sublistIterator = null;

  public SublistIterator(List ll)
  { l = ll;
    index = 0;
    if (l.size() > 0)
    { current = (List) ((ArrayList) l).clone();
      sublist = (List) ((ArrayList) l).clone();
```

```
      head = sublist.get(0);
      sublist.remove(0);
      sublistIterator = new SublistIterator(sublist);
    }
  }

  public List getCurrent()
  { return current; }

  public boolean atEnd()
  { if (l.size() == 0)
    { return true; }
    return (index == l.size() - 1 &&
            sublistIterator.atEnd());
  }

  public void advance()
  { if (l.size() == 0) { return; }  // can't move
    if (sublistIterator.atEnd())
    { if (index == l.size() - 1)
      { current = new ArrayList();
        return;
      }  // can't move
      index++;
      head = sublist.get(0);
      current = (List) ((ArrayList) sublist).clone();
      sublist.remove(0);
      sublistIterator = new SublistIterator(sublist);
      return;
    }
    sublistIterator.advance();
    List sb = sublistIterator.getCurrent();
    current = (List) ((ArrayList) sb).clone();
    current.add(0,l.get(index));
  }

  public static void main(String[] args)
  { List l = new ArrayList();
    l.add("A"); l.add("B");
    l.add("a"); l.add("b"); l.add("c"); l.add("d");
    SublistIterator si = new SublistIterator(l);
    do
    { System.out.println(si.getCurrent());
      si.advance();
    } while (!si.atEnd());
  }
}
```

3 A module design for the *Board* module could be:

```
MODULE Board
```

```
MANAGES DATA: Board, Square
CONSTRAINTS
  C5: s1 : Square &
      s2 : Square & s1.isOccupied() &
      s2.isOccupied() =>
          s2 : s1.adjacent.closure
OPERATIONS
  placeMove(b: Board, m: Move)
  // pre: { All squares under the new moves are free }
  //    lm : m.letterMoves =>
  //       b.boardSquare[lm.x,lm.y].squareLetter = {}
  // pre: { either board is empty, or a new move
  //         is adjacent to an existing one }
  //    (b.boardSquare.squareLetter = {}) or
  //    (LM : m.letterMoves &
  //       b.boardSquare[LM.x,LM.y].adjacent.squareLetter /= {})
  // post:
  //    lm : m.letterMoves =>
  //       b.boardSquare[lm.x,lm.y].squareLetter =
  //                                    lm.letter

  isOccupied(b: Board, i: 1..15,
             j: 1..15) : Boolean
  // post:
  //    result =
  //       b.boardSquare[i,j].isOccupied()

  getSquare(b: Board, i: 1..15, j: 1..15): Square
  // post: result = b.boardSquare[i,j]
END
```

4 The *B* and *C* classes are similar enough to suggest the creation of a common superclass, *BorC*, to which the *r* role is directed. The many-many association could also be eliminated. Figure D.18 shows the new model.

5 Figure D.19 shows an object diagram for this interface.

6 The classes *A*, *B*, *C*, *D* are amalgamated as shown in Figure D.20.

7 This is shown in Figure D.21.

8 The classes could be:

```
public abstract class Person
{ private int consumed = 0;

  public void consume(int units)
  { consumed += units;
    if (overLimit(consumed))
    { System.out.println("You are over your limit!"); }
```

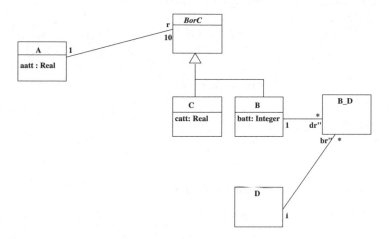

Figure D.18: Improved class diagram

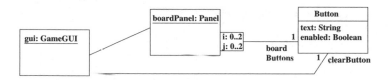

Figure D.19: Object diagram of OXO GUI

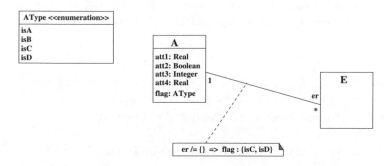

Figure D.20: Class diagram after amalgamation

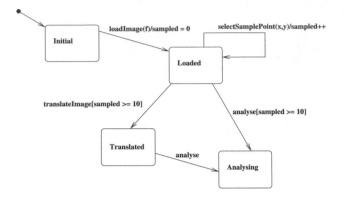

Figure D.21: Statechart of face recognition system

```
  }

  public abstract boolean overLimit(int x);

  public void reset()
  { consumed = 0; }
}

class Male extends Person
{ public boolean overLimit(int x)
  { return x > 28; }
}

class Female extends Person
{ public boolean overLimit(int x)
  { return x > 21; }
}
```

9 There is multiple inheritance of C on A and B. Both A and C have an abstract operation but are not abstract themselves. These problems could be corrected by:

- Either amalgamating A and B into a single class, or replacing the inheritance of A by C by a 0..1 to 1 association from C to A.
- Making A (or the amalgamated AB class) and C abstract.

10 The view for player number p would contain the invariant

$$i : 1..g.players[p].playerRack.rackSize \Rightarrow$$
$$rackButtons[i].text =$$
$$g.players[p].playerRack.rackLetters[i].symbol$$

and

$$i : g.players[p].playerRack.rackSize + 1..7 \Rightarrow$$
$$rackButtons[i].text = \text{“} - \text{”} \& rackButtons[i].enabled = false$$

D.5 Solutions: Chapter 6

1 These could be:

```
import java.util.*;

public class Branch
{ private String name;
  private String sortCode;
  private List customers = new ArrayList(); // of AccountHolder
}

import java.util.*;

public class AccountHolder
{ private String name;
  private Map personalAccounts = new HashMap(); // String -> Account
}

public abstract class Account
{ private int balance;
  private int maxOverdraft;
}

public class PremiumAccount extends Account
{ private int interestRate;
  private int minBalance;
}

public class OrdinaryAccount extends Account
{ }
```

2 These could be:

```
public interface I
{ public int op1(int x); }

public class B
{ private String n; }

public class A implements I
{ private int x;
  private int y;
  private List br = new ArrayList(); // of B
```

```
  public void setx(int xx)
  { x = xx;
    y = 10*xx;
  }
}
```

3 In Java, the specification of the lottery system can be directly coded up
using the *Set* data structure, which discards duplicate elements:

```
import java.util.*;

public class Lottery
{ private Set lotteryNumbers = new HashSet(); // of Integer
  private Set guesses = new HashSet(); // of Integer
  private Set correct = new HashSet(); // of Integer
  private int score = 0; // score = correct.size()

  public void generateNumbers()
  { Random rand = new Random();
    while (lotteryNumbers.size() < 6)
    { int index = rand.nextInt(29) + 1;
      lotteryNumbers.add(new Integer(index));
    }
  }

  public void addGuess(int x)
  { if (guesses.size() >= 6) { return; }
    guesses.add(new Integer(x));
  }

  public void calculateScore()
  { correct = (Set) ((HashSet) lotteryNumbers).clone();
    correct.retainAll(guesses);
    score = correct.size();
    System.out.println("You guessed: " + guesses);
    System.out.println("Lottery numbers were: " + lotteryNumbers);
    System.out.println("correct: " + correct);
    System.out.println("score = " + score);
  }

  public static void main(String[] args)
  { Lottery lott = new Lottery();
    lott.generateNumbers();
    lott.addGuess(3);
    lott.addGuess(10); lott.addGuess(3);
    lott.addGuess(13); lott.addGuess(23);
    lott.addGuess(30); lott.addGuess(13); lott.addGuess(31);
    lott.calculateScore();
  }
}
```

4   The Java code for this system is:

```
public class Person
{ private String name;
  private Person boss;
  private Company employer;

  public void setEmployer(Company c, Person newboss)
  { // pre: newboss.employer == c
    employer = c;
    boss = newboss;
  }
}

public class Company
{ }
```

5   This could be as shown in Figure D.22.

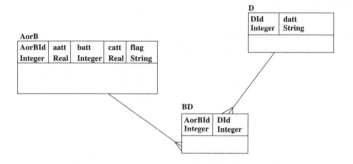

Figure D.22: Relational database schema

6   This is shown in Figure D.23.

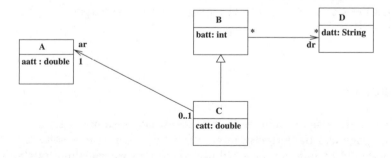

Figure D.23: PSM for Java

7   The DTD could be:

```
<!ELEMENT order (date,orderline*,customer*)>
<!ELEMENT date (#PCDATA)>
<!ELEMENT orderline (quantity,note,product)>
<!ELEMENT quantity (#PCDATA)>
<!ELEMENT note (#PCDATA)>
<!ELEMENT product (description,price,productFlag)>
<!ELEMENT productFlag EMPTY>
<!ATTLIST productFlag value (Assembled | SelfAssembly)>
<!ELEMENT description (#PCDATA)>
<!ELEMENT price (#PCDATA)>
<!ELEMENT customer (name,address)>
<!ELEMENT name (#PCDATA)>
<!ELEMENT address (#PCDATA)>
```

An order could be represented as:

```
<order>
  <date>3-5-03</date>
  <orderline>
    <quantity>4</quantity>
    <note>white</note>
    <product productFlag = "Assembled">
      <description>kitchen chair</description>
      <price>35</price>
    </product>
  </orderline>
  <orderline>
    <quantity>1</quantity>
    <note>brown</note>
    <product productFlag = "SelfAssembly">
      <description>kitchen table</description>
      <price>75</price>
    </product>
  </orderline>
  <customer>
    <name>Blossom Willowby</name>
    <address>13 Privet Drive, Little Whinging, Surrey</address>
  </customer>
</order>
```

D.6   Solutions: Chapter 7

2 The heading of the page should be in an appropriate heading tag, so the structure of the page can be correctly interpreted by screen-reader software. The image tag should include an alt attribute to explain the meaning of the image to blind users. The table should have a caption and summary, and the column headings should be in *th* tags, to emphasise that they are headings and not data.

An improved version is:

```
<html>
<head><title>Furry Friends Pet Store</title></head>
<body>
<h1>All our pets in stock</h1>

<img src="fido.jpg" alt="Image of a pet"><p>

<table summary="List of pets">
<caption><strong>List of pets</strong></caption>
<thead>
<tr><th>Name</th><th>Breed</th><th>Age</th><th>Price</th></tr>
</thead>
<tbody>
<tr><td>Fido</td><td>daschund</td>
<td>4 months</td><td>$30</td></tr>
<tr><td>Loca</td><td>siamese</td>
<td>6 months</td><td>$50</td></tr>
<tr><td>Manuel</td><td>rat</td>
<td>3 months</td><td>$20</td></tr>
<tr><td>Felix</td><td>collie</td>
<td>1 year</td><td>$35</td></tr>
</tbody>
</table>
</body>
</html>
```

3 This could be:

```
public class MagPage extends BasePage
{ private HtmlForm form = new HtmlForm();
  private HtmlInput button = new HtmlInput();
  private HtmlText textarea =
    new HtmlText("Address","textarea");


  public MagPage()
  { super();
    textarea.setAttribute("cols","20");
    textarea.setAttribute("rows","8");
    HtmlItem para = new HtmlItem("p");
    form.setAttribute("method","POST");
    button.setAttribute("type","submit");
    button.setAttribute("value","subscribe");
    body.add(form);

    HtmlText surnameLabel = new HtmlText("Surname","strong");
    form.add(surnameLabel);
    HtmlInput surnameField = new HtmlInput();
    surnameField.setAttribute("type","text");
    surnameField.setAttribute("name","surname");
    form.add(surnameField);
```

```
form.add(para);

HtmlText nameLabel = new HtmlText("First name","strong");
form.add(nameLabel);
HtmlInput nameField = new HtmlInput();
nameField.setAttribute("type","text");
nameField.setAttribute("name","name");
form.add(nameField);
form.add(para);

HtmlText phoneLabel = new HtmlText("Phone","strong");
form.add(phoneLabel);
HtmlInput phoneField = new HtmlInput();
phoneField.setAttribute("type","text");
phoneField.setAttribute("name","phone");
form.add(phoneField);
form.add(para);

HtmlText addressLabel = new HtmlText("Address","strong");
form.add(addressLabel);
form.add(textarea);
form.add(para);

HtmlInputGroup magboxes = new HtmlInputGroup("checkbox","magazine");
magboxes.addOption("Airgun World","airgunworld",false);
magboxes.addOption("Viz","viz",true);
magboxes.addOption("Granta","granta",false);
magboxes.addOption("Readers Digest","readersdigest",false);
magboxes.addOption("Time","time",false);
magboxes.addOption("Cosmopolitan","cosmo",false);
form.add(magboxes);
form.add(para);

HtmlText emailLabel = new HtmlText("Email address","strong");
form.add(emailLabel);
HtmlInput emailField = new HtmlInput();
emailField.setAttribute("type","text");
emailField.setAttribute("name","email");
form.add(emailField);
form.add(para);

HtmlText faxLabel = new HtmlText("Fax","strong");
form.add(faxLabel);
HtmlInput faxField = new HtmlInput();
faxField.setAttribute("type","text");
faxField.setAttribute("name","fax");
form.add(faxField);
form.add(para);

form.add(button);
```

```
    }
    public static void main(String[] args)
    { MagPage cp = new MagPage();
      System.out.println(cp);
    }
}
```

Figure D.24 shows the resulting web page.

Figure D.24: Magazine order web page

4 A statechart for this system could be as shown in Figure D.25.

5 This could be:

```
<html> <head>
<title>Factorial form</title>
<script language = "JavaScript">
function factorial()
{ var x =
    parseInt(document.form1.field1.value);
  document.writeln("<h1>The factorial is: " + fact(x) + "</h1>");
}

function fact(x)
{ if (x <= 1)
  { return 1; }
  return x*fact(x-1);
```

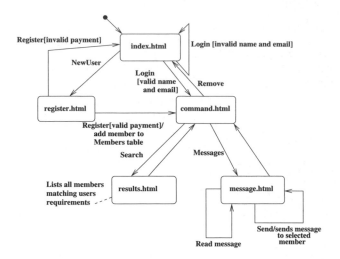

Figure D.25: Interaction statechart of dating agency system

```
}
</script>
</head>

<body>
<form name = "form1" action = "">

<p>
<strong>Enter integer:</strong>
<input name = "field1" type = "text"></p>

<p><input type = "button"
 value = "Factorial" onclick = "factorial()"></p>
</form>
</body>
</html>
```

6 This could be:

```
<html> <head>
<title>Postcode check form</title>
<script language = "JavaScript">
function check()
{ if (isLetter(document.form1.field1.value.charCodeAt(0)) &&
     (isLetter(document.form1.field1.value.charCodeAt(1)) ||
      isDigit(document.form1.field1.value.charCodeAt(1))
     )
   )
  { window.alert("Ok, it is a postcode"); }
  else
  { window.alert("ERROR: not a postcode!"); }
```

```
}

function isLetter(chr)
{ if (chr >= 65 && chr <= 90)
  { return true; }
  else
  { return false; }
}

function isDigit(chr)
{ if (chr >= 48 && chr <= 57)
  { return true; }
  else
  { return false; }
}
</script>
</head>

<body>
<form name = "form1"
 action = "">

<p>
<strong>Enter postcode to be checked:</strong>
<input name = "field1" type = "text"></p>

<p><input type = "button"
 value = "Check" onclick = "check()"></p>
</form>
</body>
</html>
```

7 Figure D.26 shows the interaction statechart, and Figure D.27 the system architecture.

8 The client-side checks could be:

```
<html> <head>
<title>NI check form</title>
<script language = "JavaScript">
function check()
{ if (isLetter(document.form1.field1.value.charCodeAt(0)) &&
      isLetter(document.form1.field1.value.charCodeAt(1)) &&
      isDigit(document.form1.field1.value.charCodeAt(2)) &&
      isDigit(document.form1.field1.value.charCodeAt(3)) &&
      isDigit(document.form1.field1.value.charCodeAt(4)) &&
      isDigit(document.form1.field1.value.charCodeAt(5)) &&
      isDigit(document.form1.field1.value.charCodeAt(6)) &&
      isDigit(document.form1.field1.value.charCodeAt(7)) &&
      isLetter(document.form1.field1.value.charCodeAt(8)) )
```

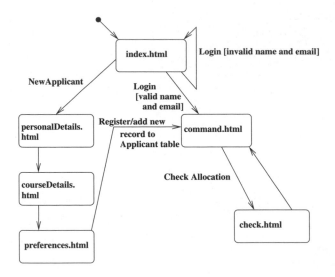

Figure D.26: Interaction statechart of accommodation system

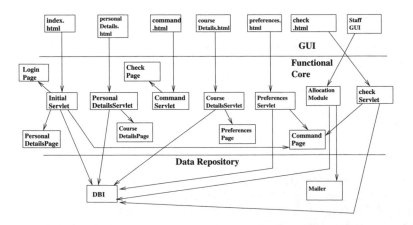

Figure D.27: Architecture of accommodation system

```
  { window.alert("Ok, it is an NI number"); }
  else
  { window.alert("ERROR: not an NI number"); }
}

function isLetter(chr)
{ if (chr >= 65 && chr <= 90)
  { return true; }
  else
  { return false; }
}

function isDigit(chr)
{ if (chr >= 48 && chr <= 57)
  { return true; }
  else
  { return false; }
}
</script>
</head>

<body>
<form name = "form1"
 action = "">

<p>
<strong>Enter NI to be checked:</strong>
<input name = "field1" type = "text"></p>

<p><input type = "button"
 value = "Check" onclick = "check()"></p>
</form>
</body>
</html>
```

The corresponding server-side checks on a string *ni* would be:

```
Character.isLetter(ni.charAt(0)) &&
Character.isLetter(ni.charAt(1)) &&
Character.isDigit(ni.charAt(2)) &&
Character.isDigit(ni.charAt(3)) &&
Character.isDigit(ni.charAt(4)) &&
Character.isDigit(ni.charAt(5)) &&
Character.isDigit(ni.charAt(6)) &&
Character.isDigit(ni.charAt(7)) &&
Character.isLetter(ni.charAt(8))
```

9 A disadvantage is that credit card numbers are normally printed and written as separate groups of four digits, so users of a web system will expect to enter data in this format. In addition some blocks have a particular meaning, eg, the first group of four digits identifies which kind of card it is. So if the digits were entered in separate groups this can be used for error checking.

An advantage of the 16 digit format is that it simplifies the form and data handling: only one value is input instead of four.

10   This could be:

```
<html>
<head><title>Property Image Map</title>
<body>

<map name = "mymap">
<area shape = "poly"
 coords = "68,41,62,36,55,36,51,41,56,45,62,45"
 href = "london.html"
 alt = "Greater London" />
<area shape = "poly"
 coords = "51,41,40,100,50,150,60,150,60,45,56,45"
 href = "sc.html"
 alt = "Sussex, Surrey, etc" />
<area shape = "poly"
 coords = "60,45,60,150,150,130,130,100,68,41,62,45"
 href = "kent.html"
 alt = "Kent" />
</map>

<img src= "areas.jpg" width= "400" height = "200"
 alt = "Image of property search areas" usemap = "mymap"/>
</body>
</html>
```

11   Some plausible constraints are:

$$arrival \ <= \ departure$$
$$noOfRooms > 0$$
$$name.size > 0$$
$$address.size > 0$$

The arrival date must also be in the future:

$$now \ <= \ arrival$$

if *now* denotes the current date.

12   The design is shown in Figure D.28. The forms are shown in Figure D.29. *propertyId* could also be supplied in the *CreateProperty* form – properties are often given a unique id reference by the estate agency staff.

The interaction sequence is shown in Figure D.30.

13   Figure D.31 shows the design class diagram of this system.
Figure D.32 shows the architecture.

```
┌─────────────────────────┐
│     <<persistent>>      │
│        Property         │
├─────────────────────────┤
│ propertyId: String      │
│              {identity} │
│ price: Integer          │
│ area: String            │
│ freehold: Boolean       │
│ detached: Boolean       │
│ position: String        │
│ type: String            │
└─────────────────────────┘
```

Figure D.28: Estate agency design model

```
┌────────────────────────┐
│     CreateProperty      │
├────────────────────────┤
│ price: Integer          │
│ area: String            │
│ freehold: Boolean       │
│ detached: Boolean       │
│ position: String        │
│ type: String            │
├────────────────────────┤
│ create() <<create>>     │
└────────────────────────┘
```

```
┌──────────────────────┐      ┌──────────────────────────┐
│    ListProperties     │      │     DeleteProperty        │
├──────────────────────┤      ├──────────────────────────┤
│ listAll()   <<list>>  │      │ propertyId: String        │
│                       │      ├──────────────────────────┤
│                       │      │ delete() <<delete>>       │
│                       │      │                           │
│                       │      │                           │
└──────────────────────┘      └──────────────────────────┘
```

Figure D.29: Estate agency forms

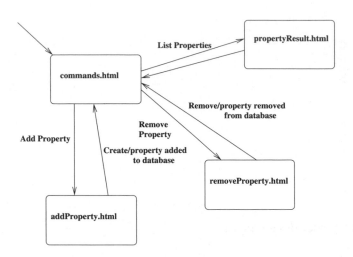

Figure D.30: Estate agency interaction statechart

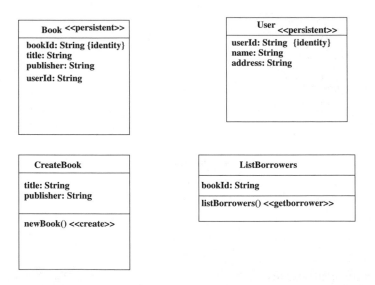

Figure D.31: Library design model

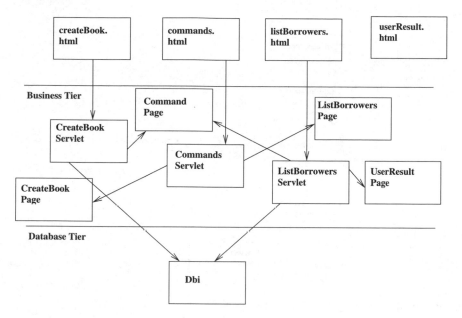

Figure D.32: Library architecture

14 Figure D.33 shows the statechart.

Figure D.34 shows the servlet architecture.

15 The message is shown every time the user puts the mouse into the field, so preventing them from entering any data.

The problem can be corrected by using a global variable var informed = false;

This is set to true after the message has been displayed once, and *areaMessage*() is redefined as:

```
function areaMessage()
{ if (informed == false)
  { window.alert("Enter a postcode, eg:\n" +
           "SW19 or EC1R");
  }
  informed = true;
}
```

D.7 Solutions: Chapter 8

1 This is shown in Figure D.35.

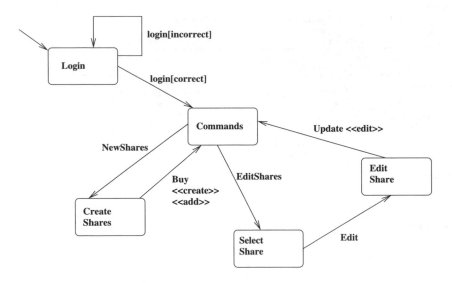

Figure D.33: Share system interaction

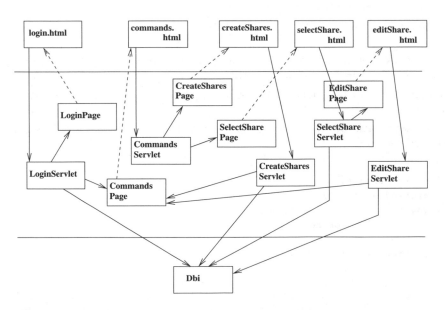

Figure D.34: Share system architecture

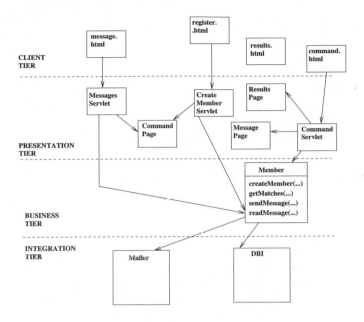

Figure D.35: Dating agency in J2EE architecture

2 The class diagram is shown in Figure D.36 and the architecture in Figure D.37.

The web pages of the system would consist of (Figure D.38):

- An initial login page with text fields for login name and password.
- A command page, with options to view sensor record, set polling, and logout.
- The sensor record page, which has a table with columns *Area*, *Last detection* (time), *Detecting* (boolean) and a link to a cam for that area (if one exists). This link will show the cam image as a live streamed feed in a new web page.
- The polling/panning setting page, which includes text fields or selection lists to modify these system parameters.

For WML, the same web structure could be used, however the sensor report page would need to be subdivided into groups of five rows, each group would be shown on successive pages.

3 This could be:

```
public static void sendMessage(String myAlias,
                               String toAlias,
                               String text)
{ String mailhost = "mail.datingagency.co.uk";
  Properties prop = System.getProperties();
  prop.put("mail.smtp.host",mailhost);
```

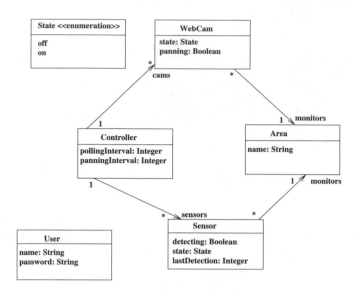

Figure D.36: Cat monitor class diagram

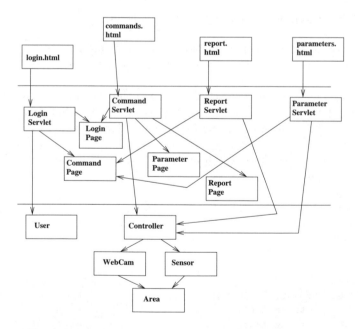

Figure D.37: Cat monitor architecture

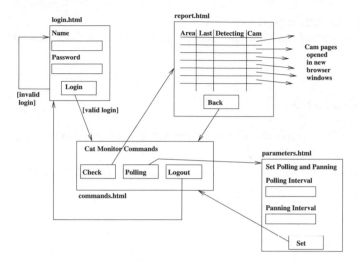

Figure D.38: Web pages of cat monitor system

```
PropSysAuthenticator auth = new PropSysAuthenticator();
Session sess =
  Session.getDefaultInstance(prop,auth);
MimeMessage mess = new MimeMessage(sess);
try
{ mess.setSubject("Message from " + myAlias);
  mess.setText(text);
  Address from =
    new InternetAddress(myAlias +
                          "@datingagoncy.co.uk");
  mess.setFrom(from);
  ResultSet res = dbi.getMember(toAlias);
  while (res.next())
  { String nme = res.getString("memberName");
    String eml = res.getString("email");
    Address to = new InternetAddress(eml,nme);
    mess.addRecipient(Message.RecipientType.TO,to);
    mess.saveChanges();
  }
  Transport.send(mess);
  res.close();
}
catch(Exception e)
{ handleException(e); }
}
```

4 The *Bill*, *Payment* and *BillItem* classes belong in a single EJB, since *Payment* and *BillItem* are subordinates of *Bill*.

Similarly, *Table*, *OrderItem*, *Variation* and *Ingredient* are subordinates of

Order and belong in an EJB with it.

Finally, the classes *Staff* and its subclasses, and *Shift*, can be grouped together.

D.8   Solutions: Chapter 9

1   The classes A and B are represented by themselves in the new model, as is br, so the mappings are:

$$\overline{m_2.A} = \overline{m_1.A}$$
$$\overline{m_2.B} = \overline{m_1.B}$$
$$\overline{m_2.br} = \overline{m_1.br}$$

i is interpreted by $br[index]$:

$$\overline{m_2.i}(a) \;=\; (\overline{m_2.br}(a))(\overline{m_2.index}(a))$$

2   A relationship defined using a foreign key is inherently many-one, because, given a particular value for the foreign key, $b.akey$, there can be at most one A object with that key value, due to the *identity* property of the key.

4 $\overline{C} \subseteq \overline{A}$ and $\overline{C} \subseteq \overline{B}$, so $\overline{C} \subseteq \overline{A} \cap \overline{B}$.

Index

373